Leadership for Follower Commitment

Leadership for Follower Commitment

David J. Cooper

OXFORD   AMSTERDAM   BOSTON   LONDON   NEW YORK   PARIS
SAN DIEGO   SAN FRANCISCO   SINGAPORE   SYDNEY   TOKYO

Butterworth-Heinemann
An imprint of Elsevier Science
Linacre House, Jordan Hill, Oxford OX2 8DP
200 Wheeler Road, Burlington MA 01803

First published 2003

British Library Cataloguing in Publication Data
A catalogue record for this book is available from the British Library

Library of Congress Cataloguing in Publication Data
A catalogue record for this book is available from the Library of Congress

ISBN 0 7506 5688 3

For information on all Butterworth-Heinemann publications
visit our website at www.bh.com

Composition by Genesis Typesetting Limited, Rochester, Kent
Printed and bound in Great Britain

Contents

Preface

This book reflects the view that leadership is not leadership unless followers willingly follow. However, our response to the notions of leadership and followership is likely to suffer paradox. For instance, ask most employees what they want of their senior management, and they will respond by saying that they want leadership. However, ask people who their leader is and they will most likely be offended that you think 'they need to be lead'. Implying that employees should be followers is equally emotive. Consequently, it is important that readers do not attach inappropriate connotations to the leadership or follower role. Leaders are not super all-knowing and special beings, and followers are not 'others' like sheep waiting for the leader 'sheep-dog' to give them some ideas as to what to do and where to go. Readers are requested to accept the view that the potential for improved relationships in organizations is more important than the titles 'leader' or 'follower'.

My interest in leadership for follower commitment has been generated over 25 years. For example, I was involved in a major exercise to form a 'winning culture' from the merger of two disparate organizations with polarized styles of management. Two major surveys encompassing 25 000 employees representing all levels within the merged company explored employee attitudes to the company. The important issue arising from the surveys was that many employees reported a lack of commitment. Poor leadership and inadequate concern for employees evolved as the broad-brush cause for poor manager–employee relationships and lack-lustre performance. Consequently, an essential focus of this book concerns the senior manager–leader role. While not denying the importance of leadership or the need for followership at other organizational levels, if leadership is not demonstrated 'from the top', then wishing for leadership qualities at other levels in the organization is inherently problematic. None the less, analysis, conclusions and recommendations provided within the text are of equal importance to supervisors and managers at all levels within the organization, including leaders of project and cross-functional teams. Potential followers should also find the narrative of interest while judging leadership qualities in their current manager, and perhaps other managers they have known.

Many employees today find themselves in situations of being both a follower and leader at different times and in different work settings. For this growing category of managers/employees, the text should have extra benefits. For example, it will provide employees in leader roles with process helpful to engaging potential followers, while in a potential follower role, employees will feel more confident to provide information to the leader as to what they need in order to willingly follow.

The underlying principle and basis for the book is that organizations and students of organizational behaviour require current and 'joined-up' support to help understand leadership from a leader and follower perspective. In preparation, literature and current research revealed many related and interrelated areas of interest. Included were aspects of organizational structure, business management and applied business, social and developmental psychology. Key areas used for investigation and further analysis focused on organizational behaviour and occupational psychology. While acknowledging the influence of leadership theory, most theoretical and conceptual approaches miss the importance of follower perceptions. Emphasis is therefore given to psychological forces, employee motivation and perceptions of cognitive environmental cues that stem from management action. I have attempted to integrate a substantial number of meaningful references to literature and research. It is hoped that this approach provides significant information to aid further study, and gives students, tutors and managers confidence that conclusions are well informed. A selection of research-based case studies follows each main chapter together with important questions to assist discussion.

It is acknowledged that the major complaint of students, lecturers and managers is that books dealing with academic disciplines do not often sufficiently link theory with recommended action. From my perspective, what was not required was another book that simply regurgitated conventional theory without considering how leadership and the interface between organizational leaders and employees might be improved.

Equally inappropriate, would be to offer limited and perhaps over-simplified recommendations without reasoned and well-founded underpinnings based on literature and research. Consequently, this book attempts to bring literature, research and practical managerial experience together. The work offers informed practical ideas, techniques and guidelines that should assist students to feel comfortable analysing leadership and employee commitment, and help managers consider behaviour and action conducive to the continuous development of the leader–follower process.

The book is organized in five chapters. The first chapter commences with an introduction and rationale for the book. It also utilizes contextual issues such as organizational theory, globalization and the knowledge-based economy as a backdrop for further analysis. Chapter 2 contains a literature review relating to management and leadership. The third chapter explores followership, commitment and motivation. Working definitions are explored. Previous research findings are introduced and discussed from a potential follower perspective. Informed by literature, theory, analysis, research and experience, Chapter 4 offers process and technique to form a leadership strategy based on recognition of followers. Chapter 5 provides consolidation by reviewing conventional theory and reflecting on the need for process to guide continuous learning.

David J. Cooper

The leadership context

Introduction

This chapter aims to provide a contextual backdrop to leadership and followership. It does so by highlighting underlying managerial approaches related to the historic and evolving nature of organizational design. The chapter also introduces themes such as globalization and the rise of the knowledge economy. It offers that such developments beckon organizations to re-think the leader–follower interface.

The contextual challenge

The nature of organization

The search to discover and apply the best forms of systems and management for the good of the organization is not new. History provides useful theory as to how organizations might attempt to structure their organization and apply managerial methods conducive to changing internal and external environmental circumstances.

Literature offers several and often competing ideas to explain how organizations function:

1 Early writers on management believed in the need for control and predictability, notably Fayol (1916), Taylor (1911) and Urwick (1947).

2 The bureaucratic school emphasizes logic and technical rationality. The term 'bureaucracy', originated by Weber (1930, 1947/1964) describes the conceptual approach of this school as a label for a formal organization in which impersonality and rationality are both supported and developed.

3 The contingency school emphasizes the influence of the environment and the differences in organizations in terms of design and function. Supporters include Burns and Stalker (1961), Woodward (1958, 1965), Lawrence and Lorsch (1967) and Perrow (1970).

4 The human relations school urge interest in the significance of group behaviour. Supporters include Roethlisberger and Dickson (1939), Mayo (1949), Brown (1964) and Silverman (1970).

5 The behavioural scientists apply their ideas of how people behave in organizations rather than the way organizations are designed and functioned. Supporters of this approach include McGregor (1957/1960, 1966), Likert (1961), Herzberg *et al.* (1957) and Blake and Mouton (1964/1985).

6 Members of the systems school see the organization as a socio-technical system (Miller and Rice, 1967). This approach is basically concerned with inter-relationships and interdependence (Katz and Khan, 1966/1978). It involves the need to assess boundaries, systems, the dynamics of interaction and environmental influences on structures and processes.

7 Finally, there are post-modernists, who include those who analyse the new flexible and responsive organization operating in a chaotic world where rationality, logic and scientific management are both unreal and inappropriate due to the speed of change, competition and environmental chaos.

The produce of organizational theory has been developed at the interface of capitalist theory and capitalist practice (Clegg, 1977). The emphasis has been on order, formality and control. Goldman and Van Houten (1980) suggest that the most strategically important managerial need is the design and implementation of the most effective form of control over the labour process in the capitalist mode. From these overriding principles, the need for stability, a formal structure, coordination and clear lines of authority were derived. Firth (1964), states that an organization infers 'a systematic ordering of positions and duties which define a chain of command'. March and Simon (1958) refer to explicit and stable roles that make for a high degree of predictability and coordination in organizational behaviour.

Formal organizations have been established for the explicit purpose of achieving certain goals. They possess clear lines of authority by which communication occurs within a formal status

structure (Silverman, 1970). However, some post-Weberian studies have shown that many organizations have no clear hierarchy
of authority (Burns and Stalker, 1961). 'Officials can have very
diffuse functions' (Gouldner, 1954), and act 'in a far from
impersonal manner' (Crozier, 1964). Although selecting certain
organizations with no formal lines of authority seems possible, for
example a partner consultancy, nevertheless such an organization
may be the exception rather than the rule.

Roles in bureaucratic organizations can be seen as specific,
effectively neutral and collectivity orientated (Weber, 1964).
Weber went on to suggest that this role pattern was the most
efficient mode. This ideal type, however, has come under most
criticism from psychologists because of its alleged failure to take
account of 'human needs', and its simplistic view that motivation
is implicit within the approach. Reed (1985) writes, 'Organizational theory has gradually acquired the intellectual trappings of
social science but retains a parasitic dependence upon the
managerial requirements on monopoly capitalism which has
determined the character of its central problematic.' It seems the
'informal' aspect of organization, which is normally associated
with an organization's workforce, should not be ignored.

Many organizations have purposely altered the formal nature of
their organization. While maintaining absolute authority at the
top of the organization, they have reduced the number of levels of
hierarchical authority. It would appear that the prime reason for
doing this is economic. Nevertheless, other reasons may be
offered, for example, the need to devolve responsibility to be more
responsive to market and customer needs, and to provide a degree
of flexibility as to product or service. Kettley (1995) found that
middle and line management favour employee involvement
schemes and devolving responsibility; nevertheless, they prefer
those that do not directly challenge their authority.

Management, and in particular senior management, have
attempted to transform their organization to compete successfully
in the future by turning to a variety of improvement initiatives.
Each has had demonstrable success stories, champions, gurus and
consultants. In contrast, many have yielded disappointing results.
New change programmes follow in rapid succession and become
'flavours of the month'. The programmes have often been
fragmented. Morgan (1994) states that when senior management
waves the flag saying 'we're restructuring' or 'we're going to
revolutionize quality and service', it is those who fear the
consequences that take the most interest. Andrews (1995) comments that mistrust can potentially ruin the implementation of any
programme. It has been argued that mistrust occurs because the
implementation of such initiatives has generally focused upon

functional, operational and political inferences rather than improvement of the worker–organization relationship. Covey (2001) comments that 'Even though tens of thousands of organizations are deeply involved in quality initiatives . . . the fundamental reason why most quality initiatives do not work is a lack of trust in the culture – in the relationships between people'. He adds, 'It is impossible to fake high trust. It has to come out of trustworthiness.' Clearly, control and maintenance of corporate culture is the responsibility of senior management. Moreover, an essential difference between management and leadership might be the successful negotiation, implementation and maintenance of 'trustworthiness'. Trust, that is, between leaders and followers.

Senior management

Literature often refers to senior management or the senior management team as 'top management or company directors'. Stoner (1978) adds that top management is responsible for the overall management of the organization. Arguing that the roles of direction and management have different legal foundations is possible. Nevertheless, in most organizations senior level managers are the directors and leaders of the organization.

The term 'corporate governance' reflects the primary role of the 'Board' or senior management team (Coulson-Thomas, 1992). The function of a senior management team is summarized as follows:

- To define the company's purpose.
- To agree the strategies and plans for achieving that purpose.
- To establish the company's policies.

Importantly, the role involves certain standards (Institute of Directors, 1995):

1 The Board is expected to be focused on the commercial needs of the business, while acting responsibly towards its employees, business partners and society as a whole.
2 The Board is responsible for specific tasks, including:
   (a) Policy formulation – based on long-term views and externally orientated thinking.
   (b) Strategic thinking – based on long-term internally orientated thinking.
   (c) Supervision of management – based on short-term internally orientated thinking.
   (d) Accountability – based on short-term externally orientated thinking.

Management operates at many levels. Stating that every manager reports to a more senior figure seems fair. In this book, the identification and location of senior management are more to do with the substance of their behaviour and actions as perceived by employees than it is to do with the title 'senior manager.' None the less, the term 'senior management' will be used to describe those within the organization who establish and hold influence over strategic and policy decisions. Policy and strategic decisions are seen as involving the efficient and effective utilization of organizational resources, including employees, money and physical resources. The work adopts the premise that organizational change is best instigated from above. It is also argued that values that may not have been recognized, acknowledged, or supported by senior management are unlikely to enter the psyche of the organization.

Cadbury (1990) simply states that in all, 'the function of the senior management team is to be the driving force of the company'. Reflection suggests that the driven message from a decade of process improvement is 'get the processes right, and the company will manage itself'. However, Hout and Carter (1995) offer that 'in fact, process-focused companies need more top-down management – not less' adding, 'senior management must become more activist and interventionist'. Senior management has the authority to go to the heart of any problem. Consequently, they are able to provide superior solutions for the organization, 'solutions which are inspirational as well as computational' (Thompson, 1967).

Hendry (1998) criticizes senior management leadership; he states that 'when chief executives talk about the importance of people, they are often referring to their top team'. Pickard (1998) questions management intentions, asking 'do they really believe that all the people make a difference or just some of them?' Garratt called his book *The Fish Rots from the Head: Crisis in our Boardrooms* (1995). Critical of the training and competence among those who direct organizations – public and private, Garratt suggests there has been an assumption that the title 'director' immediately makes managers omniscient. He cynically adds, 'they suddenly know everything about the complex integration of their organization, they are immediately aware of all political problems, and they need no reliable internal sources of information'. However, there is little, if any, training and development for directors. The Institute of Directors report 'Development of the Board' (1990) showed that 92.4% of UK directors had no training and development for the job. Amazingly, most respondents admitted that they did not know what the job entailed – not a good start.

Management–employee relationships

The management–employee relationship is likely to be one that has built up over many years. The roots of the relationship may be historic, and involve different players. Moreover, the relationship may not be of a personal and interactive nature. Communication and understanding of the relationship will be based on perceptions of the two parties. Importantly, two entities must have a relationship before communication becomes valid.

Drucker (1973) comments that the role of senior management must move toward the identification of overall strategy, and thereafter, they must provide support coupled with reward systems. Evans (1996) comments that managers need to create an environment in which people enjoy their work by offering them guidance, feedback and reward. Lock and Farrow (1988) state that the senior manager of the future will be a spokesperson and representative of the business. They add that 'senior management will talk and think less about "subordinate" employees and more about "colleagues" and "teams", never underestimating the contribution of others'. Marchington (1996) asserts that a significant element in the relationship between senior management and employees is the perception that employees receive about management appreciation of the contributions of its workforce. However, Guest (1991) warns that the pursuit of commitment by senior management is really a means of gaining compliance – employees are expected to be committed to what the organization wants them to do.

Why leadership is becoming more important to gaining competitive advantage

Organizations seek improved performance and sustained competitive advantage as a response to increased market and other external pressures. Ignoring this fact may put an organization's survival in jeopardy. Change is generic, constant, all around us, and for most organizations, it provides a 'white water' context. This is true for all sectors, business, government, health care, social, non-profit etc. Organizations need to produce goods and services in a fast, consistent, flexible and responsive way that reflects value for money and gains customer satisfaction.

The need for change urges organizational leaders to make internal adjustments that inherently pressure people to respond. The response they require is for employees to dedicate their physical and mental energies for the benefit of the organization. Worman (1996) offers that 'employers will need to gain the willing contribution of a diverse workforce in order to target new markets and distinguish their products and services from the competition'. However, employees feel insecure, lack confidence and are less loyal to management (Wallace, 1997).

What is required is leadership that encourages employees to follow willingly. A workforce that is not only empowered, but encouraged and rewarded so as to provide talent and commitment for the good of the organization and its leadership. However, Gratton (2000) asserts that 'until organizations face up to the gap between rhetoric as to the importance of people and organizational priorities, they are doomed to create organizations that break the soul and spirit of its members'. More positively, many human resource professionals continue to express confidence that 'attention devoted to people issues will grow' and that, 'HR professionals will have unparalleled opportunities to make a difference' (Griffiths, 2002).

Globalization

The need for rapid radical change confronts an increasing range of organizations. Developments such as liberalization, deregulation, globalization and the call for effective development and utilization of knowledge, demand that companies reposition in markets and products. Firms wishing to transfer skills or to develop an international marketplace for their products, brands, services and image normally establish sales outlets in other countries. Liberalization and deregulation have opened new market opportunities while attracting new competitors to the marketplace. Globalization has resulted in the development of multinationals by means of expansion, strategic alliances, takeovers and mergers. Some multinationals are now so large that they have a turnover that is the envy of small countries, and therefore have both economic and political influence.

Managers of organizations working in or towards establishing global presence for products and services are requested to respond to the opportunities provided by the global market, to seek out new business, to exploit technology and take advantage of efficiencies. Torrington and Weightman (1994) suggest that most global companies should adopt a strategy of acting locally while planning globally. This is to ensure local or regional changes are considered and to adapt to local market conditions, while attempting to view the whole world as one marketplace.

Organizations who instigate a global strategy are most often attempting to make economies. For example, production, marketing and perhaps product development might be undertaken in advantageous locations. The prime motive is profit by reducing costs and creating new markets via regionally based ventures. However, this strategy may attract adverse comment on ethical grounds. For instance, less developed countries may suffer from the fast changing, exploitative and competitive nature of global enterprise. Aspects not common to all countries include national deeply rooted cultures, world position, history and stage of development. Hofstede (1980) provides reasoned research as to difference in national cultures. Consequently, a single managerial approach, or the imposition of a conventional and often Western corporate or organizational culture, may be inappropriate. Castells (1996) also notes that a great beneficiary of the global economy is global crime.

Capitalism is perhaps the best economic system to create wealth. However, the power of capitalism also holds the propensity to encroach on human rights. For example, a potential conflict of interest exists between the organizational need to minimize operational costs in the interests of shareholders and the wider interests of other stakeholders. Consequences might include poor pay leading to inadequate employee housing, poor schooling and poor standards of human decency including 'sweat shops' and slave labour. Millionaires and 'fat cat' directors often appear to ride on the backs of millions of people who have uncertain access to food.

The business challenge is clear. Management need to embrace the advantages offered by free trade and liberalized free markets, extend business activity, establish appropriate decentralized structures, adopt an appropriate business and market strategy, and customize products and services. The people and social challenge is less clear. Gaining agreement as to the importance of business objectives and market goals will need to be properly managed and balanced. Management will need to understand new cultures, political frameworks and work practices, build new relationships, and develop skills to manage by cooperation not coercion. Balancing skills will be aimed at agreeing and acting in accordance with specific needs of different countries as well as the needs of employees. A balance of values will need to be declared and monitored that acknowledges leadership accountability to those who have put money in the company but also openly accepts responsibility to those who are affected by the company. This is a special challenge given that such a notion has not yet been generally established in many organizations that work solely within a domestic marketplace.

Organizations will look to senior management for direction and vision. However, Kets de Vries (1996) casts doubt on senior management ability to understand aspects of individual and organizational behaviour. He states 'most executives have a notoriously underdeveloped capacity for understanding and dealing with emotion. All but the best are reluctant to ask themselves why they act the way they do; as a result most fail to understand both their own managerial behaviour and the behaviour of others.' Moreover, Strebler (1997) asserts that top management culture 'has not, to this day, been open to disclosure, so changing senior management behaviour will take time'. Nevertheless, Conger (1998) comments that leadership will become even more important for successful organizations in the next century, but comments that 'hardly anyone understands the capabilities we need to start developing now'.

The knowledge economy

The knowledge economy is a term used to describe the importance of 'know-how' as being key to wealth creation in the future. The notion suggests companies will progressively rely on employees' existing knowledge and their ability to innovate, acquire and exploit new knowledge – to optimize intellectual capital.

A firm's intellectual/knowledge capital is seen as the sum of employees' ability multiplied by their willingness to dedicate their energies towards organizational goals and objectives (after Quinn, 1992; Quinn *et al.*, 1996; Ulrich, 1998). People and their intellectual capital is the firm's only appreciable asset (Ulrich, 1998). More certainly, intellectual capital is an appreciable asset, and perhaps more so than a firm's physical and financial assets. For example, intellectual capital is capable of converting all assets, including inanimate factors, into meaningful wealth-related outcomes. Unfortunately, although the collective brainpower of an organization generate the wealth of that organization, it is invisible and much more difficult to identify, develop and measure than physical assets (Lank, 1997). Nevertheless, organizations have become increasingly concerned with mentofacture, 'creation using the mind', rather than manufacture, 'creation using physical tools'. Gibson (1997) writes 'up ahead . . . we see a world of chaos and uncertainty. A world where economics will be based not on land, money or raw materials but on intellectual capital.' However, Stewart (1997) warns that 'trying to identify and manage knowledge is like trying to fish barehanded. It can be done . . . but the object of the effort is damnably elusive.'

Knowledge, be it technical, philosophical, or academic, has always had value. In many ways, the idea of knowledge capital is not new. It has always been important to organizations, regardless of sector, to exploit knowledge. New knowledge is generated and provided via many organizations and institutions, including nation-state research and development programmes, science policies and higher education funding. Many corporate organizations also have research and development functions and maintain collaborative partnerships with industry and institutions that result in product development, service innovations and improved cost management. In most circumstances, economic life is driven by a need to exploit knowledge to gain competitive advantage for profit. Lank and Thompson (2002) assert, 'Knowledge is now seen as a critical business asset ... interest in the topic has grown despite the understandable bursts of cynicism that are generated by any well-hyped new management jargon.'

To put this argument in context, it is often followers of leaders who are the creative element that results in successful scientific, technical or social development and/or financially rewarding commercial outcomes. This is nothing new. Leaders throughout history have relied on the knowledge gained, maintained and developed by followers to be successful. This seems as true of followers in the workplace as followers of leaders on the battlefield.

The outcome of the knowledge economy might be best thought of in collective terms. For example, innovation is often a sequence of using existing knowledge, knowledge transfer, of gathering, re-interpretation, development and re-development by people, groups or organizations over time who share similar interests or work on similar problems. Identifying leaders and followers in this complex and often virtual environment is problematic. None the less, innovation and development will remain the product of people's ability and willingness to improve and advance products, services, systems and/or processes. All aspects to some extent are owned by people who are overseen by more senior people.

There is likely to be a difference between potential intellectual capital that the firm might be able to exploit, and available intellectual capital. Current intellectual capital would consist of 'current' employee competence multiplied by 'current' employee commitment to the organization. Potential intellectual capital is probably infinite, but it will rely on the development of competence through learning, and the development of employee commitment to the organization. Unfortunately, at an operational level, experience suggests that vital knowledge often appears to 'walk out the company door' as employees become disillusioned, jobs become redundant, employees decide to retire early, or even worse − retire their mind while still employed. Movements towards establishing work practices around the knowledge economy adds to the complexity that challenges leaders of industry.

The introduction of knowledge management systems and processes has been the response of many organizations to help capture, develop and maintain information. The best organizations will provide due process, procedure and management practice that enables the organization to innovate, capture and exploit knowledge – wherever it may be held or developed. However, such interventions often miss the vital point that training people to understand and use knowledge management systems and process is only part of the solution. Gaining people's willingness to involve themselves and openly offer their knowledge and ideas to others in the organization is key. It might be worth reminding ourselves that the best system of memory and reflective use of knowledge is still the human brain. It is up to leaders to promote and foster human capital. Leaders in organizations therefore need to apply a form of leadership that helps, or at least does not hinder individuals and groups of individuals to use this vital organ. To use and manage knowledge competitively, managers need to provide broad-based incentives as well as systems and procedure to manage knowledge. A high performance outcome will require leadership that has a better understanding of people.

To result in continuously effective and equitable outcomes, leaders and followers at all levels within an organization must play their part and be committed to act accordingly within the process. Followers should realize the opportunity the global and knowledge economy provides. Essentially, acknowledgement of the need to manage the knowledge economy provides followers with an opportunity to demonstrate their full worth and potential. Perhaps for the first time, employee knowledge, ability and flexibility will be accepted by most organizations as key to their current and future competitive position.

Human resource practitioners continue to communicate the need for a different form of leadership focused on leadership that encourages cooperation. Importantly, continuous improvement of the leader–follower relationship will become increasingly essential as the need to exploit knowledge develops. It will be about establishing an effective, trusting, workable and possibly enjoyable process by which the skills, knowledge and attributes of all concerned are willingly honed and applied. Leaders will need to adjust and develop behaviour conducive to this outcome. The alternative is for organizations to ignore the promise of wealth creation via the application of employee and organizational 'know-how', innovation and creativity. Leadership characteristics, behaviour and process are the subject of the following chapter.

References

Andrews, G. (1995) The Importance of Trust, *HR Management*, 39 (9), p. 14.

Blake, R.R. and Mouton, J.S. (1964) *The Managerial Grid*, Houston, TX: Gulf Publishing Company (*The Managerial Grid III*, 1985).

Brown, J.A.C. (1964) *The Social Psychology of Industry*, Harmondsworth: Penguin.

Burns, T. and Stalker, G.M. (1961) *The Management of Innovation*, London: Tavistock.

Cadbury, A. (1990) *The Company Chairman*, London: Director Books.

Castells, M. (1996) *The Rise of the Network Society*, Oxford: Blackwell.

Clegg, S. (1977) Power, Organizational Theory, Marx and Critique, in S. Clegg and D. Dunkerley (eds), *Critical Issues in Organizations*, London: Routledge and Kegan Paul.

Conger, J. (1998) Learner-leaders, *People Management*, 4 (21), p. 35.

Coulson-Thomas, C. (1992) Developing Competent Directors and Effective Boards, *Journal of Management Development*, 1 (11), pp. 39–49.

Covey, S.R. (2001) Four Roles for Leaders, *Sixth Annual Worldwide Lessons in Leadership Series,* Kentucky: Wyncom Inc.

Crozier, M. (1964) *The Bureaucratic Phenomenon*, Chicago: University of Chicago Press.

Drucker, P.F. (1973) *Management, Tasks, Responsibilities, Practices*, London: Heinemann.

Evans, D. (1996) Rewards and Recognition, *Management Training*, November/December, p. 32.

Fayol, H. (1916) *Administration Industrielle et General* (trans. by C. Toors as *General and Industrial Management*, London: Pitman, 1949).

Firth, R. (1964) *Essays on Social Organizations and Values*, University of London.

Garratt, B (1995) '*The Fish Rots from the Head*': *Crisis in our Boardrooms*, London: HarperCollins.

Garratt, B. (1996) Directing and managing are not the same thing, *People Management,* 2 (15), p. 19.

Gibson, R. (1997) *Rethinking the Future*, London: Nicholas Brealey, Chapter 1.

Goldman, P. and Van Houten, D. (1980) Bureaucracy and Domination: Managerial Strategy in Turn-of-the-Century American Industry, in G. Salaman and D. Dunkerley (eds), *International Yearbook of Organizational Studies*, London: Routledge and Kegan Paul.

Gouldner, A.W. (1954) *Patterns of Industrial Bureaucracy*, Glencoe, IL: Free Press.

Gratton, L. (2000) A Design For Life, Academic Focus: London Business School, *People Management*, 6 (20), pp. 48–51.

Griffiths, W. (2002) Viewpoint: A Chance to Grow with the Flow, *People Management*, 8 (4), p. 27.

Guest, D.E. (1991) Personnel Management: The End of Orthodoxy, *British Journal of Industrial Relations*, 29 (2), pp. 149–76.

Hendry, C. (1998) quoted in J. Pickard, Top Bosses Accept 'People are most Valuable Asset', *People Management*, 4 (6), p. 15.

Herzberg, F.W., Mausner, B. and Snyderman, B. (1957) *The Motivation to Work*, New York: Wiley.

Hofstede, G. (1980) *Culture's Consequences: International Differences in Work Related Values*, London: Sage Publications.

Hout, T.M. and Carter, J.C. (1995) Getting it Done: New Roles for Senior Executives, *Harvard Business Review*, Nov–Dec, pp. 133–45.

Institute of Directors (1990) *Development of the Board*, IoD publication.

Institute of Directors (1995) *Standards for the Board*, IoD publication.

Katz, D. and Kahn, R. (1966/1978) *The Social Psychology of Organizations*, New York: Wiley.

Kets de Vries, M. (1996) The Leader as Analyst, *Harvard Business Review*, Jan–Feb, p. 158.

Kettley, P. (1995) *Is Flatter Better? Delayering the Management Hierarchy*, Institute for Employment Studies.

Lank, E. (1997) Translating Intellectual Capital into Real Money, *People Management*, 3 (11), p. 43.

Lank, E. and Thompson, M. (2002) Knowledge Management: Head to Head, *People Management*, 8 (4), pp. 46–8.

Lawrence, P. and Lorsch, J. (1967) *Organization and Environment*, Boston, MA: Harvard Business School Division of Research.

Likert, R. (1961) *New Patterns of Management*, New York: McGraw–Hill.

Lock, D. and Farrow, N. (1988) *Managing Information*, New York: McGraw–Hill.

McGregor, D. (1957/1960) *The Human Side of Enterprise*, New York: McGraw–Hill.

McGregor, D. (1966) *Leadership and Motivation*, Cambridge, MA: MIT Press.

March, J.G. and Simon, H.A. (1958) *Organizations*, New York: Wiley.

Marchington, M. (1996) Translating Theory into Good Practice, *People Management*, 2 (14), p. 42.

Mayo, E. (1949) *Hawthorne and the Western Electric Company: The Social Problems of an Industrial Civilization*, London: Routledge.

Miller, E. and Rice, A. (1967) *Systems of Organization*, London: Tavistock.

Morgan, G. (1994) The 15-per-cent Solution, Canada, *The Globe and Mail*, p. 3. See also extract provided by Dr Gareth Morgan to attenders of the Salford University Seminar held on 19 January 1996 and G. Morgan (1988) *Riding the Waves of Change: Developing Managerial Competencies for a Turbulent World*, London: Sage.

Perrow, C. (1970) *Organizational Analysis. A Sociological View*, London: Tavistock.

Pickard, J. (1998) Natural Lore: An Interview with Arie de Geus, *People Management*, 4 (20), pp. 41–3.

Quinn, J.B. (1992) *Intelligent Enterprise*, Free Press.

Quinn, J.B., Anderson, P. and Finklestein, S. (1996) Managing Professional Intellect: Making the Most of People, *Harvard Business Review*, Mar–Apr.

Reed, M. (1985) *Redirections in Organizational Analysis*, London: Tavistock, pp. 20–36.

Roethlisberger, F.J. and Dickson, W.J. (1939) *Management and the Worker*, Cambridge, MA: Harvard University Press.

Silverman, D. (1970) *The Theory of Organizations: A Sociological Framework*, London: Heinemann.

Stewart, T.A. (1977*) Intellectual Capital: The New Wealth of Organizations*, London: Nicholas Brealey, p. 14.

Stoner, A.F. (1978) *Management*, Hemel Hempstead: Prentice-Hall, p. 16.

Strebler, M. (1997) Soft Skills and Hard Questions. Report on the DfEE commissioned study 'Changing Roles for Senior Managers', *People Management*, 3 (11), pp. 20–4.

Taylor, F.W. (1911) *The Principles of Scientific Management*, New York: Harper.

Thompson, J.D. (1967) *Organizations in Action*, New York: McGraw–Hill.

Torrington, D. and Weightman, J. (1994) *Effective Management: People and Organization*, Hemel Hempstead: Prentice Hall International, p. 338.

Ulrich, D. (1998) Intellectual Capital = Competence × Commitment, *Sloan Management Review*, 39 (1).

Urwick, L.F. (1947) *Dynamic Administration*, London: Pitman.

Wallace, N. (1997) *The Changing Nature of the Employment Relationship: Implications for People Practitioners towards the Millennium*, address to the Northern Partnership Conference, IPD, p. 2, April 1997, Leeds.

Weber, M. (1930) *The Protestant Ethic and the Spirit of Capitalism*, London: Allen & Unwin.

Weber, M. (1947/1964) *The Theory of Social and Economic Organization*, New York: Free Press.

Woodward, J. (1958) *Management and Technology*, London: HMSO.

Woodward, J. (1965) *Industrial Organizations: Theory & Practice*, Oxford: Oxford University Press.

Worman, D. (1996) Take It or Leave It, *People Management*, 2 (21), p. 53.

Leaders and managers

Introduction

People refer to the process of leadership, what leaders say and do, and refer to typical leadership characteristics while assuming that all share one common understanding. However, the following definitions help illustrate different perspectives:

Leadership is the activity of influencing people to cooperate toward some goal which they come to find desirable. (Tead, 1935)

The functions of leadership include: providing equipment, materials and supplies, development of personnel, planning work, directing activities, selecting methods, checking results. (Walter, 1949)

Leadership is a system of organized methods of operation in controlling work performance. (Heinrich (1951)

Leaders in various ways guide, control, direct, counsel, advise, teach, influence, and help others in the conduct of their public and private lives. (Lindgren, 1954)

Leadership on the job is summed up in the effect that everything a leader says and does has on the workforce. . . . Leadership involves securing [followers'] willing cooperation, their interest, and their desire to do the job the way [the leader] wants it done . . . being ahead of the group, showing the way, finding the best path to [the leader's] objective. (Brown, 1956)

Leadership is principally a task of planning, coordinating, motivating and controlling the efforts of others toward a specific objective. (Lundy, 1957)

Leadership is not an abstract essence. It is a function, an influence, and a relationship. (Blakely, 1959)

A leader is a person who is appointed, elected, or informally chosen to direct and coordinate the work of others in a group. (Fieldler, 1995)

For some writers and/or observers, leadership is more of a skill, or is it a task, or a series of functions, or a system of control, or more of a process; perhaps it is to do with decisions, or an expression of personal qualities, or is it a service, or a relationship? It would seem that a definition of leadership might depend on:

- The theoretical stance of the writer.
- The managerial approach that might be in vogue at the time.
- The managerial approach favoured by the writer.
- The organizational level on which the writer may wish to focus.

Definitions may also contain an element of personal experience. Georgiades and Macdonell (1998) comment that 'images of leadership are entirely personal'. Commonsensical similarities and dissimilarities will depend on our own experience and views. Consequently, it is more common today for academics and observers to acknowledge that leadership is a multi-faceted 'back-box' concept on which few, yet, agree on one definition.

Readers might agree that to lead is a role of guiding or showing the way, or of going in front. A leader might therefore be defined as one who is followed by others (*The Oxford Encyclopaedic English Dictionary*, 1991). Generally, leadership is the process of motivating as well as directing other people to act in particular ways to achieve specific goals. Consequently, leadership is not leadership unless followers willingly follow. Importantly, followers permanently, or at least temporarily accede to the preferences and goals of the leader in exchange for rewards they expect to receive as a result of following. It can be asserted therefore, that leaders who are able to attain desired outcomes do so by effective encouragement of followership. Perhaps it is best to accept that most definitions tend to have some merit. None the less, like most observers, the author has a few preferences:

Leadership implies two directions in the relationship [follower and leader], and the effective leader receives as well as leads. His

*leadership indeed may include his fitting in or integrating the needs
and wants of his employees with the needs and wants of his
company. (Calhoon and Kirkpatrick, 1956)*

   *Leadership is a skill . . . involved in a process of two-way
communication, a continuous feedback. This interaction sustains the
working morale and the feeling of personal worth of each member of
the team, and is in turn sustained by them. . . . True leadership is
characterized not by domination, but by service. (Marrow, 1957)*

Theories of leadership

People can manage without leaders. Yet, whenever a group of
people get together to perform a task, a leader normally emerges.
What a group appears to require is a clear process of handling
responsibility. Group formation and exchange theory (Thibaut
and Kelley, 1959) would suggest that leaders are recognized by
followers because they provide more benefits and rewards than
burdens or costs for followers. For an effective leader–follower
relationship, there needs to be a positive and appropriate
exchange between leader and followers. Motivation theory in
Chapter 3 provides detailed discussion as to essential characteristics of this exchange. Other theories of leadership fall into
categories such as great man, trait, type, style and contingency
theories.

Great man (person) theory

Historical biographies of great men and women such as Alexander
the Great, Joan of Arc and Winston Churchill provide enticing
support for the view that leadership characteristics may be
inherent in certain people. Supporters of this explanation are
closer to the nature rather than nurture end of the personality
development debate as they point to genetic inferences. They
would subscribe to the view that leaders are born and not made.
They would also suggest that some people possess a natural, if not
innate ability, to rise out of any situation and become great
leaders.

   In a classroom setting, it is common when enquiring as to the
characteristics of leaders for prominent figures to be used to justify
the importance of great vision and achievement. However, critics of
great man theory argue that, in human behavioural terms, any
simple connection between genes, biological influences and
behaviour cannot explain the complexity of social behaviour.
Analysis based on a handful of key historical personalities is

over-simplified and tends to ignore the impact of experience, self-development and context. Examples of the theory also tend to concentrate on military or political figures rather than leaders of industry.

From an organizational perspective, the theory is intriguing and sufficiently simple to be generally accepted. However, it may also be dangerously misleading. If leadership ability were inherent and possibly inherited, then selection and recruitment of potential leaders would need to focus on the candidate's parents and ancestors. In an organizational context, evidence of work experience would be less valued. The importance of development would also be devalued. Put simply, if leaders are born and not made – why bother with management development programmes? Absolute adherence to this theory would suggest that great leaders will emerge regardless of the context and willingness of organizations to recruit, select, develop, coach, mentor, train, develop and appraise employees. However, we might accept that historical 'Great Leaders' are probably fair examples of good leaders who have been lucky enough to find themselves in the right place at the right time, and who have used appropriate behaviour toward followers. From an organizational perspective, potential leaders who learn to understand and act upon what is considered by followers as effective behaviour might prove to be a simple and significant step forward. Great man theory evolved into what is commonly known as the trait theory of leadership.

Leadership: trait theory

Several researchers have found and argued the prevalence of personal characteristics (Shore and Martin, 1989; Brooks and Seers, 1991). In 1937, Allport published *Personality: A Psychological Interpretation* in the USA. It was the first theory of personality outside clinical psychodynamic Freudian traditions. In his book, Allport reviewed about fifty definitions of personality and then arrived at his own: 'Personality is the dynamic organization within the individual of those psychophysical systems that determine his characteristic behaviour and thought' (Allport, 1937, 1961). He built his theory around the concept of traits, which he saw as the means of consistency in behaviour; inner personality dispositions or mental constructs (Allport, 1937) do nothing less than determine behaviour.

Trait theory is based on the assumption that the determining factor in an effective leader is a set of personal characteristics. Consequently, research has centred on establishing universal traits possessed by leaders. Davies, quoted by Torrington and

Weightman (1994), believes that there are four general traits related to successful leadership.

1 *Intelligence.* Leaders usually have a slightly higher level of general intelligence than the average among those who would be regarded as followers.
2 *Social maturity.* Leaders have self-assurance and self-respect.
3 *Achievement drive.* Leaders have a strong desire to get things done.
4 *Human relations attitudes.* Knowing that they rely on other people to get things done, leaders are interested in their subordinates and work at developing subordinate response.

There is some evidence to suggest that empathy or interpersonal sensitivity and self-confidence are desirable leadership qualities (Reitz, 1987). Yukl (1981) includes skills such as creativity, organization, persuasiveness, diplomacy and tactfulness, knowledge of the task and the ability to speak well. Stodgill's (1974) research discovered that the average person occupying a position of leadership exceeds the average member of the group with regard for characteristics such as scholarship, intelligence, socio-economic status, originality, dependability and social participation. Additional to the need for a leader to be intelligent and decisive, Ghiselli (1971) simply suggests that the ability to supervise other people is important. However, Luthans (1992, p. 274) comments that the results of voluminous research effort were generally disappointing. Only intelligence seemed to hold up with any degree of consistency. It is disappointing therefore to discover that there does not appear to be any agreement as to what intelligence is, apart from a general acceptance that the concept is somewhat slippery. Moreover, the 'jury is still out' as to whether intelligence occurs through cognitive and volition or connate process – for example, a product of thinking or the exercising of the will, or as nativists believe, something that is inherited and exists from birth.

From experience, the prominence of certain traits tends to differ over time and in relation to situational factors. The work environment appears to help shape both behaviour and abilities. Consequently, siding with empiricists, it is common today for human resource specialists to accept that specific traits can be nurtured and developed. For example, personality-profiling instruments are used for recruitment, selection, employee development, team development, career planning etc.

Allport found nearly 18 000 adjectives that describe personality characteristics (Allport and Odbert, 1936). Nevertheless, they believed that relatively few basic traits produce key variations seen in human behaviour. Similarly, several adjectives can be applied to the personality characteristics of a 'leader'. Unfortunately, researchers and observers do not yet agree as to which 'traits' are the most appropriate. That does not mean that the search should be discontinued, simply that caution is strongly recommended.

Type theory

Type theories start from the premise that it is a personality type to which a person belongs that is important. Personality is seen by many as something that is consistent; it is something that each of us has inside and which helps us explain why someone is consistent in their behaviour across different situations and over quite long periods. The term 'personality' often carries value judgements about the competence of the individual. More certainly, organizations tend to favour some personalities while others struggle for recognition.

Kretschmer (1925) discovered a systematic correlation between people's physical build and the propensity to develop certain psychiatric disorders. Sheldon (1940) worked out a threefold typology of temperament related to physiques. Here we find the short, fat and jolly person; the tall, thin thinker; with the energetic, assertive athlete somewhere between. Such research says a lot about our wish to stereotype people. The approach might be expanded, for example by suggesting that nurses have a caring personality and all salespeople are extroverts.

Eysenck's (1953) theory is based upon the idea that personality 'types' are distinguished by fundamental differences in the neurophysiology of nervous systems, differences that are probably inherited. For instance, he suggests that the personality dimension introvert–extrovert is caused by the level of arousal in the brain and that genetically determined individual differences exist that affect levels of arousal. Through their behaviour, people tend to adjust these levels of arousal to a comfortable optimum. Introverts, being chronically over-aroused, will behave in a way that attempts to reduce their arousal level. In contrast, extroverts are chronically under-aroused and will tend to behave in a way that increases their arousal level. Eysenck's work provides partial evidence that personality and behaviour might be controlled by biological make-up.

Moreover, it has long been established, using questionnaires, that people usually have political beliefs and attitudes that can range on a single axis corresponding to a radical–conservative dimension (political 'left' versus political 'right'). As with

Eysenck's personality dimensions, there is likely to be a normal distribution of people along the radical–conservative dimension, with most clustering in the middle. Eysenck (1972) has contributed the idea that there is a second dimension, independent of the first, which corresponds to general social attitudes. He has called this dimension the tough-mindedness–tender-mindedness dimension. It encourages the view that shared values would be expressive of the middle ground between tough-mindedness and tender-mindedness and between the radical and conservatism dimension. For example, senior management decision might balance tough-minded task issues similar to those of traditional rational economic factors with tender-minded process factors, which focus upon, people, social and psychological factors. Thus, the middle ground could be used to integrate values. Perhaps leaders do this particularly well.

Conceptually, it is possible to accept the notion that 'committed' behaviour focused on the goals of the organization will generally move individuals displaying such behaviour toward more responsible organizational positions. Clearly, certain 'high flyers' have characteristics that organizations value. In contrast, low achievers may only merit inclusion at lower levels of the organizational hierarchy. For example, some managers might possess 'type' capabilities that make them more worthy of senior 'leadership' positions. Moreover, certain employees may hold a biological or innate propensity that results in a determination to 'follow'. This being so, leaders will become leaders regardless of individual or organizational interventions, and the same would apply to followers. Indeed, from a pure functional perspective, separation of individuals into certain levels of the organization is simply an extension of natural selection.

Type theory goes against our view of ourselves as possessing self-will, or having the ability to reason and make value judgements that may result in our 'typed' behaviour being different to others' expectations. Type theories might be viewed as possessing common sense. However, it is worth remembering that common-sense views are not always commonly held. Moreover, when exposed to debate – they are not totally sensible.

Style theories

This perspective suggests that it is the style of a leader that is fundamental in achieving desired outcomes. Leadership style refers to how leaders behave towards potential followers. Handy (1976) suggests that while a supportive style of leadership leads to greater subordinate satisfaction, lower grievance rates and less conflict, the gain in productivity is not substantial. However, Gaertner and Nollen (1989) found that participative management styles strongly and positively enhance organizational commitment. Similarly, Savery (1994) found that a democratic leadership style leads to higher levels of employee commitment. This may be preferable to an authoritarian style where power is exercised solely by the manager. However, as McGregor explains:

> *I believed that a leader could operate successfully as a kind of advisor to his organization. I thought I could avoid being a boss . . . I thought that maybe I could operate so that everyone would like me – that 'good human relations' would eliminate all discord. I couldn't have been more wrong. It took a couple of years, but finally began to realize that a leader cannot avoid the exercise of authority any more than he can avoid the responsibility for what happens to his organization. (McGregor, quoted in Handy, 1976)*

Other notable leadership styles, expressed as poles of a continuum, might include:

- Process orientation *v.* Technical orientation
- Distant *v.* Approachable
- Totally involved *v.* Laissez-faire
- Hard management *v.* Soft management

Wooldridge (1995) states that 'Organizations are demanding more loyalty and commitment from those they employ, while undermining employee support structures and creating job-insecurity.' In support of the creation of a new psychological contract between employer and employee, he suggests that managers have to find ways to engage higher-order employee needs. This seems especially important in response to changes in the organizational internal and external environment, including the impact of global competition and the move toward a knowledge-based economy. To this end, it has been argued that a person-centred leadership style will be more effective. However, the need for rapid decisions may be a major part of the organization's function and therefore task-centred methods may sometimes be essential.

Many supporters of the human relations perspective may continue to think that by adopting their preferred approach all would be well. This seems a little naive. Similar to McGregor's conclusion, Rogers (1978) highlights that 'soft' appreciative methodologies may not be always appropriate. What is likely to be most effective is some balanced criteria, weighted to cater for the effects of organizational factors, for example, a mixture of a 'task-centred' leadership style and 'person-centred' leadership style. Blake and Mouton (1964) illustrate this by representing styles by way of a 'Managerial Grid'. They use axes labels 'concern for people' and 'concern for production'. The labelling used in the grid is similar to traditional polarized 'scientific' and 'social relations' styles of management. Figure 2.1 illustrates leadership represented by a team manager grid position (9,9) and by an equal high concern for people and results. Balanced leadership styles may bring the best results. Perhaps this is why employees often describe a good manager as being firm but fair. The Grid figure strongly suggests a connection between leadership and commitment from people, and that a relationship of trust and respect is built on shared purpose.

Leaders do not exist in a vacuum; they are clearly affected by circumstance. Moreover, it is probable that leader style is affected by the performance of the organization. For example, Barrow (1976) found that poor productivity had a greater impact on

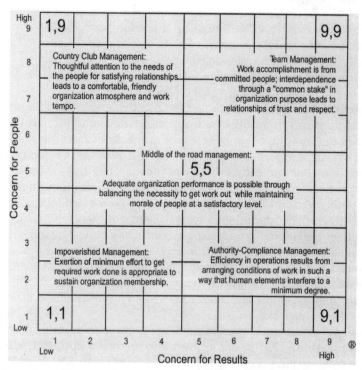

Figure 2.1 The Leadership Grid® figure from *Leadership Dilemmas – Grid Solutions* by Robert R. Blake and Anne Adams McCanse (formerly *The Managerial Grid* by Robert R. Blake and Jane S. Mouton). Houston: Gulf Publishing Company, Copyright 1991 by Grid International, Inc.)

leadership style than style had on productivity. None the less, if followers notice changes in leadership style, some may feel manipulated. Rogers (1978) points out that being congruent and autocratic may be better than apparently people-centred and incongruent. The need for leader integrity and consistency seems important to establishing follower trust.

Contingency theories

Contingency theories are based on the idea that there is no single best style of leadership but that the most effective style depends upon the factors contained within specific circumstances. It is a general theory that suggests all organizations and people are different in so many ways that generalizing leadership styles or attempting to isolate leadership traits is inherently problematic. Consequently, supporters of the contingency approach would argue that there does not appear to be a single pattern of leadership, nor consistent leader behaviours that are effective in all situations. Therefore, it is best to view leadership as a process that requires adaptation in view of the specificity of the situation; the leader assesses the situation and acts accordingly – a continual dynamic process.

With a view to providing general guidelines, Fielder's (1967) contingency theory utilizes central themes of 'task' and 'process' while overlaying situational-specific considerations. The theory focuses on the degree of structuring in the task and the leader's organizational power. He finds that where the task is highly structured and the leader is liked, trusted and powerful, then the most effective leadership style is a directive 'task-orientated' style. Where the task is ambiguous and the leader is in a weak position, then the same 'task-orientated' directive is most effective. However, in intermediate situations where the task is ambiguous and the leader liked and respected then a participative 'person-centred' style is most effective. Unfortunately, there is some doubt about Fieldler's original sampling in that it focused on American football team coaches.

Path–goal leadership theory is a development of the contingency approach (House, 1971; House and Mitchell, 1974). It is an approach to understanding and predicting leadership effectiveness in different situations (Hannagan, 1998, p. 51). The manager/leader identifies 'goals', available rewards and the 'paths' that must be taken to achieve goals. Consequently, this approach makes linkages between management/leadership style and subordinate motivation. House offers four styles of leadership:

1 *Directive:* The leader gives specific directions and the subordinate does not participate.
2 *Supportive:* The leader is friendly and shows concern for subordinates.
3 *Participative:* The leader asks for suggestions but still makes decisions.
4 *Achievement-orientated:* The leader sets challenging goals and shows confidence in subordinate ability and willingness to perform well.

To smooth the path toward achieving their goals, the manager attempts to influence potential follower perceptions by practising the different styles of leadership in different circumstances.

Generally, approaching leadership from a contingent perspective seems logical because organizational internal environments will require incremental adjustments. Importantly, the theory gives credence to the notion that managers need to consider the personal characteristics of employees, the situation and the work to be carried out before deciding the most appropriate leadership style. It is perhaps best to think of leadership as situationally specific, but none the less accept that the situation is mostly contingent on the current relationship between leaders and followers. Comments made earlier concerning the need for leaders to maintain integrity in order to encourage follower trust equally apply to the contingency approach to leadership.

Douglas McGregor

McGregor's Theory X and Theory Y is well known. The popularity of the theory often means that simply stating the theory or the theorist's name is seen as sufficient coverage. McGregor (1957/1960) argues that the style managers adopt is a function of their attitudes to employees, and attitudes are based on managers' view of human nature and behaviour. The two theories provide oversimplified, extreme but recognizable managerial philosophies. Theory X is offered as a traditional 'carrot and stick' approach to management, its assumptions are:

1 People are inherently lazy and dislike work.
2 People's natural goals run counter to those of the organization.
3 Because of their irrational feelings, people are incapable of self-discipline and self-control.

4 People can be divided into two groups. The first group fit the above assumptions, prefer to be directed, lack ambition but value security. The second group consist of those who are self-motivated, self-controlled and not dominated by their feelings. Therefore, they must assume management responsibility for the former.

According to Theory X, management is responsible for organizing the elements of production, money, materials, equipment and people – in the interest of economic ends. Without the interventions of management, people would be passive or even resistant to organizational needs. The management of people must involve a process of directing, controlling and modifying employee behaviour. Management must therefore persuade or coerce employees to conform. This is achieved by means of reward (primarily financial) and punishment.

The human side of enterprise today is fashioned from prepositions and beliefs such as these. (McGregor, 1960)

Theory X assumptions are inconsistent with the growing need for organizations to harness the creativity and goodwill of employees. As mentioned in Chapter 1, jobs have become more complex and organizations have come to expect and even rely on employee judgement, creative capacity, loyalty and increased commitment. Unfortunately, personal experience would suggest that although not openly discussed, several Theory X assumptions are still 'alive and kicking'.

McGregor's alternative Theory Y approach to man-management and human nature can be encapsulated by the following:

1 Individuals seek to be mature in their job.
2 People can learn to take responsibility, and are capable of self-direction, self-control and self-development.
3 Motivation is normally at levels above security needs.
4 Given the chance, employees will voluntarily integrate their own goals with those of the organization. There is no inherent conflict between self-actualization and organizational performance.

The management implications of adopting a Theory Y approach are substantial. With this theory, the management role and style changes to one of helping employees in finding meaning in their work and in making most use of their abilities. Consequently, it may be more fruitful to imagine employees not as an unavoidable consequence of the process of the organization, but conversely, as the organization itself.

Transformational leadership

Burns (1978) contrasted two types of political leadership: transactional and transformational leadership. Transactional leadership might be viewed as a traditional managerial process. Rules and standards are used to guide leader behaviour. It involves the leader in exercising legitimate authority in order to achieve organizational goals. The relationship with employees is likely to reflect a traditional 'mutually dependent' exchange whereas rewards are given for satisfactory completion of the work task. In contrast, transformational leaders are those who display the following characteristics: charisma, inspiration, intellectual stimulation and individual consideration (Bass, 1990; Bass and Aviolo, 1993). Transformational leaders inspire and motivate followers through personal vision and energy. Tichy and Devanna (1986) describe transformational leaders as sharing the following characteristics:

1 They identify themselves as change agents.
2 They are courageous.
3 They believe in people.
4 They are value-driven.
5 They are lifelong learners.
6 They have the ability to deal with complexity and uncertainty.
7 They are visionaries.

Research finds that transformational behaviour augments the impact of transactional forms of leadership because followers feel trust and respect toward the leader and are motivated to do more than they are expected to do (Yukl, 1989). Examples of transformational leadership include the research work of Bass *et al.* (1987); Boal and Bryson (1988); House *et al.* (1988, 1991); Howell and Frost, 1989; Shamir *et al.* (1993). Although approaches differ somewhat from each other, they share a common perspective. By fostering acceptance of group goals, effective leaders change the basic values, beliefs and attitudes of followers to a point at which followers are willing to perform beyond the minimum levels specified by the organization.

Armstrong (1991) requests that management provide transformational leadership 'from the top' that can inspire people with a vision for the future: 'Management has to demonstrate that it knows where it is going, that it knows how to get there and that it can turn its vision into reality.' Vision is seen by Armstrong as the first step towards the implementation of a value-based commitment approach. He suggests that the vision must:

1 Integrate the values and needs of all stakeholders.
2 Be clearly communicated.
3 Be implemented in such a way as to validate itself as perceived by all stakeholders.

From experience, vision and mission statements often stress instrumental organizational values and the importance of the customer but not always the values and needs of employees. Clearly, individual employee needs must have room for fulfilment within overall company strategies and objectives. However, my own research of a cross-section of employees reveals that although subjects understood the values and objectives of their organization, they none the less disagreed that those objectives covered their work needs. Findings also suggested that employees who did not feel that their own objectives were adequately integrated were more inclined to indicate that their commitment to the company was comparatively low. This evidence may illustrate that transactional management and not transformational leadership was in practice.

In a separate survey, I asked junior and middle managers attending MBA and MSc part-time study whether their wish to gain a higher education qualification related to their wish to develop their own objectives in line with their companies. Over 90% suggested they were studying to help their own career. However, all answered negatively to the question 'Do you feel that your organization tries to understand your own needs?' and 'Do you feel that your organization attempts to integrate your needs into company objectives?' Given that the above simple polls and surveys contain a degree of validity, one could surmise and project the following views.

1 In practice, companies mainly display/communicate company values and objectives and expect employees to be committed to setting their own objectives in line with those of the organization.
2 Employee needs and objectives may not be assimilated and integrated into company objectives. The development of commitment to shared objectives seems unlikely.
3 If employees do not envisage their own values and needs are satisfactorily included as part of company objectives, then this is likely to affect employee commitment to the organization.

Adopting the 'balanced scorecard' (Kaplan and Norton, 1996) terminology, Templeton College interviewed board level executives from 23 leading multinational companies across several industry sectors. They found that 80% of the more successful companies involved the use of broad 'transformational scorecards'. The scorecard aim was to monitor customer performance and 'soft' areas such as behaviour and attitudes of employees as well as financial measures and indicators. Commenting on the Templeton study, Bird (1997) asserts that transformational leaders need to combine transformational customs with transformational style and process. Littlefield (1996) comments on the Halifax's move towards the adoption of the balanced scorecard assessment process. He offers, 'The organization should, of course, be aware of financial performance and internal controls, but in future these should be balanced with the needs of customers and staff.'

Management and leaders

Hannagan (1998, p. 39) suggests that 'Management implies leadership, and in fact the success or failure of managers can be judged on their leadership qualities.' In this sense, leadership can be viewed as a subset of management. Most practising managers and academic observers would suggest that management is concerned with bringing together resources, developing strategies, planning, organizing, coordinating and controlling activities in order to achieve agreed objectives. This sounds very similar to the notion of a transactional leader. Leaders, they suggest, select the goals and objectives of an organization and motivate people to achieve same. This sounds a little like transformational leadership. However, Kotter (1990a) argues that we must not confuse leadership with management.

Atkinson (1990) suggests that the difference between managers and leaders is that leaders do the right things and managers do things right. Typically, managers would use the power of a logical mind; leaders would use the power of intuition. Consequently, we might see managers as analytical, structured and deliberate, while leaders are flexible, experimental, visionary, innovative and even creative. Lower level management may be interested in doing the right things as well as doing things right. However, power relationships, operational necessities and perhaps time constraints mean they are normally constrained within the parameters of 'top management's' definition of what are the right things.

Organizational behaviour lecturers often refer to Bennis (1989) as having provided a means to promote discussion as to difference between management and leadership. Generally, Bennis appears to utilize characteristics from both trait and style theory (Table 2.1).

Kotter's (1990b) comparisons also help sum up the conceptual difference between leaders and managers (Table 2.2).

Attempting to single out what makes a good leader while avoiding references to any theoretical approaches, I conducted an enquiry with directors attending the Institute of Director's Diploma in Directorship between 1993 and 2002, at the University

Table 2.1 Manager and leader characteristics (Bennis)

Manager characteristics	Leader characteristics
Administers	Innovates
A copy	An original
Maintains	Develops
Focuses on systems	Focuses on people
Relies on control	Inspires trust
Short-range view	Long-range perspective
Asks how and when	Asks what and why
Eye on the bottom line	Eye on the horizon
Imitates	Originates
Accepts the status quo	Challenges the status quo
Classic good soldier	Own person
Does things right	Does the right thing

Source: Bennis (1989, p. 7)

Table 2.2 Manager and leader activities (Kotter)

Manager activities	Leader activities
Plan and budget	Establish direction
Organize and staff	Align people
Control and problem solve	Motivate and inspire
Focus on order and predictability	Focus on change

of Salford. The following were the recurring recorded characteristics of a good leader of an organization.

- Able to maintain integrity/ honesty
- Interpersonal skills
- Good communicator
- Risk taker (measured)
- High stamina/energy
- Astute as to internal politics
- Visionary
- Charismatic
- High intellect
- Approachable
- Financial awareness
- Trustworthy
- Credible
- Friendly
- Quick learner
- Team builder
- Able to get the best out of people
- Motivated
- Enthusiastic
- Sense of humour
- Strategic thinker
- Good 'time manager'
- Challenging
- Able to delegate
- Maintains integrity
- Decisive

Characteristics identified by directors confirm essential traits such as intelligence, quick learner, motivated etc. Director views also suggest an appropriate leadership style, for example, to be approachable, friendly and able to maintain integrity. Moreover, the list confirms the importance of transformational characteristics such as challenging, visionary and charismatic enthusiasm. One characteristic that is seemingly missing, is the ability of leaders to integrate needs and values of followers. The following list therefore adds potential abilities that leaders need to develop to encourage followership.

- Nurture a positive yet flexible culture
- Be positive
- Serve and support people
- Search for cohesive solutions
- Behave as a partner not a boss
- Elicit creativity
- Be inspirational
- Use emotional intelligence
- Develop people
- See simplicity
- Seek out potential in others
- Use empathy

The sub-set of characteristics offered above acknowledges the follower perspective. Similarly, Adair (1973) offers a model of leadership that encompasses the importance for leaders to look after three interlocking, interdependent and equally key aspects, those of addressing and attending to *task needs*, *group needs* and *individual needs*. Importantly, as pointed out by Adair, if any need is neglected then one of the others will suffer. What would develop follower commitment is an understanding that one's own needs are an integral component of the organization's value system. Such consideration introduces ethical dimensions of 'Rights' and 'Universalism' (Weiss, 1996):

> *Rights – Managers who overlook the rights of even one individual or group may jeopardize the implementation of a decision, policy, or procedure.*

> *Universalism (The Golden Rule) – Moral authority is based on the extent to which the intention of an act treats all persons as ends (not means) in themselves and with respect.*

What do followers seek from potential leaders? Taylor's (1962) survey work and listing below still appears to have a fair degree of face validity. He recorded characteristics that a majority of shopfloor workers wished to see in supervisor behaviour. Behaviour, that is, that workers require in order for them to follow a person they would regard as a leader. Taylor's listing appears to have greater scope than the supervisor–shopfloor worker relationship. Perhaps potential followers, regardless of level or position would welcome them.

1 *Thoughtfulness:* Treat followers with courtesy and with regard for their feelings.
2 *Impartiality:* Treat followers with equal consideration and avoid favouritism.
3 *Honesty:* Behave with a sense of fair play and trustworthiness.
4 *Proficiency:* Illustrate and display technical and people related skills.
5 *Person-knowledge:* Understand follower needs and behaviour.
6 *Control:* Accept the power the leadership position offers.
7 *Courage:* Be positive and committed.
8 *Directness:* Provide feedback regarding follower performance – but always with tact.
9 *Decisiveness:* When the occasion fits, 'call the shots'.
10 *Dignity:* Do not over-socialize.
11 *People interest:* People need and expect to be 'put ahead' of the task.
12 *Helpfulness:* In the eyes of followers the only real justification for a leader's existence is their ability and willingness to help followers attain goals and satisfy worker needs.

(after Taylor, 1962)

Taylor's twelfth and final comment seems to capture an obvious conclusion. Before organizational leaders can expect their workforce to be committed to the organization and follow, they must first consider the goals and needs of all stakeholders to ensure that they are the basis of objective setting activities. Leadership occurs when leaders integrate the needs of followers within the goal (Kakabadse *et al.*, 1988). Importantly, if an organization does not integrate the goals and needs of potential followers, how can the vision of the future be anything more than unacceptable to them?

Leadership, organizational culture and climate

Cultures can be identified as several individuals holding or sharing the same 'meanings' that influence or determine their behaviour. For example, groups of individuals may have a preferred way of doing things; they may share assumptions or agree dominant moral or instrumental values. They may also covertly or overtly acknowledge what is acceptable and what is not acceptable behaviour.

Organizational culture can be perceived as the sum of the various organizational sub-cultures. Importantly, a culture exists because it has worked well enough to be considered valid. Individuals may simply refer to their group or organizational culture as 'the way we do things around here'. However, Edgar Schein (1980) defines culture as a 'pattern of basic assumptions that a given group has invented or developed in learning to cope with the problems of external adaptation and internal integration'.

Schein (1980) suggests that the strength of a culture can be defined in terms of the stability of group membership and the intensity of the shared experience of the group. The advantage of creating a strong organizational culture is that it can be beneficial if complementary to the organization's environmental context. However, Legge (1989) suggests that 'if the strong culture is inconsistent with company ideology, commitment of members will be misdirected'. Handy (1989) advocates the development of a 'culture of consent'. The task for management can therefore be seen as working towards ensuring that people behave in a way that both complements the corporate direction of the company and adds value to the organization.

Peters and Waterman (1982) and Smircich (1983) see culture as a variable that can be changed within a short period. A cultural change activity might be effectively communicated through an organizational development programme. This is a normative and re-educative cultural change strategy. Some organizations claim some success, many would suggest that the process has been less rewarding than the outcome originally envisaged. Chin and Benne

(1976) suggest that an appropriate cultural change strategy must take account of the complexity of cultural factors and ignore the need for a 'quick fix', top-down and relatively 'mechanical' methodology.

Mintzberg (1988) is an exponent of the view that culture is subject to evolution over decades, is embedded in the context of organizational/social life or organizational context, and requires 'incremental' emergent managerial interventions, at strategic and operational levels. Therefore, cultural change must be strategic, for example, must be integrated with the organization's goals and corporate objectives (Quinn, 1982).

Georgiades and Macdonell (1998) comment that covert cultural issues are a little like the nine-tenths of the iceberg that remains under water. Consequently, this area is often viewed by senior management as one over which they have little or no control. Unfortunately, elements of organizational culture contain the very essence of competitive advantage.

The managerial or leadership culture, which might best be described as the 'corporate or overt culture' will predominantly reflect senior managerial values and interpretations. The characteristics and content of corporate culture are controlled and directed by leaders of the organization. It is an important element of organizational culture because it openly provides a declaration as to the norms and aims of the organization. Consequently, it is also the phenomenon that may hold the key to follower understanding and/or perceptions as to what leaders say, do and value. Moreover, because it is openly communicated, potential followers have the opportunity to relate their values to those of potential leaders.

Cultural values are provided to others through communication and interaction. Communication can be overt or covert and is contained within spoken, written language and non-verbal systems of symbolic representation. Managers, and potential leaders communicate by means of decision and behaviour influenced by accepted organizational values and priorities. The leadership group's development of long-standing policies and their adopted management style enforce shared understanding and provide 'meanings and values' that may affect follower behaviour. These building blocks of the organization's corporate culture affect the organizational climate.

Organizational climate might be viewed as less encompassing than organizational culture and seems more to do with people's perception of their environment. French *et al.* (1985) comment that organizational climate is a 'relatively persistent set of perceptions held by organization members concerning the characteristics of culture'. It is the atmosphere felt by members of the organization. Climate relates to the strength of feelings held by employees and is connected to the need for care and goodwill. Mullins (1996) comments that 'the organizational climate is characterized by the nature of the people–organization relationship and the superior–subordinate relationship'. Tagiuri and Litwin (1968) define climate as:

A relatively enduring quality of the internal environment of an organization that: (a) is experienced by its members; (b) influences their behaviour; and (c) can be described in terms of the values of a particular set of characteristics (or attributes) of the organization.

More recently, the attributes of organizational climate have been used as a benchmark for assessing the health of the organization, a topic which I believe will grow in importance. Mullins' (1996) features of a healthy organizational climate include:

1 The integration of organizational goals and personal goals.
2 Democratic functioning of the organization with full opportunities for participation.
3 Justice in treatment with equitable personnel and employee relations policies and practices.
4 Mutual trust, consideration and support among different levels of the organization.
5 Managerial behaviour and styles of leadership appropriate to the particular work situation.
6 Acceptance of psychological contract between the individual and the organization.
7 Recognition of people's needs and expectations at work, and individual differences and attributes.
8 Equitable systems of rewards based on positive recognition.
9 A sense of identity with, and loyalty to the organization, and a feeling of being a valued and important member.

A common-sense reaction to the above immediately suggests that many organizational leaders may have some difficulty substantiating the prominent existence of such features within their company's internal environment. However, the culture and climate of the organization is at the heart of the needs and expectations of the people that work within the organization. Hence, it should be managed to avoid dysfunction, low morale and poor performance from dissatisfied personnel. My own recommendation is that potential leaders should attempt continuous rather than spasmodic cultural management toward establishing a climate appropriate to potential followers.

A look at current management practice, priorities and values

As Kets de Vries (1996) suggests 'Leadership is like pornography. It's hard to define, but easy to recognize. Leadership is both a process and a quality.' Theory suggests that leadership is a process involving management abilities such as those listed in Table 2.1. It is also a quality that is informed by the leader characteristics listed in Tables 2.1 and 2.2. Importantly, from a follower perspective, both leadership process and quality should be informed by emotional intelligence – the ability of leaders to be self-aware, to understand the impact of their behaviour, and to 'work with' and incorporate understanding of people. This seems such an obvious aspect of leadership, that it is intriguing to ask the question why managers might fail to incorporate the view within their behaviour and actions. Consequently, in addition to looking for management behaviour that might encourage follower-ship, I have looked for behaviour in management that might not be conducive or may even be detrimental to followership. Key to a better understanding was the identification of quite common characteristics and possible consequences of potential leaders' theory-of-action. Analysis of the literature provides focus, and particular acknowledgement is given here to the casework and writings of Argyris and Schön.

Theory-of-action

Argyris and Schön (1974, 1978) suggest that a person's theory-of-action is that which determines all deliberate human behaviour. The theories we accept as valid are those that primarily determine the way we act. A fundamental idea is that human beings have theories-of-action in their heads as to how to behave. This is true of leaders and followers.

It is common to refer to theory-in-use when commenting on behaviour. Theory-in-use is defined as the 'theory-of-action constructed from observation of actual behaviour' (Argyris and Schön, 1974, p. 25; Argyris, 1997). Theories-of-use are said to maintain a person's 'field of constancy' (Argyris and Schön, 1974, p. 16). They specify the governing variables and their critical relationship to one another. Simply, theory-of-use specifies the variables used by a person that they are interested in, and to which they give priority. They determine action.

It seems feasible that senior management adopting similar roles will also adopt a theory-of-use that has similar characteristics. The dangers of generalizing are acknowledged. However, what characteristics might be shared? Based on research, characteristics of what the author terms a conventional theory-of-action are explored by reference to scientific management, the rational-economic model and leadership decisions and values. When combined, they provide evidence as to why management may often be viewed as managers and not leaders. Readers may wish to consider each of the following three sections as to whether they apply to managers and organizations known to them.

Scientific management

Scientific management was an attempt to uncover aspects of work and organization that would inevitably produce efficiency. The concept is generally associated with Taylor (1911). Several others contributed to the development of scientific management principles, including Fayol (1949) and Gilbreth (1908).

Taylor suggested that management could not demand efficiencies, as they have no idea about how much they could expect if the job were done efficiently. To achieve what he described as 'externalizing knowledge', scientific research methods would be required. Jobs, he suggested, need to be broken down into component parts, and this would make it easier to study them – scientifically. Consequently, industrial age companies created distinctions between groups of employees. The intellectual elite and engineers were separated from employees who produced products and delivered services. Readers may note the similarity between several Theory X assumptions and scientific management.

Today, technological improvement has meant that the percentage of people who do traditional work functions has reduced. Kaplan and Norton (1997) add that, 'machines are designed to run automatically, the people's job is to think, to problem-solve'. Moreover, a mass of information comes from all directions. Consequently, even individuals still involved in direct production and service delivery are asked for their suggestions on how to improve quality, reduce costs, decrease cycle times, etc. Such activities would have quite easily been interpreted as a function of elite management and not the responsibility of 'the workers'.

Organizational structures have been reshaped so that more workers are closely involved in day-to-day decisions. Organizational change now encompasses the move towards autonomous groups with greater managerial responsibilities and devolved budgetary control. The term empowerment is used to describe the process of devolving responsibility to its lowest possible level within the organization. It is seen as crucial if organizations wish to be flexible and responsive to market needs. Moreover, Litchfield (1996) reports that empowerment programmes can lead to major reductions in cost. The approach is also seen as motivational in the sense that incumbents who possess it are inherently satisfying their need for self-esteem. However, Morton (1998) is critical of the process. He states that 'the born again senior manager tells the workforce that they are empowered. What is left of middle management is bypassed and self-managed teams are created. This leaves top management to concentrate on pacifying shareholders. Unfortunately, either the corporate engine will not start or it is badly tuned; in any event, it still cannot compete.' Quality suffers and top management criticizes the empowered workforce, only to find that 'empowerment means no controls, no system, no ownership, no instruction and no improvement'. From experience, empowerment is viewed by employees as a notion devolving responsibility. However, many perceive that they still have little real authority and receive very little support from senior managers when things go wrong. Moreover, the idea is sometimes related to a reduction in staff numbers.

Morton comments that 'it is no wonder that employees try to keep their heads down when such initiatives are introduced'. Wooldridge (1995) confirms this view; he states 'As we put our organizations through processes of downsizing and de-layering, the simultaneous exhortations for teamwork, empowerment, partnership and shared vision seem hypocritical.' Arie de Geus (in Pickard, 1998) comments that downsizing (sometimes referred to as rightsizing) is anathema to him because it disturbs the sense of identity that is vital to the organizational community. Research suggests that organizational change such as rightsizing can have a detrimental impact on employee wellbeing and motivation. Cameron *et al.* (1993) suggest that 70 per cent of managers had commented that morale and trust (and eventually productivity) suffered following company downsizing.

Scientific management is also based on the following assumption:

Scientific management . . . has for its very foundation the first conviction that the true interests of employer and employee are one and the same. (Taylor, 1911, p. 10)

Taylor's statement clearly displays a unitary view of organizations. However, unitary goals will be difficult to achieve if we accept that for many purposes organizations are more usefully thought of as pluralistic entities – that is, they characteristically contain a rich variety of groupings with distinctive attitudes, interests and concerns. All human behaviour is self-interested so that achieving cooperation towards collective objectives is inherently problematic (Olson, 1965). The presence of inter-group or inter-departmental conflict reflects the fact that an organization is composed of multiple collectives with distinct goals to which individuals can become committed (Lawrence and Lorsch, 1967; Walton and Dutton, 1969). Managers may wish to convince employees that there is little conflict between the goals of employees and those of the organization. However, so often efficiencies and productivity are obtained by employees having to work harder and not necessarily smarter. There is logic in management suggesting to employees that by being committed to the organization, employees should help secure their own employment. In reality, organizational improvements often result in a need for employees to be re-trained, re-deployed or for the firm 'to have to let employees go' – to make their jobs redundant.

The above extracts clearly show a potential gap between espoused rhetoric, for example 'empowerment', and senior management theory-in-use based on classic principles. Morgan (1994) states that employees get disillusioned because rhetoric is contradicted by processes that continue to reinforce the status quo. Appeals to cast off the heritage of Taylorist principles are not new. What has given them fresh bite has been the message that the control and compliance model, though highly relevant for a post-war era dominated by a mass production system, is inappropriate for the modern world (Sabel, 1982). The requirement for an increase in employee knowledge, skill and application suggests that Taylorist principles may not be sufficient for organizations that are increasingly reliant on employee commitment. It would seem that scientific management principles worked well enough when management attention is drawn to physical responses of employees, less well when the organization is paying for the contents of the employee's mind.

The rational-economic model

An important element leading to the adoption of a conventional theory-of-action was thought to be the influence of rational-economic thinking. Biddle and Evenden (1990) suggest the use of this popular notion should relate to a framework and guide to analysis rather than be a 'straitjacket stereotype'. Unravelling the notion, it can be argued that when scientific management theory and capitalist economics are combined, the result is a rational-economic approach to managing.

Rational-economics is related to the economic or econological model and offers conventional wisdom based on the ideals of Taylor (1911) and Gilbreth (1908). The view sees people and organizations as individuals 'mainly motivated by economic incentives, [who] will always act in a calculating way to maximize economic gain for themselves' (Biddle and Evenden, 1990).

The economically rational doctrine is essentially the same as that advocated by Adam Smith (1759). When Smith's theory of the operation of economic markets is used as a basis for management, it leads to a very strong emphasis on the role of money. It is often assumed that economic incentives primarily motivate people, and that offering or withholding financial rewards can effectively control people. The ideology in practice gives management what appears to be a rational argument. The inference of the approach suggests that any human behaviour that may involve feelings or emotion is irrational. This means that organizations need to be designed and managed in a way that neutralizes and controls people's feelings. The analogy of the well-oiled machine offered by Mintzberg (1988) comes to mind. Because of the success of the scientific approach, managers still tend to put total reliance upon the need of 'workers' for an adequate amount of pay – pay for conformance to standards associated with efficient performance. However, Murlis (1996) categorically states that 'pay is usually way down the list of what is most important to people'.

In organizations, the performance maximization measures of return on investment (ROI) and return on capital employed (ROCE) and their derivative financial ratios are perceived as quantitative, endowed with mathematical reason, and they help reduce uncertainty. They are techniques associated with the rational-economic management approach and its overriding philosophy, and therefore are likely to be perceived by management as wholly desirable.

Economic priorities in the private sector relate to the objective of maximizing chosen corporate economic objectives and managing by means of a strong preference for financial performance indicators. From a public sector viewpoint, poor budgetary control may lead to a greater burden on public expenditure, a possible increase in the nation's borrowing requirement and interest payable by government. Consequently, public services have been directed to concentrate on conventional private sector approaches, for example, tight control of expenditure. It now seems reasonable to state that 'the genericist argument that all organizations function with similar economic and financial goals can still be supported' (Cooper, 1993). To test this assertion, I conducted a survey with Directors attending the Institute of Directors Diploma programmes at Salford University between 1993 and 2002. Over one hundred Directors were simply requested to clarify the key objectives used by them in their organization. Organizations ranged in size, industry and sector, although the majority represented the private sector. More than

80% identified the essential objective of the company as the need to maximize profit or for tight cost control. More than 30% added the need for growth or stability. Only two organizations suggested that they were in business to enjoy themselves and to make work an enjoyable experience for other employees. Both organizations had turnovers below £5 million and fewer than 50 employees. Referring to the importance of customers and employees as the true assets of an organization, Reichheld (1997) comments that owners of smaller businesses deal face to face with true assets and are deeply and constantly involved in improving the flow of value to and from their customers and employees. He comments, 'that small business owners do not use accounting statements to run their businesses, they use them only to calculate their taxes or deal with bankers'.

Armstrong (1996, p. 182) confirms that 'the overriding goal of most organizations is to maximize profitability'. Moreover, during my own survey it was common for Directors who identified the need for the maximization of profit to question the judgement of organizations (mostly small business owners) who suggested the need to satisfy other stakeholders. One Director humorously commented that 'Director's need on the one side to ensure a happy, contented and a well-paid workforce, and on the other side – make enormous profits', adding with a wry smile, 'I bet you can't figure out which one really predominates my thinking!'

It is likely that one reason an individual is chosen to be a manager relates to his or her ability to internalize and be successful in relation to using economically rational ideals. This would include behaviour that may emphasize the overall import-ance of company profit. Ellen Van Velsor and Jean Brittain Lesley (1994) of the Centre for Creative Leadership, Greensboro, North Carolina, conducted a study of 15 'Fortune 500' manufacturing and service companies in the United States, and 24 large companies in Belgium, France, Germany, Italy, Spain and the UK. A total of 62 executives were asked to talk about managers they knew who had been successful and risen to the top of their organization. The authors noted that 'people who are successful in their early careers seem proficient in task-based profit-related leadership but are presented with a challenge when job demands begin to require a balance with a more employee-based relation-ship-orientated style of leadership'.

While analysis supports the view that short-term financial indicators are likely to form an essential part of senior manage-ment theory-of-action, potential followers may not have intern-alized the managerial profit motive. For example, Wheeler and Sillanpaa conducted a detailed survey of 2200 Body Shop employees as part of a wider social audit. The survey found that while most employees endorsed the group's values, they had reservations about the everyday realities of working for the company. Fewer than half the employees agreed that the company's commitment to being a caring company was apparent to them on a day-to-day basis (also see Arkin, 1997). They offer that the development of loyal, inclusive stakeholder relationships will become one of the most important determinants of commercial viability.

Failure to appreciate attributes other than financial imperatives may adversely affect morale, loyalty, trust, motivation and commitment. Such an environment would not be conducive to followership. Arie de Geus quoted by Pickard (1998) states that management should be 'concerned with ensuring long-term survival [rather] than with making a quick buck, after all, a person's number-one priority is survival'. He adds, 'We do not live to make a profit, in contrast, we make profit in order to live.' The recent success of his book *The Living Company* asserts that profits are a symptom of success and not an end in themselves.

Reichheld (1997) states that the current approach to management might simply be called the profit theory. He suggests that a new theory should see the fundamental mission of business not as profit, but as value creation – a means rather than an end, a result as opposed to a purpose. Reichheld differentiates between virtuous and destructive profit. Virtuous profit can be seen as the result of an organization's ability to build and develop the assets of the company. It is the result of creating value. Destructive profit does not come from value creation and value sharing; it comes from exploiting assets, from selling off a business's true balance sheet.

Profits and budgets alone seem an unreliable measure of organizational performance. The maximization of owner wealth is probably a more credible organizational purpose. It is only maximization of wealth that takes account of both return and risk simultaneously. Wealth maximization also balances short- and long-term benefits in a way that profit-maximizing goals cannot (McLaney, 1994). Moreover, owners or influential bodies who control the financing of an organization are not likely to be impressed with management who do not maximize wealth from all resources, including human.

The need to understand social behaviour in organizations and maximizing wealth should not be viewed as in conflict. For example, Guest (1998) supports Huselid's (1998) view that traditional sources of competitive advantage, such as access to capital or economies of scale, are becoming less important and that people instead increasingly provide the key. In a survey involving 31 chief executives, Price and Dauphinais (1998) assert that the get-rich quick routes to profitability have been exhausted – people have taken precedence.

Adshead (1997) comments that potential owner investors should ask two key questions of senior management. First, is the Board fit for the purpose; is it competent, focused and acting together? Second, has the company really engaged and motivated its people successfully? He asserts that enquiry relating to the latter question is pursued less often. However, both questions relate to the maximization of wealth.

Like financial resources, one can perceive people as an opportunity. Their knowledge, skills and potential application are an essential source of revenue. In many ways, thinking of employees as a cost is not rational. However, it would seem that the absolute importance of economic concerns might often override social and moral obligations and judgements. Given this backdrop, management may implicitly treat employees as a problem resource. After all, employees are costly to maintain and because they are human, complex and unpredictable, management cannot easily use experience to help them man-manage. It is offered that such a view may become part of management thinking.

Trist (1963) and his associates at the Tavistock Institute carried out extensive studies about the effects of technological 'change'. Their findings suggest that change dictated by economic thought alone can disrupt the social organization of employees. The result is decreased efficiency, social difficulties and a psychological loss of 'meaning'. Moreover, Glautier and Underdown (1994) state that if management use only conventional measurements of revenues, expenses, profit, cost variances and output, it is possible that short-run economic gains may be achieved at the expense of long-run goals.

Studies by Hutchinson, Kinnie and Purcell (1996) suggest that one main reason senior management are readier to adopt 'flavour of the month' and 'one-off' improvement programmes, is because it has always been difficult to establish a clear link between good practice people management and improved business perform-ance. However, 'research is starting to establish links between increased employee job satisfaction and improved organizational profitability' (Sheffield University, 1998). Moreover, Huselid's (1998) work finds that firms with significantly above-average scores on an index of high-performance (or high-commitment) work practices provided an extra market value per employee of between £10 000 and £40 000. On this basis, continuous invest-ment in people pays off handsomely. More pessimistically, challenges to conventional theory-of-action and rational-econom-ics still seem limited.

Borrowing from scientific management principles, rational-economic management can be seen as a unitary goal-oriented belief system that is scientific in its approach. It assumes that priorities are always understood, consequences are always known and official goals are unitarily agreed. The notion urges managers to use, where feasible, computational methods based on hard data. Kets de Vries (1996) comments that 'our society and most of our business life is organized around airtight logic, numbers, and explanations that make sense'. He adds, 'senior management are sensitive to numbers and figures but treat people as anonymous entities'. If true in practice, potential followers will obviously sense and object to such an approach.

Rational-economics is at the extreme end of a rational-social continuum of decision making behaviour (Luthans, 1992, p. 497). The notion is also linked with what is called T-type management. It is management bias stemming from 'interest, indeed success, in the technical aspects of their function'. Logical with a technical focus, it attempts to discover objective 'best means' solutions towards perceived agreed ends. Biddle and Evenden (1990) comment, 'when people are promoted to senior management, they find it difficult to take off their technical blinkers and this creates problems'. The implication is that leaders of organizations need a different approach toward solving problems and making decisions.

Leadership decisions

Argyris and Schön (1974, p. 13) state an organization is a theory-of-action. It is a 'cognitive enterprise undertaken by individual members'. Theory-of-action is embedded in decisions that members take on behalf of the organization, and 'decisions are governed by collective rules for decision'. From the author's perspective, an organizational corporate theory-of-action is the theory-of-action which has been adopted by senior management. It contains the determinates by which senior management manage their organization. These determinates are also associated with follower perceptions of senior management. They are therefore crucial as to analysis of the leader–follower process.

Most publications on decision making usually include and suggest the following sequence of events:

1 The problem is clearly identified and defined.
2 Data is collected.
3 The data is analysed and alternatives are evaluated.
4 A decision is made based on analysis and evaluation.
5 The decision is implemented.

This common approach complements rational-economic think-ing and suggests applying logic can successfully accomplish decision making based on a rigid and well-defined series of activities. For instance, Lindblom (1959) points out that the first way by which the administrator might try to make a policy decision is to aspire to a rational-deductive ideal. Such an approach follows 'the ideal of science; a complete deductive system transferred to the field of "values" and application'. However, the idea attracts important questions. For example:

1 Can problems be easily identified and defined?
2 What data should be collected, and should behavioural data related to potential followers as well as technical and financial data related to shareholders and customers enter the senior management decision-making process?

Three associated issues are worth consideration. First, the conventional model of decision making suggests that effective problem definition should specify the standard according to which a situation is considered a problem (above which it is satisfactory). Consequently, the first step in decision making is the manager's perception that a situation or organizational process is in a state of disequilibrium. Disequilibrium can be described as an aspect of the company that is 'not what it ought to be' or does not conform to what decision makers would like to see as to desired outcomes. Before recognition of a state of disequilibrium, senior management decision makers will need to be aware that a problem exists. Adherence to economically rational issues may provide some blind spots. Moreover, in some circumstances management may be reluctant to admit a problem exists.

Second, decision making is often considered to consist of problem solving, or planning, or organizing, and is sometimes extended to include all aspects of thinking and acting. However, Hitt *et al.* (1996) suggest that many decision makers either 'overlook or do not fully complete the first step in the decision-making process', i.e. determine objectives. They argue that the objective is likely to focus on 'solving the problem'; therefore, only converse thought may take place or, at best, diverse thinking may be limited.

Third, literature on organizational decision making suggests that 'choice making' is an essential management function (Bross, 1953; George, 1964; Feldman and Kanter, 1965). 'To make a decision means to make a judgement regarding what one ought to do in a certain situation after having deliberated on some alternative courses of action' (Ofstad, 1961). However, Kluckholm

(1951) warns of a tendency to evaluate and make choices rather than analyse as a basic human characteristic.

Lindblom (1959, 1968) terms the decision process as the strategy of disjointed incrementalism. The decision process proceeds by successive limited comparisons. Lindblom's view is that decision is most often incremental, restricted, means oriented, reconstructive, serial, remedial and fragmented. This practice limits information, restricts choices and shortens horizons. The problem will worsen as competitive pressure creates continuous environmental and contextual turbulence surrounding organizations. Instability, unpredictability and constant change are descriptions commonly used by Directors (Institute of Directors, 1993–2002) while attempting to characterize work pressure, their organization and market. Consequently, senior management may not have sufficient time for 'intricate reckoning' associated with the complexity that surrounds some problems.

Pettigrew (1977, 1985) accounts for incrementalism as the result of social and political processes in organization. Research studies show the extent to which strategic decisions are characterized by high degrees of bargaining and solicitation (Mintzberg *et al.*, 1976; Fahey, 1981; Lyles, 1981). Such activity emphasizes masculine features within the decision-making process, for example, the need to compete and achieve in an atmosphere of high energy. Such a climate may not be conducive to widening the decision making process to include consideration of organizational behavioural issues.

The more a situation might be defined as 'technical', the greater the possibility that, over time, one situation might be seen as similar to another. Consequently, past knowledge and experience can more easily be used and change more easily managed. It should not be surprising, therefore, that many managers favour this approach. However, the hard decision-making approach has critics. Notably, Checkland (1988) has done much to overcome technical and positivistic thinking by arguing against the extremes of technical rationality and, in his view, applying reductionist science to human situations:

> *Human affairs call for a problem and process orientation, rather than a technique-orientated approach.* (Checkland, 1988, p. 27)

The soft systems method aims to integrate all aspects of the environment inside and outside the problem boundary. In this way, the approach widens and encompasses aspects that may have been poorly considered if the hard systems approach had been adopted. Checkland's problem-solving process seems suitable for messy, people-related problems. Unfortunately, his soft systems approach is sometimes viewed by management as somewhat cumbersome, over-elaborate, time-consuming and costly. This is unfortunate, because in most organizational problems someone is involved. It could even be suggested that all problems to some degree are human problems no matter whether the problem can be labelled 'technical', 'economic', or 'human' in nature.

Simon (1960) suggests that management is synonymous to decision making and decisions most often fall within two polarized categories. He differentiates decisions from those that are repetitive and routine requiring programmed responses in a habitual manner, to non-programmed decisions which are those situations that are not cut-and-dried, require new strategies and rely on the intellectual capacities of the organization's decision makers. Senior management are typically involved in non-programmable decision-making activities. They create policy and make decision that relates to the achievement of corporate strategy. Consequently, they need to exercise choice in compli-cated situations involving conflicting goals and values, many minds, and high expenditure in terms of money and time. Selection among alternatives is an important concept of decision making. Similarly, prioritizing stakeholders is also a function of senior management choice.

When a manager [or management team] decide, they will have reflected on personal experience to provide a frame of reference *vis-à-vis* the situation. As Allport explains, 'the way a man [person] defines his situation constitutes for him its reality' (Allport, 1955). It seems likely those parties viewed by senior management as influential stakeholders will form an essential part of a manager's understanding of the realities of their situation. Stakeholder analysis can be revealing as to which stakeholder yields the most power and influence. Arkin (1997) comments that stakeholder analysis is not a new idea. He quotes Tony Blair as saying stakeholding is one of the oldest strategies for creating value. However, stakeholder power may not be equally distributed. For example, in the private sector, shareholders are important because they supply the company with capital. They expect a good return for their investment. In the public sector, government are important because they provide funds. Custom-ers, regardless of sector, are also important because they supply the company with income or consume a service. However, some suppliers and employee-potential followers may be viewed as less important because they can be viewed as taking funds out of the company. This is a simplistic viewpoint, but none the less commonly recognized (Institute of Directors, 1993–2002). Pugh *et al.* (1983) assert that 'decisions should not be taken without an intricate reckoning of the interests involved and the demands of all who are interested'. Pugh's democratic notion may not be very practical in many organizations today. Nevertheless, according to Dennis and Dennis (1991) senior management must take a strategic overview on behalf of the whole organization. They have overall responsibility for consideration and integration of all stakeholders needs.

Unfortunately, it is not easy for aspiring leaders; scripts exist within the organization that contain those aspects the organization promotes as important. They may not be in written form but can be witnessed in rituals and ceremonies which assist in maintaining previously held paradigms (Meyer and Rowan, 1977; Trice and Beyer, 1984). Wilkins calls them organizational stories that do nothing short of controlling the organization. There is also an acceptable language within an organization which may limit factors beyond the present paradigm from consideration (Meyer, 1982). All act to legitimize and preserve core beliefs, power relationships, priority values and what are regarded as acceptable assumptions.

Values are at the core of management thinking, priority setting and decision making. They provide normative standards and represent enduring beliefs that a specific type of conduct or end state is preferred (after Jacob *et al.*, 1962). Values act as guidance systems. Consequently, values inform every stage of the senior management decision-making process. Argyris and Schön (1974, 1978), Argyris (1994) and Schön (1996) refer to a 'Model-One' managerial theory-in-use. They argue that despite continued research all over the world, the model's values in organizations seem to have no variance.

Governing values held by those applying a 'Model-One' theory-of-use typify:

1 A desire to be in unilateral control of situations.
2 A need to win.
3 A need to suppress negative feelings in self and others.
4 Behaviour that is as rational as possible.

The model's values reinforce previous sections by first suggesting that a conventional senior management theory-of-action is likely to contain a propensity for classical principles based on a rational and scientific foundation of the need for control. Second, the overall management objective still appears to be that management wish to be seen as achieving by acting rationally. Third, such an approach may not be overly conducive to the leader–follower relationship. For instance, it has been argued that organizations today rely on employee willingness to apply their knowledge as well as their physical abilities in order for the organization to 'win' via increases in efficiency, productivity and profitability. Accepting that people have emotions, suppressing rather than addressing feelings may not be conducive to a firm's overall performance.

Values held by managers may be unconsciously adhered to. They may have remained unchallenged for such a lengthy period that they have become automatic. Sparrow and Pettigrew (1988) point to the need to look in more depth at what senior management (potential leaders) are doing in terms of shaping the behaviour of people. More positively, Kakabadse (1995) suggests that until recently it would have been unusual for chief executives to be making value statements about people. It is common today for organizations to state that it values its people. This seems a step in the right direction if managers are to be perceived as leaders and employees are to become more willing to follow. However, Guest (1991) comments that analysis must go beyond espoused values of the organization to what really happens. Importantly, Paine (1994) suggests that company leaders must be personally committed, credible and willing to act on the values they espouse. Moreover, if employees see potential leaders promoting very distinctive value statements, but behaving in different ways, then employees will cease to trust them and followership will become less likely. Handy (1995) states that 'If it is true that organizations do not trust their people, then there is a piquant irony in the fact that they expect people to trust them absolutely.'

To state the obvious, if senior management do not make decisions that secure the interests of the most powerful stake-holders in the organization, then they risk losing their position. For senior management, it would appear that self-interest can be obtained by conforming to expectations. This will be achieved by allowing parameters and paradigms to become set within the decision-making processes that subdue issues not related to a given specification, measurement, or satisfaction of key stake-holder groups. Thompson (1967) asserts that organizations act rationally to increase their evaluations or ratings by others on whom they are dependent. It follows that senior management will 'act rationally' on behalf of the owners.

Weber's 'typology of domination' is based on the various strategies which 'rulers' implement through the promulgation of certain beliefs and their partial and provisional acceptance by followers (Reed, 1985). The implementation of dominant values is not new. It would also seem that conflict is expected between dominant values and social needs. From this perspective, 'fol-lowers' may be urged or perhaps coerced to subordinate their own values in preference for the rulers. Generally, the organization can be seen as buying the services and obedience of its employees and avoiding the irrational side of their nature by a system of authority, power and controls.

McGregor (1966) and Argyris (1964) criticize the unidirectional 'common-sense assumptions' which they suggest so often govern managerial behaviour. Richard Finn, Director of Strategic HR Consultancy at Crane Davies comments, 'even managerial common sense tends to be anything but common. Senior management best practice in relation to the management of people in organizations is simply not happening' (Finn, 1998). As the application of employee knowledge becomes more important, a means of countering what he terms 'the power paradox' must be found. Reed provides a possible clue to alleviating difficulties:

The function of management is to maintain equilibrium so that individual needs and organizational demands neatly coincide (Reed, 1985, p. 23).

Reed's view confirms the 'Leadership Grid' notion that leadership means balance in terms of people and production. A key reason for adopting a balanced criterion of individual and organizational issues within the decision-making process is simply that validation of the decision and the decision process rests on whether the decision can be successfully implemented. Perhaps a preferred definition of a quality decision would be that it includes employee acceptance. In particular, Vroom (1964, 1966, 1974) comments that the acceptance or commitment by subordinates to execute the decision effectively will be a key factor as to the effectiveness of decisions. It is unfortunate that the word subordinates demerits the importance of employees as essential stakeholders in the organization.

Physical separation of senior management from many employees begs the question 'how is senior management theory-of-action communicated to employees?' The answer is that the decision-making process acts as a conduit communicating dominant and priority aspects. Just as management is synonymous with decision making, potential follower perception of managers as leaders may be synonymous with decisions management take. Followers will judge management as leaders based on the repercussions and implications that decisions have on them.

To summarize, decisions are the theory-in-use outcome of senior management theory-in-action, and outcomes reflect governing managerial or leader values and priorities – the effects of which all stakeholders feel. Clearly, for managers to be viewed as leaders by followers, they need to make decisions in such a way that employees feel their interests are included. Moreover, managers who do not consider the implementation of each decision and its consequence on subordinates take the risk that potential followers will simply remain employees.

Leadership: a need for change?

Definitions of leadership record different viewpoints and interests. The most appropriate support the idea that leadership is an influencing process involving two or more persons, a leader and a follower, or followers. Leadership theory recorded in this chapter provides useful explanation and an essential backdrop for discussion. From an academic rigour perspective, the author may have some concerns about sampling, and that some theories work to establish extremes and some tend to over-simplify. As a practising manager, the author has far fewer worries. Most leadership theories seem to have stood the test of time, and several offer reasonable and helpful explanations for leadership behaviour.

Based on experience, some people appear more predisposed to behaviour that would be perceived of as portraying leadership characteristics, and some may prove to have biological beginnings, although absolute links with ancestry and genealogy seem a step too far. The effects of the environment and the possibility for leaders to evolve and develop leadership abilities should not be precluded. Contingency theory highlights the importance and effect of the environment. Path–goal theory also provides benefit in that it acknowledges followers' need for rewards. As for trait theory, although personality may be relatively stable, behaviour can be changed and so certain behavioural dimensions might be subdued or enhanced. Although personality instruments can be abused, the use of profiling might assist in ensuring employees feel comfortable in certain roles and job positions.

It was the author's experience while working as a personnel/ human resource practitioner that many employees commented that the 'style' of their manager affects their performance, so much so that pragmatically this theory should not be ignored. Supportive and participative styles rather than autocratic task-centred styles seem the most practical. However, a personal preference would be for leaders to balance styles rather than work to polarized extremes.

Transformational or charismatic leadership emphasizes the effect leaders can have on followers. Its focus on senior management vision and the need to motivate in order to revitalize organizations has been well received in most academic and managerial quarters. It is a shame that to illustrate this concept observers often recall 'Great Man' political and military figures as examples, thus giving a feeling of *déjà vu*.

This chapter also suggests that managers, especially senior managers wishing to become leaders of followers, might review their own theory-of-action. Behaviour expected by followers typified in Jack Taylor's listing will be difficult to achieve without so doing. Unfortunately, 'rational-economic management techniques have been incredibly influential in the way private and public sector managers approach their responsibilities. Colleagues reinforce this behaviour due to the approach's perceived logic' (Cooper, 1993).

Manifestations of rational-economic management practice suggest that the philosophy is pervasive and becomes a dominant paradigm. Moreover, concentration on economic/financial concerns moves emphasis to what might best be referred to as 'economic-rationality'. This notion clearly provides an inviting ideology that managers find easy to justify, endorse and maintain. Few managers would admit to using a Theory X style of management, adhering to scientific management principles and of acting economically rational. None the less, many assumptions contained therein appear to have survived in what the author describes as a conventional theory-of-action. In the shadow of Argyris and Schön, the notion might be seen as the legacy of scientific management and rational-economics.

It is acknowledged that the needs of the company and its owners pressure management to achieve good financial results. Thus, to concentrate on economic performance indicators seems a natural managerial response. Consequently, criticism of management for managing the only way they can seems arrogant and inappropriate. Unlike managers, however, leaders must influence all stakeholders: customers, shareholders, superiors, suppliers, employees etc. Influencing all simultaneously would appear exceptionally difficult. None the less, despite obvious difficulties of conflicting values and objectives, Kakabadse *et al.* (1988) strongly suggest that leadership is an influencing process and thus leaders must influence all interested parties. We might add that employees will only recognize managers as leaders if they can be seen to be representing their needs.

Management, in particular senior management, is all about making decisions in response to identified environmental problems or opportunities. However, what seems fundamental to decision making is the decision process itself – the act of thinking. There is an implicit if not explicit human dimension in every decision. Acknowledgement immediately begs the question that if humans are an integral part of every problem, leaders should integrate the human element into their thinking process. The leadership process should therefore involve making decisions that incorporate behavioural as well as technical aspects.

Support for the above conclusion is partially found in post-modernist notions that suggest rationality, logic and scientific management is inappropriate (if not unreal) due to the speed of change, competition and environmental chaos surrounding organizations. An environment where McHale (1993) categorically states that there is now a strong case for putting ethics first and managerial economics second. Connock and Johns (1995) state that ethical values should embrace an organization's vision, its core values and its operational code of conduct, and in particular the way it treats its employees. However, Johns (1995) states that 'Business ethics is good business, but some organizations adopting ethical concerns are jumping on a fashionable bandwagon rather than acting from real conviction.' O'Brien (1995) provides evidence that little has changed concerning employee perception of ethical management. Results from her studies of six major UK companies revealed that only 13% of employees felt valued by their company, and only 9% of employees believed that top management had a sincere interest in them. Moreover, only 8% of employees considered management could be counted on to give employees a fair deal. This is not a good environment to develop improved leader–follower relations!

Leaders must find ways of influencing all stakeholders by means of both instrumental and psychological means. Thus, support is provided for the idea that psychological contracts with potential followers must go beyond rational-economic thinking and the simple use of instrumental rewards. Curnow (1995) states that the re-engineered world of work cries out for a re-engineering of the psychological contract between corporations and their senior talent. Bower (1996), describing the psychological contract for the twenty-first century, comments, 'there seems little doubt that there is now a call for greater balance between what employees contribute to the organization and what they get out of it'. Armstrong (1996, p. 327) describes several principles relating to a mutual commitment firm. Included is the need for top management to value commitment, that there is an effective voice for human resources in strategy making and governance, and there is a climate of cooperation and trust. Levering's (1988) quid pro quo 'partnership' model supports the argument that employee commitment to the organization should be balanced by employer commitment to the employee. In support of Levering, Eisenberger *et al.* in two studies (1986, 1990) comment that individual employees within organizations form common beliefs as to the extent to which their contributions are valued by the organization.

They add, 'Individuals support organizations when they perceive that the organization is actively supporting them'.

To conclude, leaders need to accept that without followers leaders do not exist – only managers remain. Moreover, followers who merely lead without dedicating a high degree of energy towards the organization are unlikely to be 'following leaders'. Perhaps they are following managers. In the light of analysis, the author would suggest that organizational leadership is both a quality and a process; it involves managerial efficiency but concentrates on leader effectiveness that results in the provision of willing followers.

Complementary to the findings of leadership theory, Bennis (1989) suggests that leaders inspire trust and confidence from subordinates; they focus on people, develop them and do the right thing in the eyes of people. He adds, 'to survive in the twenty-first century, organizations and other institutions are going to need a new generation of leaders – leaders not managers.' It is difficult to disapprove of the philosophy behind his thinking.

Followers are extremely unlikely to follow someone they do not trust. Trust is something that cannot be requested – only given. Moreover, trust must be earned. The way leaders can earn the trust of employees is to behave with integrity, never forgetting the needs of those that follow. Confidence in leaders will be built over a long time. Unfortunately, it is also easily destroyed. This chapter has argued that managers may have become glued to an outdated mindset. They need to think outside the conventional theory-of-action box. While the content of this box provides a comfort zone for managers, unthinking acceptance is likely to subdue the development of the leader–follower relationship. Importantly, findings suggest that if conventional theory-of-action notions permeate organizations, managerial thinking, and therefore guide and dominate management behaviour, potential followers are unlikely to view their management as potential leaders.

Bennis's suggestion that leaders must do the right things in the eyes of people is clearly good advice. However, this raises the question as to how leaders know what is right in the eyes of potential followers. The following chapter provides some answers by considering the second essential element, that of potential follower commitment and work motivation.

Case study 1: Sven-Goran Eriksson

The appointment of Sven-Goran Eriksson as coach to the England soccer team took the world of English football by surprise. A Swede from a modest background, he had risen to make his mark as a successful coach in Europe but was almost unknown in England when he was chosen to coach the national football team, which at the time was seen as under-performing. Sven's appointment prompted criticism and controversy the moment it was announced. The selection of a foreigner was an unprecedented act. Moreover, his appointment was set against a BBC poll that suggested 40% of online voters expected Terry Venables to take the England coaching position. Observers argued that an England coach should be English. Yet within months Sven was being hailed as the saviour of English football. Five goals scored against Germany in Munich shocked the English nation (or at least anyone who was half interested in football). Clearly admired and respected by potential members of the England team, hopes were high that England could do well in the 2002 World Cup. Moreover, interest in the success of Sven the manager moved into interest in Sven the man. How was it that this quiet, unassuming, dignified man had achieved so much in so short a time? Such an impact was manna from heaven for the media, academics and all those people searching for an answer as to what makes an effective leader.

Before Eriksson, English coaches had come and gone. All seemed to go through a cycle of welcome, high expectation, disappointment, a decline in results and finally, following a media onslaught, sad scenes of another English coach 'leaving the field'. In contrast to previous coaches, who showed their passion for the game and for the job in different ways, Sven's behaviour might be characterized as thoughtful, considered, calm and even disconnected, at least from the training activity. He is a manager who tends to keep players at 'arm's length'; preferring quiet one-to-one talks with individual players when required. In interviews it is clear that Sven is very supportive of his squad, their abilities, his staff, the English nation, its football credentials, qualities and potential. None the less, when England have under-performed in parts of the game, he quickly acknow-ledges problems and indeed some obvious weaknesses in player ability or fitness levels. He is said to be a man that can handle immense pressure, or at least, does not tend to show the strain that inherently comes from the position. Very laid back and relaxed, he tends to take each day as it comes. Perhaps differently from previous English managers, he tends not to raise his voice but prefers to remain reserved and to exercise emotional control – thinking before reacting and displaying quiet confidence in a diplomatic manner. His behaviour on the touchline is impeccable; during his time in Italy he was referred to as the 'Iceman'. The outcome is that Sven has won the respect and (up to the time of writing) an excellent reputation as a progressive coach in world football.

His record of accomplishment in club football boasts winning five championships in three countries, Sweden, Portugal and Italy. Leaving Lazio Football Club was a big decision. In a news conference in Rome, Eriksson commented that the decision to leave Lazio was taken as he was travelling in the car to the club's training ground, adding, 'the players were the first to know about it'. The president of the club, Sergio

Cragnotti, mentioned how much the club owed Eriksson, but his position as coach at Lazio had been thrown into doubt following a 1–0 home defeat in the Rome derby match against Roma and a shock 2–1 home defeat to lowly positioned Napoli. This result left Lazio with six defeats in their previous nine games, and 11 points behind the divisional leaders. Crisis talks resulted in the chairman declaring that Eriksson could stay with the club until the end of the 2001 season. The next day Sven resigned.

Some observers suggest that the Sven 'softer' style of leadership might be replacing the 'big, loud and often in your face' charismatic leaders of the past. For instance, despite similarities as to the single-minded need for an effective end-result, Sven can be viewed as different in that he appears quietly charismatic, unflappable, modest and pragmatic. Others suggest that leadership will still be governed by the situation, and that several styles of leadership might be effective given the appropriate context.

Questions

1 What does the Sven case suggest in relation to great man (person), trait, style and contingency theories?
2 Could Sven be classed as a charismatic or transformational leader?
3 What characteristics (if any) might be conducive to members of the England team perceiving Sven as a leader?

For discussion of the case see Appendix D.

Case study 2: Conventional theory-of-action?

One piece of research as to whether senior management employed a conventional theory-of-action was conducted by the author on the senior management board of a UK national 'brown goods' supplier.

The aim of the study was to monitor senior management decisions and the aspects they normally considered as important factors relating to each decision. Besides observation, various instruments were used relating to group processes, personality profiling and team roles. The researcher also conducted in-depth interviews with each member of the senior management team.

In terms of Belbin's team type roles, board members of the senior management team were fundamentally 'shapers'. Shapers can be described as dynamic, outgoing and challenging; people who pressurize and maintain direction of the team towards agreed goals. Of interest was the comparatively lowly position of team-worker, the type characterized by Meredith Belbin as the role that supports members, improves communications within the team and fosters team spirit.

Using a well-known Saville and Holdsworth Ltd personality profiling instrument, four of the five full-time senior managers self-assessed themselves as having comparatively high achievement related traits as compared with a norm of managerial professional people (n = 728). Standard ten (sten) scores of 7 (1 = low, 10 = high) and above were recorded for the traits: competitiveness, achieving, independence, assertiveness and controlling. The trait 'achieving' was above sten 9 for all board members. Low sten scores of 4 or below were recorded on three senior management profiles for empathy, modesty, caring and affiliative. The mean score (10 subjects) for 'affiliative' was sten 5. The median was sten 4.

The result of observational studies was that the board made twice as many references to task-related aspects during their decision-making processes as they did for 'people/employee'-related aspects. Task aspects centred on performance indicators with a strong productivity and profit centred focus.

Questions

1 In what way does this case suggest that a conventional theory-of-action is in operation?
2 Accepting that traits and behaviour of senior managers might change in relation to context, what traits and behaviour might be witnessed in two years' time if a Sven-Goran Eriksson type of manager took over as Chief Executive?

For discussion of the case see Appendix D.

References

Adair, J. (1973) *The Action-Centred Leader*, McGraw–Hill: London.

Adshead, J. quoted in MacLachan, R. (1997) When It Pays to Look at the People Inputs, *People Management*, 3 (1), p. 24.

Allport, G.W. (1937) *Personality: A Psychological Interpretation*, New York: Rhinehart and Winston, p. 289.

Allport, G.W. (1955) *Becoming: Basic Considerations for a Psychology of Personality*, New Haven, CT: Yale University Press.

Allport, G.W. (1961) *Patterns and Growth in Personality*, New York: Holt, Rinehart and Winston, p. 28.

Allport, G.W. and Odbert, H.S. (1936) A Psycho-Lexico Study, *Psychological Monographs*, 1 (47), p. 211.

Argyris, C. (1964) *Integrating the Individual and the Organization*, New York: J. Wiley and Sons.

Argyris, C. (1994) *On Organizational Learning*, Cambridge, MA: Blackwell.

Argyris, C. (1997) A Yearning for Learning, *People Management*, 3 (5), pp. 34–5.

Argyris, C. and Schön, D. (1974) *Theory and Practice: Increasing Professional Effectiveness*, San Francisco: Jossey–Bass.

Argyris, C. and Schön, D. (1978) *Organizational Learning: A Theory of Action Perspective*, Reading, MA: Addison–Wesley, ch. 1, pp. 8–29.

Arkin, A. (1997) Stakeholding Guide is a Blair Necessity, *People Management*, 3 (8), p. 11.

Armstrong, M. (1991) *A Handbook of Personnel Practice*, 4th edn, London: Kogan–Page.

Armstrong, M. (1966) *A Handbook of Personnel Management Practice*, 6th edn, London: Kogan–Page.

Atkinson, P.E. (1990) *Creating Culture Change: The Key to Successful Total Quality Management*, Bedford: IFS, p. 87.

Barrow, J.C. (1976) Worker Performance and Task Complexity as Causal Determinants of Leader Behaviour Style and Flexibility, *Journal of Applied Psychology*, 61, pp. 433–40.

Bass, B.M. (1990) *Handbook of Leadership*, New York: The Free Press. See also B.M. Bass (1990) *Bass and Stogdill's Handbook of Leadership Theory, Research, and Managerial Implications*, 3rd edn, New York: Free Press.

Bass, B.M. and Aviolo, B. (1993) *Improving Organizational Effectiveness through Transformational Leadership*, Thousand Oaks, CA: Sage Publications.

Bass, B.M., Waldman, D.A., Avioli, B.J. and Bebb, M. (1987) Transformational Leadership and the Falling Dominoes Effect, *Group and Organization Studies*, No. 12, pp. 73–87.

Bennis, W.G. (1989) Managing the Dream: Leadership in the 21st Century, *Journal of Organizational Change Management*, 2 (1), p. 7.

Biddle, D. and Evenden, R. (1990) Human Aspects in Management, *Institute of Personnel and Development*, pp. 19–46.

Bird, J. (1997) Human Aspects of Transformation, *Management Skills and Development*, 1 (March), p. 19.

Blake, R.R. and Mouton, J.S. (1964) *The Managerial Grid*, Houston: Gulf Publishing Company (*The Managerial Grid III*, 1985).

Blakely, R.J. (1959) *Strategies of Leadership*, New York: Harper and Brothers.

Boal, K.B. and Bryson, J.M. (1988) Charismatic Leadership: A Phenomenological and Structural Approach, in J.G. Hunt, H.P.

Baliga and C.A. Schriesheim (eds), *Emerging Leadership Vistas*, Lexington, MA: Lexington Books, p. 528.

Bower, D. (1996) The Psychological Contract, *The Institute of Personnel and Development National Conference* (conference notes), p. 10.

Brooks, J.L. and Seers, A. (1991) Predictors of Organizational Commitment: Variations Across Career Stages, *Journal of Vocational Behavior*, 38 (1), pp. 53–64.

Bross, I.D.J. (1953) *Design for Decision*, New York: Macmillan.

Brown, M. (1956) *Effective Supervision*, New York: Macmillan.

Burns, J.M. (1978) *Leadership*, London: Harper and Row.

Calhoon, R.P. and Kirkpatrick, C.A. (1956) *Influencing Employee Behaviour*, New York: McGraw–Hill.

Cameron, K.S., Freeman, S.J. and Mishra, A.K. (1993) Downsizing and Redesigning Organizations, in G.P. Huber and W.H. Glick (eds), *Organizational Change and Redesign*, Oxford: Oxford University Press.

Checkland, P. (1988) Soft Systems Methodology: An Overview, *Journal of Applied Systems Analysis*, 15, pp. 27–30.

Chin, R. and Benne, K. (1976) *General Strategies for Effecting Changes in Human Systems*, in W.G. Bennis, K.D. Benne, R. Chin and K.E. Corey (eds), *The Planning of Change*, New York: Holt, Rinehart and Winston.

Connock, S. and Johns, T. (1995) *Ethical Leadership*, London: IPD.

Cooper, D.J. (1993) *Health Care Management – Philosophical and Managerial Implications*, Strategic Issues in Health Care Management: Setting Priorities in Health Care, Second International Conference, August 1993, University of St Andrews.

Curnow, B. (1995) Two Worlds that Need Each Other's Expertise, *People Management*, 1 (14), p. 25.

Dennis, L.B. and Dennis, T.L. (1991) *Management Science*, St Paul, MN: West Publishing, p. 3.

Eisenberger, R., Huntington, R., Hutchinson, S. and Sowa, D. (1986) Perceived Organizational Support, *Journal of Applied Psychology*, 71 (3), p. 500.

Eisenberger, R., Fasolo, P. and David-LaMastro, V. (1990) Perceived Organizational Support and Employee Diligence, Commitment, and Innovation, *Journal of Applied Psychology*, No. 75, pp. 51–9.

Eysenck, H.J. (1953) *The Structure of Human Personality*, London: Methuen.

Eysenck, H.J. (1972) Conditioning, Introversion, Extraversion and the Strength of the Nervous System, in V. D. Nebylitson and J. A. Grey (eds), *Biological Bases of Individual Behaviour*, New York: Academic Press.

Fahey, L. (1981) On Strategic Management Decision Processes, *Strategic Management Journal*, No. 2, pp. 43–60.

Fayol, H. (1949) *General and Industrial Management*, London: Pitman.

Feldman, J. and Kanter H.E. (1965) Organizational Decision Making, in G. James and R. March (eds), *Handbook of Organizations*, Chicago: Rand McNally.

Fieldler, F.E. (1967) *A Theory of Leadership Effectiveness*, New York: McGraw–Hill.

Fieldler, F.E. (1995) Cognitive Resources and Leadership Performance, *Applied Psychology: An International Review*, 44, p. 7.

Finn, R. (1998) quoted in J. Walsh, HR Strategy, *People Management*, 4 (18), p. 15.

French, W.R., Kast, F.E. and Rosenzweig, J.E. (1985) *Understanding Human Behaviour in Organizations*, New York: Harper and Row.

Gaertner, K.N. and Nollen, S.D. (1989) Career Experiences, Perceptions of Employment Practices, and Psychological Commitment to the Organization, *Human Relations*, 11.(42), pp. 975–91.

George, C. Jr (1964) *Management in Industry*, Hemel Hempstead: Prentice–Hall.

Georgiades, N. and Macdonell, R. (1998) *Leadership for Competitive Advantage*, New York: John Wiley, p. 147.

Gilbreth, F.B. (1908) *Field Systems*, New York: Myron. C. Clark.

Glautier, M.W.E. and Underdown, B. (1994) *Accounting Theory and Practice*, 5th edn, London: Pitman Publishing, p. 646.

Guest, D.E. (1991) Personnel Management: The End of Orthodoxy, *British Journal of Industrial Relations*, 29 (2), pp. 149–76.

Guest, D.E. (1998) Bundling: Combine Harvest, *People Management*, 4 (21), pp. 64–6.

Ghiselli, E. (1971) *Explorations in Managerial Talents*, Pacific Palisades, CA: Goodyear Publishing.

Handy, C.B. (1976) *Understanding Organizations*, Harmondsworth: Penguin.

Handy, C.B. (1989) *The Age of Unreason*, London: Business Books.

Handy, C.B. (1995) Trust: A New Concept in the Management of People?, *People Management*, 1 (11), p. 53.

Hannagan, T. (1998) *Management Concepts and Practices*, London: Pitman Publishing.

Heinrich, H.W. (1951) *Formula for Supervision*, National Foreman's Institute, Hemel Hempstead: Prentice–Hall.

Hitt, M.A., Lei, D. and Bettis, R. (1996) Dynamic Core Competencies Through Meta-learning and Strategic Context, *Journal of Management*, 22 (4), pp. 549–69.

House, R. (1971) A Path–Goal Theory of Leadership Effectiveness, *Administrative Science Quarterly*, September.

House, R. and Mitchell, T. (1974) Path–Goal Theory of Leadership, *Journal of Contemporary Business*, Autumn.

House, R.J., Spangler, W.D. and Woycke, J. (1991) Personality and Charisma in the U.S. Presidency: A Psychological Theory of Leadership Effectiveness, *Administrative Science Quarterly*, No. 36, pp. 364–96.

House, R.J., Woycke, J. and Fodor, E,M, (1988) Perceived Behavior and Effectiveness of Charismatic and Non-charismatic US Presidents, in J. Conger and R. Kanungo (eds), *Charismatic Leadership and Management*, San Francisco: Jossey-Bass, p. 100.

Howell, J.M. and Frost, P.J. (1989) A Laboratory Study of Charismatic Leadership, *Organizational Behavior and Human Decision Processes*, No. 43, pp. 243–69.

Huselid, M. (1998) in D.E. Guest, Bundling: Combine Harvest, *People Management*. 4 (21), p. 64.

Hutchinson, S., Kinnie, N. and Purcell, J. (1996) 'The People Management Implications of Leaner Ways of Working', A Report by the University of Bath, London: Institute of Personnel and Development.

Institute of Directors, University of Salford (1993–2002), Discussions with Directors attending the Diploma in Directorship, unpublished work.

Jacob, P., Flink, J. and Schuchman, H. (1962) Values and Their Function in Decision Making, *American Behavioural Scientist*, 5, Suppl 9, pp. 6–38.

Johns, T. (1995) Don't be Afraid of the Moral Maze, *People Management*, 1 (23), p. 32.

Kakabadse, A., Ludlow, R. and Vinnicombe, S. (1988) *Working in Organizations*, Harmondsworth: Penguin Books, p. 186.

Kakabadse, A. (1995) When Won't Values Work? *People Management*, 1 (16), p. 23.

Kaplan, R.S. and Norton, D.P. (1996) Using the Balanced Scorecard as a Strategic Management System, *Harvard Business Review*, Jan–Feb, pp. 75–87.

Kaplan, R.S. and Norton, D.P. (1997) *The Balanced Scorecard*, Boston, MA: Harvard Business School Press, p. 5.

Kets de Vries, M. (1996) The Leader as Analyst, *Harvard Business Review*, Jan–Feb, p. 158.

Kluckholm, C. (1951) *Mirror for Man*, New York: McGraw–Hill, p. 149.

Kotter, J.P. (1990a) What Leaders Really Do, *Harvard Business Review*, 1 (47), pp. 59–67.

Kotter, J.P. (1990b) *A Force for Change: How Leadership Differs from Management*, New York: Free Press.

Kretchmer, E. (1925) *Physique and Character* (trans. W.J.H. Sprott), New York: Harcourt Brace and World (originally published in 1921).

Lawrence, P. and Lorsch, J. (1967) *Organization and Environment*, Boston, MA: Harvard Business School Division of Research.

Legge, K. (1989) *Human Resource Management: A Critical Analysis*, in J. Storey (ed.), *New Perspectives in Human Resource Management*, London: Routledge.

Levering, R. (1988) *A Great Place To Work: Why Are Some Employees So Good (And Some So Bad)*, New York: Random House.

Lindblom, C.E. (1959) The Science of Muddling Through, *Public Administration Review*, No. 19, pp. 79–88.

Lindblom, C.E. (1968) *The Policy Making Process*, Englewood Cliffs, NJ: Prentice–Hall.

Lindgren, H.C. (1954) *Effective Leadership in Human Relations*, Edinburgh: Nelson and Sons.

Litchfield, D. (1996) Be Prepared to Blow your own Trumpet, *People Management*, 2 (7), p. 12.

Littlefield, D. (1996) Halifax Employees to Assess Management, *People Management*, 2 (5), p. 5.

Lundy, J.L. (1957) *Effective Industrial Management*, New York: Macmillan.

Luthans, F. (1992a) *Organizational Behaviour*, 6th edition, McGraw-Hill.

Lyles, M.A. (1981) Formulating Strategic Problems – Empirical Analysis and Model Development, *Strategic Management Journal*, No. 2, pp. 61–75.

McGregor, D. (1957, 1960) *The Human Side of Enterprise*, New York: McGraw–Hill.

McGregor, D. (1966) *Leadership and Motivation*, Cambridge, MA: MIT Press.

McHale, J. (1993) Successful Companies Set an Example for Employees, *People Management*, 1 (20), p. 52.

McLaney, E.J. (1994) *Business Finance for Decision Makers*, London: Pitman Publishing, pp. 15–20.

Marrow, A.J. (1957) *Making Management Human*, New York: McGraw–Hill.

Maslow, A.H. (1954) *Motivation and Personality*, New York: Harper (2nd edn, Harper and Row, 1970).

Meyer, A.D. (1982) How Ideologies Supplement Formal Structures and Shape Responses to Environments, *Journal of Management Studies*, 1 (19), pp. 45–61.

Meyer, J.W. and Rowan, B. (1977) Institutional Organizations: Formal Structures as Myth and Ceremony, *American Journal of Sociology*, 83, pp. 340–63.

Mintzberg, H. (1988). Crafting Strategy, *The McKinsey Quarterly*, Summer, pp. 71–89.

Mintzberg, H., Raisingghani, D. and Theoret, A. (1976) The Structure of Unstructured Decision Processes, *Administrative Science Quarterly*, 21, pp. 246–75.

Morgan, G. (1994) The 15-per-cent Solution, Canada, *The Globe and Mail*, p. 3. See also extract provided by Dr Gareth Morgan to attenders of the Salford University Seminar held on 19 January 1996.

Morton, C. (1998) Water Proof, *People Management*, 4 (12), p. 48.

Mullins, L.J. (1996) *Management and Organizational Behaviour*, 4th edn, London: Pitman, pp. 716–17.

Murlis, H. (1996) Pay 'Less of a Factor', *People Management*, 2 (9), p. 14.

O'Brien, R.C. (1995) Employees Involvement in Performance Improvement: A Consideration of Tacit Knowledge, Commitment and Trust, *Employee Relations*, 17 (3), p. 110.

Ofstad, H. (1961) *An Inquiry into the Freedom of Decision*, Oslo: Norwegian Universities Press.

Olson, M. (1965) *The Logic of Collective Action: Public Goods and the Theory of Groups*, Cambridge, MA: Harvard University Press.

Oxford Encyclopaedic English Dictionary (1991) Oxford: Clarendon Press.

Paine, L. (1994) Managing for Organizational Integrity, *Harvard Business Review*, Mar–Apr, pp. 106–17.

Peters, T. and Waterman, R.H. (1982) *In Search of Excellence, Lessons from America's Best Run Companies*, New York: Harper and Row.

Pettigrew, A.M. (1977) Strategy Formulation as a Political Process, *International Studies of Management and Organization*, 2 (7), pp. 78–87.

Pettigrew, A.M. (1985) *The Awakening Giant*, Oxford: Blackwell.

Pickard, J. (1998) Top Bosses Accept 'People are Most Valuable Asset', *People Management*, 4 (6), p. 15.

Pickard, J. (1998) Natural Lore: An Interview with Arie de Geus, *People Management*, 4 (20), pp. 41–3.

Price, C. and Dauphinais, W. (1998) *Straight from the CEO*, London: Nicholas Brealey.

Pugh, D.S., Hickson, D.J. and Hinings, C.R. (1983) *Writers on Organizations*, Harmondsworth: Penguin Books.

Quinn, J.B. (1982) Managing Strategies Incrementally, *Omega: The International Journal of Management Science*, 10 (6), pp. 613–27.

Reed, M. (1985) *Redirections in Organizational Analysis*, London: Tavistock, p. 71.

Reichheld, F.G. (1997) *The Loyalty Effect*, Boston, MA: Harvard Business School Press, p. 6.

Reitz, H.J. (1987) *Behaviour in Organizations*, 3rd edn, Homewood, IL: Irwin, p. 469.

Rogers, C.R. (1978) *Carl Rogers on Personal Power*, London: Constable.

Sabel, C. (1982) *Work and Politics*, Cambridge: Cambridge University Press.

Savery, L.K. (1994) Attitudes to Work: The Influence of Perceived Styles of Leadership on a Group of Workers, *Leadership and Organization Development Journal*, 15 (4), p. 12.

Schein, E.H. (1980) *Organizational Psychology*, Englewood Cliffs, NJ: Prentice–Hall, pp. 106–33.

Schön, D.A. (1996) *Organizational Learning*, Reading, MA: Addison Wesley.

Shamir, B., House, R.J. and Arthur, M.B. (1993) The Motivational Effects of Charismatic Leadership: A Self-concept Based Theory, *Organization Science*, No. 4, pp. 1–17.

Sheffield University (1998) 'A link between improved profitability and increased job satisfaction has been found', BBC Radio 4 *Today* programme, 4 October.

Sheldon, W.H. (1940) *The Varieties of Human Physique: An Introduction to Constitutional Psychology*, New York: Harper and Row.

Shore, L.M. and Martin, H.J. (1989) Job Satisfaction and Organizational Commitment in Relation to Work performance and Turnover Intentions, *Human Relations*, No. 7, pp. 625–37.

Simon, H.A. (1960) *The New Science of Management Decision*, New York, Harper and Row.

Smircich, L. (1983) Concepts of Culture and Organizational Analysis, *Administrative Science Quarterly*, No. 28, pp. 339–58.

Smith, A. (1759) *A Theory of Moral Sentiments*, London Press.

Sparrow, P.R. and Pettigrew, A. (1988) Contrasting HRM Responses in the Changing World of Computing, *Personnel Management*, 2 (20), pp. 40–5.

Stodgill, R.M. (1974) *Handbook of Leadership*, New York: Free Press.

Tagiuri, R. and Litwin, G.H. (eds) (1968) *Organizational Climate*, Boston, MA: Graduate School of Business Administration, Harvard University, p. 27.

Taylor, J.W. (1962) *How to Select and Develop Leaders*, New York: McGraw–Hill, pp. 42–3.

Taylor, F.W. (1911) *The Principles of Scientific Management*, New York: Harper. See also F.W. Taylor (1947) *Scientific*

Management, New York and London: Harper and Row; Taylor's testimony to the House of Representatives' Special Committee (1912) in F.W. Taylor (1967) *Principles of Scientific Management*, New York: Norton, p. 48.

Tead, O. (1935) *The Art of Leadership*, New York: McGraw–Hill.

Thibaut, J.W. and Kelley, H.H. (1959) *The Social Psychology of Groups*, New York: Wiley.

Thompson, J. D. (1967) *Organizations in Action*, New York: McGraw–Hill.

Tichy, N. and Devanna, M.A. (1986) *Transformational Leadership*, New York: Wiley.

Torrington, D and Weightman, J. (1994) *Effective Management: People and Organization*, Hemel Hempstead: Prentice–Hall, p. 338.

Trice, H.M. and Beyer, J.M. (1984) Studying Organizational Cultures through Rites and Ceremonies, *Academy of Management Review*, 4 (9), pp. 653–9.

Trist, E.L., Higgin, G.W., Murray, G.W. and Pollack, A.B. (1963) *Organizational Choice*, London: Tavistock.

Van Velsor, E. and Leslie, J.B. (1994) Why do Managers Derail?, *Harvard Business Review*, 3 (73), p. 10.

Vroom, V.H. (1964) *Work and Motivation*, New York: John Wiley.

Vroom, V.H. (1966) Organizational Choice: A Study of Pre- and Post-Decision Processes, *Organizational Behaviour and Human Performance*, No. 1, pp. 212–25.

Vroom, V.H. (1974) A New Look at Managerial Decision Making, *Organizational Dynamics*, No. 5, pp. 66–80.

Walter, L.R. (1949) *Business Organization*, New York: McGraw–Hill.

Walton, R.E. and Dutton, J.M. (1969) The Management of Interdepartmental Conflict: A Model and Review, *Administrative Science Quarterly*, 14, pp. 73–84.

Weiss, J.W. (1996) *Organizational Behavior and Change*, St Paul, MN, West Publishing, pp. 192–3.

Wheeler, D. and Sillanpaa, M. (1997) *The Stakeholder Corporation*, London: Pitman.

Wooldridge, E. (1995) Time to Stand Maslow's Hierarchy on its Head, *People Management*, 2 (11), p. 17.

Yukl, G.A. (1981) *Leadership in Organizations*, Englewood Cliffs, NJ: Prentice–Hall, p. 70.

Yukl, G.A. (1989) Managerial Leadership: A Review of Theory and Research, *Yearly Review of Management*, No. 15, pp. 251–89.

Followership, employee commitment and motivation

Introduction

Chapter 2 provided an overview of leadership. It also considered leader characteristics conducive to encouraging followership. This chapter utilizes conceptual, theoretical and research evidence to help clarify the type of 'follower' commitment most useful to leaders in organizations, and what this means to followers as to satisfaction at work. Consequently, the chapter looks on leadership from the perspective of the psychological forces of those who might be encouraged to be lead – the needs, values, motives and drives of potential followers.

According to the *Oxford Encyclopaedic English Dictionary* (1991), a follower is an adherent or devotee who follows or comes after a leader. Such a definition does not capture the essence of what followership might mean from an organizational perspective. Jacobson (2000) defines followership as 'the commitment to collectively act with courage, intelligence, responsibility, and self-reliance to accomplish the organization's purpose and goals'. Perhaps followership is simply about people who willingly seek and enthusiastically accept direction, guidance and leadership of another. Follower traits might include commitment, enthusiasm, responsibility, dependability, accountability, self-discipline and dedication. Importantly, from an organizational viewpoint, key to enabling and enthusing a willing followership is to gain the commitment of employees. Consequently, to understand followership we need to have knowledge of employee commitment.

€mployee commitment defined and analysed

Research shows that people use a variety of categories to type others (Abelson, 1976; Bern and Allen, 1974). One type of category that has emerged is that of the committed person (Norman, 1963). Cantor and Mischel (1979) found commitment to be an attribute on which individuals evaluate others and that it was distinct from other personal characteristics.

Commitment might be described as the Holy Grail of organizational behaviour and business psychology. The key objective of all management being to develop a positive corporate culture as manifested in values, norms and management style which combine to promote commitment (Peters and Waterman, 1982; Tichy, 1983; Armstrong, 1991, p. 869). Denton (1987) states that obtaining employee commitment is key to quality and productivity improvements. Moreover, the central plank of Human Resource Management is the development of employee commitment to the organization (Guest, 1987). The rationale behind this is that committed employees 'will be more satisfied, more productive and more adaptable' (Guest, 1987; Walton, 1991).

For Walton, commitment is an essential precursor to high performance. It represents the latest stage in the evolution of managerial practice, a successor to the 'control' characteristic of Taylorist management during the early and mid-twentieth century. Committed employees can be viewed as in contrast to those who are seen as simply conforming and compliant (Ogbonna and Wilkinson, 1988, 1990). Walton suggests that the rate of transition from control to commitment strategies continues to accelerate, 'fuelled not only by economic necessity but also by individual leadership in management and labour, philosophical choices, organizational competence in managing change, and the need for cumulative learning from change itself'. The emerging views in this area are that to create a successful workplace, an organization must concentrate its energies on both economic and social performance, and invest in promoting commitment (Daley, 1988; Brooke and Price, 1989).

A substantial amount of research effort has been invested in identifying the various causes and implications of organizational commitment. A number of commentators raise questions about the concept of commitment. These relate to three main problem areas:

1 commitment and its unitary frame of reference (Mangham, 1979; Mintzberg, 1983);
2 commitment as an inhibitor of flexibility (Legge, 1989; Coopey and Hartley, 1991); and
3 whether high commitment results in improved organizational performance (Walton, 1985; Guest, 1991).

Some researchers and observers (Martin and Nicholls, 1987; Drennan, 1989a; Armstrong, 1996; Mullins, 1996) provide steps and broad guidelines as to how management can improve employee commitment. All add to our understanding; however, evidence suggests that commitment is a complex phenomenon that operates in different directions and at different levels.

The multifaceted nature of commitment is problematic for student and manager. Nevertheless, identifying the form of commitment that 'potential leaders' would normally wish to encourage in 'potential followers' is a pre-requisite to understanding.

Definitions of commitment differ. For example, organizational commitment might be defined as 'readiness to pursue objectives through the individual job in cooperation with others' (McEwan *et al.*, 1988). Less clinically perhaps, it might be defined as a strong desire to remain a member of a particular organization, in other words loyalty to the company. According to this definition, commitment refers to an individual's psychological bond to the organization, as an effective attachment and identification (Coopey and Hartley, 1991). Salancik (1977) states that 'Commitment is a state of being in which an individual becomes bound by actions to beliefs that sustain activities and involvement.' Complementary to conclusions offered in Chapter 2 above, Hall, Scheider, and Nygren (1970) dealt more with the issues that lead to shared values. They define commitment as 'the process by which the goals of the organization and those of the individual become increasingly integrated or congruent'. However, the most widely used definition of organizational commitment in current research appears to be that of Porter, Steers, Mowday and Boulian (1974), who developed the Organizational Commitment Questionnaire (shown in Appendix B). They define organizational commitment as the strength of an individual's identification with and involvement in a particular organization, characterising it by three psychological factors: desire to remain in an organization, willingness to exert considerable effort on its behalf, and belief in and acceptance of its goals and values. In support of Porter *et al.*, O'Reilly and Chatman (1989) define employee commitment as 'a psychological attachment felt by the employee for the organization'. The Porter instrument and definition has been so widely used by researchers that Reichers (1985) asserts that the Porter approach 'is the approach to commitment'. The following definition assists in capturing the essence of the Porter *et al.* dimensions:

> *A willingness to exert high levels of effort on behalf of the organization and a definite belief in, and acceptance of the values and goals of the organization. (Martin and Nicholls, 1987)*

It can be seen that commitment can be viewed and defined in terms of attitude or behaviour. Therefore, it is not surprising that two widely known views of commitment relevant to work organizations have emerged: behavioural or continuance commitment and attitudinal or affective commitment.

Behavioural and continuance commitment

In attempting to understand the psychological and environmental process through which employees attach themselves to an organization, research has concentrated on behavioural commitment (Mottaz, 1989; Kirschenbaum and Weisberg, 1990; Klenke-Hamel and Mathieu, 1990). It is defined as the degree of an employee's intention to stay in an organization (Price and Mueller, 1981; Halaby, 1986; Halaby and Weakliem, 1989).

Behavioural commitment relates to the individual's calculation of the costs of leaving rather than the rewards of staying. Keisler (1971), Keisler and Sakumura (1966) and Salancik (1982) see commitment from this viewpoint and suggest that commitment is the process of binding the individual to behavioural acts.

There is a strong similarity between 'behavioural commitment' as discussed by Becker (1960), Keisler (1971) and Salancik (1977, 1982) and continuance commitment as described by Allen and Meyer (1990). Continuance commitment involves the need to remain in the organization because of accumulated 'side-bets' and generally the lack of alternative employment opportunities (Becker, 1960). For example, Hrebiniak and Alutto (1973) define commitment as 'a result of individual–organizational transactions and alterations in side-bets or investments over time'. Basically, side-bets refer to anything of importance that an employee has invested, such as time, effort, or money that would be lost or devalued at a cost to an employee, if he or she left the organization (Meyer and Allen, 1984). This approach suggests that commitment is the outcome of inducements and contribution between an organization and an employee (Morris and Sherman, 1981). Commitment increases as more side-bets are accumulated and if they are contingent upon continued employment in the firm (Ritzer and Trice, 1969; Hrebiniak and Alutto, 1973; Meyer and Allen, 1984). The accrual of side-bets over time should make leaving more costly and hence increase continuance commitment (Mathieu and Zajac, 1990).

Age, tenure and level of education may contribute to the development of continuance commitment (Cohen and Lowenberg, 1990; Angle and Lawson, 1993). For example, older workers or those with permanent job appointments may feel tied or reluctant to leave the organization. Moreover, employees with low education levels are less likely to possess transferable skills and knowledge (Allen and Meyer, 1990). Some research (Farrell and Rusbult, 1981; Rusbult and Farrell, 1983) has found that investments such as 'non-portable' training increased employee commitment over time. By definition, non-portable training provides knowledge and skills that are only applicable to one organization. However, findings from studies of self-rated continuance commitment surveys suggest few conclusions regarding this link (Meyer *et al.*, 1989; Shore and Barksdale, 1991; Hackett *et al.*, 1994).

Continuance commitment as perceived by the individual relates to his or her view of the commitment and energy they have provided in the past. McGee and Ford (1987) explain that continuance commitment is concerned with sunk costs. Sunk cost is a phrase borrowed from the world of accountancy and means an 'unrecoverable cost'. In business, the term is used during financial appraisal of projects. In principle, sunk costs should be ignored when making decisions about future returns from projects. In practice, managers in organizations sometimes attempt to recover costs associated with earlier and perhaps regretted decisions. Similarly, people may choose to stay with a firm in an attempt to reap the rewards of past effort.

Iles *et al.* (1990) suggest that the association between the employee and the values of the organization may be seen in compliance terms. Employees are only committed to their organization because they perceive few existing alternatives. An obvious example is employment during high-unemployment and economic recessionary periods. Fewer jobs external to the employing organization should result in greater commitment to the employing firm because a lack of opportunities increases the perceived costs of discontinuing membership (Rusbult, 1980; Farrell and Rusbult, 1981). Iles *et al.* (1990) state that compliance commitment can take two possible forms: 'instrumental-calculative', or 'alienative'. The former, as the name implies, involves an instrumental exchange of involvement in return for rewards. They see commitment as a function of an individual's evaluation of the costs and benefits of maintaining membership. Alienative commitment is a condition where:

> *Individuals perceive themselves unable to change or control their organizational experiences and also perceive a lack of alternatives. A negative attachment then exists, combining weak intentions to meet organizational demands with intentions to maintain organizational membership.* (Iles *et al.*, 1990, p.150)

Again using financial terminology, employees can choose to withdraw their investment; not simply in the sense that they can choose to withdraw their labour, but in the sense they may choose to withdraw or not apply a willingness to exert substantial effort. In response to signs of alienative commitment, the organization adopts a predominant form of compliance patterns to achieve its goals (Reed, 1985).

From a manager, and more certainly a potential leader perspective, behavioural or continuance commitment might not be overly desirable. This form leverages employees to stay with the organization. However, managers and leaders wish for more from employees than compliant behaviour set to conform in a way that aids continuous employment but which may add little to the performance of the organization. Moreover, it says little as to the development of commitment in the future.

If employees only display behavioural or continuance commitment toward the organization and its managerial leaders, they may be 'following' but the substance of their commitment will be passive – not energetic. Analysis in Chapter 2 also suggests continuance or even alienative commitment might be more commonly found in organizations where management has adopted a conventional theory-of-action. In these circumstances, employees are unlikely to follow willingly, but perhaps managers are also not leading.

When reading though the following section, it is worth while considering the function of 'organization' and 'leadership' from the perspective of employees as synonymous. For example, for many employees, their senior management leaders are the organization, and vice versa.

Normative and affective commitment

Meyer *et al.* (1989) state that when conducting research it is important to distinguish between commitment based on desire and commitment based on need. While continuance commitment is based on need, affective and normative commitment is built on desire.

Normative commitment is interpreted as the feeling that one ought to remain with the organization because of personal norms and values. Clearly, this feeling would be conducive to follower-ship. It provides a sense of moral duty or obligation and is associated with internalization of the organization's and [its leaders] norms and values, and acceptance of its goals and mission (Iles *et al.*, 1996). Affective commitment provides a deeper sense of emotional attachment. It involves the notion of wanting to remain in the organization because through experience one develops a positive attitude towards the organization and/or its leadership. This commitment is triggered when an employee can relate to and agree with the norms of the organization because they compare well with their own personal norms and value system. Mowday *et al.* (1982) characterize affective commitment as having strong ties to, and psychological identification with an organization. It is offered that this psychological connection would extend to the relationship between employee and leader, or leadership group.

Guest (1992) argues that findings point to affective commitment being linked to effort while continuance commitment is linked to low labour turnover. However, Mowday *et al.* (1982) suggest both are linked in that each reinforces the other. According to Meyer and Allen (1991) both affective and continuance commitment represent psychological states that have implications for the organization. Side-bets urge an employee to continue with the organization, and affective commitment closely relates to the possession of a positive attitude towards the organization.

The two aspects of commitment are possibly inseparable if employees are to show a strong willingness for the good of the company. Meyer *et al.* (1990) offer support for this view. They state that research findings raise the possibility that although they are distinct concepts, continuance and affective commitment might be related, suggesting a process by which one view of commitment influences the other. Nevertheless, an equal number of studies support the distinctiveness of affective and continuance commitment (Hackett *et al.*, 1994; Shore and Barksdale, 1995).

Directors attending University of Salford executive programmes were introduced to the many definitions and approaches to employee commitment. They responded by suggesting:

'It is not always advisable to retain all of the same employees'

'It is extra effort that senior management require, not simply the continuance of what has been done before'

'Compliance is only useful at certain times. When it becomes less useful is when we want employees to think for themselves or to benefit from creative ideas . . . creative ideas are becoming more important'

'If anything we need to adopt a strategy that goes all out to destroy organizational behavioural commitment and encourage individual affective commitment'

Directors' comments indicate their wish for affective rather than continuous employee commitment. Consequently, followers who display affective commitment are likely to receive encouragement from leaders. Moreover, leaders who encourage and support employees are more likely to be acknowledged as leaders and increase follower affective commitment – a win/win outcome.

Pluralism and commitment

A pluralist view of employee commitment recognizes the multi-faceted nature of the concept of commitment (Iles *et al.*, 1990). Coopey and Hartley (1991) support this view and suggest that free standing, context-free assumptions of single-commitment models may not be sufficient. According to Reichers:

> *Commitment is a process of identification with the goals of an organization's multiple constituencies. These constituencies may include top management, customers, unions, and/or the public at large. (Reichers, 1985, p. 468)*

Middle and senior management leaders, sectional leaders, project leaders and supervisory staff might be added to the list. Importantly, the pluralists' approach moves to a broad stance where from a general construct of commitment, they first ask the question 'whose goals and values serve as the foci for multiple commitments?'.

The pluralist assumption also suggests that the more constituencies the individual employee identifies with and is committed to, the potentially more fragmented becomes the possibility of global commitment for the values of the organization as expressed by senior manager leadership. This assumption asserts that commitment is a finite resource. For example, if an employee identifies with customers, unions and senior management that their available commitment level will somehow be more limited than an employee who only associates with top management values. This notion is difficult to accept.

The multifaceted approach offered by pluralists seems credible and complements earlier text about the non-unitary nature of organization. Nevertheless, it carries far too many assumptions about commitment, especially that levels may be finite.

Levels of commitment

Randall (1987) distinguishes three levels of commitment. Descriptions relate to previously stated definitions of commitment. Nevertheless, by using levels it can seen that employee commitment can occupy different stages of development:

High level
A strong belief in the organization's goals and values

Medium level
A willingness to exert considerable effort on behalf of the organization

Low level
A strong desire to continue as an organization member

Randall's high and medium levels of commitment above clearly focus on 'affective' commitment. However, high level commitment does not explicitly acknowledge that employee needs might form an integral element of organizational goals and values – perhaps it should. Low commitment levels relate to continuance commitment.

Rather than levels of commitment, Martin and Nicholls (1987) suggest that affective commitment encapsulates 'the giving of all of yourself while at work'. This entails such things as using time constructively, attention to detail, making that extra effort, accepting change, cooperation with others, self-development, respecting trust, pride in one's own abilities, continuously seeking improvement, and giving loyal support. The reality of organizational life may be different. For instance, a poll conducted by Birkbeck College commissioned by the Institute of Personnel and Development (1996), found that the typical employee feels more loyalty to their colleagues than their line manager – and much less to their senior management and the organization. Such findings limit the chance of gaining synergies from a continuously improving leader–follower relationship.

The *Guardian* survey revealed that 83% of employees from ten organizations said that they were 'very' or 'moderately' committed to their employers. However, a similar percentage thought that management attitudes toward staff had changed for the worse.

McCall (1996) interprets these results by suggesting that when people say they are committed they perceive commitment as being asked by management to do more work and working longer hours. She adds, 'when you probe beneath simple multiple choice questioning, a lot of what they are saying suggests that they do not trust their employers'.

Antecedents and consequences

Most studies of employee commitment consider correlation and are cross-sectional. Consequently, it is often difficult to establish whether the commitment identified is a cause or effect. For example, do leader actions help create and sustain commitment or does high commitment to the organization encourage employees to think of their managers as leaders? Perhaps the solution to this dilemma is to accept that establishing association between correlates is at least a step in the right direction. None the less, literature provides a number of possible antecedents and con-sequences, namely, job satisfaction, employee involvement, com-munication, job satisfaction, labour turnover, absence and stress. For purposes of comprehensiveness, the following eight sections provide an overview of research findings. First, the important link between commitment and job performance is considered.

Current research as to possible links between commitment and job performance

Senior management interest in leadership and improving and extending employee commitment centres on the assumption that greater commitment leads to improved work and organizational performance. Drennan (1989b) states that most managers believe that with real commitment from staff, the performance of their businesses could improve dramatically. 'Employee commitment' he says, 'does make a real difference.' Walton (1985) suggests that at the heart of management philosophy is the belief that employee commitment will lead to enhanced performance. He adds, 'the evidence shows this belief to be well founded.'

Some researchers have found a positive relationship between organizational commitment and company performance (DeCotis and Summers, 1987; Randall, 1990); others have found no relationship (Angle and Perry, 1981). Mathieu and Zajac (1990) found that meta-analysis (analysis across several studies) indi-cated weak relationships between organizational commitment and output measures of performance such as a change in operating profit and sales targets. They conclude 'commitment has relatively little direct influence on performance in most instances'. However, indirect associations may exist, for example, some research suggests that commitment to specific, difficult goals leads to high performance (Locke *et al.*, 1981; Hollenbeck and Klein, 1987). Becker *et al.* (1996) state that although the evidence is sketchy 'commitment based on the internalization of goals and values is likely to predict performance'. Others have argued (Salancik and Pfeffer, 1978) and demonstrated (Krackhardt and Porter, 1985) that commitment may be influenced by the statements or actions of relevant others. In an organizational setting, managers and in particular senior managers are definitely 'relevant others'.

Organizational structure and commitment

Organizational size is thought to be negatively associated with organizational commitment. As organizations get larger, the ability to be involved and visible decline. Consequently, feelings of commitment also decline (James and Jones, 1974). It is also possible that decentralized and less formalized work settings increase work commitment (Payne and Pugh, 1976; Williams and Anderson, 1991). There is support for the negative effect of centralization on commitment (Miller and Labovitz, 1973; Bluedorn, 1979; Price and Mueller, 1981). Informal settings might also assist contact between employees and senior figures, and therefore, encourage the leader–follower attribute. However, contrasting the argument for informalized environments, findings by Michaels *et al.* (1988) found that greater organizational formalization was associated with higher employee commitment. They found no evidence of a negative reaction from employees to a formalized work environment. In fact, stemming from the results of their study is the view that 'the more structured a situation, the more committed employees tend to be'.

One aspect requiring further research is the view that as organizations become larger and perhaps more formalized, there is normally a greater physical and perhaps emotional distance between leaders and potential followers. This distancing may not be conducive to improved leader–follower relationships, unless, that is, senior figures can provide appropriate systems and processes by which followers can clearly perceive that their interests form an integral part of leader behaviour and actions.

Absence, labour turnover and commitment

Research evidence suggests that the link between organizational commitment and absence is weak (Guest, 1992). This is surprising given that high commitment to the organization and its leadership should conceivably result in high attendance levels. However, items more closely related to continuance rather than affective commitment may have been used in the measurement. Steers and Rhodes (1978) have suggested that attendance is a function of motivation to attend and ability to attend. While commitment may affect motivation or vice versa, it may have little effect on ability to attend. Pluralists would argue that competing commitment, for example, to family, might negatively affect ability to attend.

Mobley (1982) suggests that organizational commitment has been found to be inversely related to employee turnover. For instance, as employee turnover increases, commitment decreases and vice versa. By definition, highly committed employees wish to remain with their employing organizations (Mowday *et al.*, 1982). Consequently, commitment is an important predictor of intention to quit, which is invariably the best predictor of actual labour turnover. However, quantitative findings (Mathieu and Zajac, 1990; Randall, 1990) suggest the relationship between organizational commitment and turnover does not provide large correlations. The strongest correlation relates to two meta-analyses of Steel and Ovalle (1984) and Carsten and Spector (1987). One explanation for lower than expected correlation is that other variables probably moderate the relationship (Mathieu and Zajac, 1990).

Generally, longitudinal research studies show that the link between commitment and labour turnover may be indirect. Clearly, employees may have multiple reasons for looking elsewhere for employment. Moreover, they may be reluctant to reveal prime motives. For example, employees often quote the lack of opportunity of improved remuneration as a reason for leaving the organization. However, personal evidence arising from conducting many 'exit interviews' has uncovered scathing comments about the way employees have been managed. Many suggest poor management and not necessarily the potential for increasing take-home pay was the main reason for 'looking elsewhere'. It was also common for interviewees to express the view that their organization did not have leaders, or even managers. Crucially, they were not following – they were leaving.

Stress and commitment

A 1996 survey by the *Guardian* newspaper of more than 11 000 readers found that 97% of respondents had experienced stress at work, compared with 77% surveyed in 1988 (Arkin, 1996). Research by Demos (1995), an independent 'think-tank', found the following indicators of stress in UK companies:

- Forty-four per cent of the workforce reported coming home exhausted.
- Time off for stress related illnesses has increased by 500% since the 1950s.
- One in three British men work a six to seven day week.
- Eighty-six per cent of women workers say they never have enough time to get things done.

Evidence (Cox and Cooper, 1985) suggests stress is a major cost to the organization. The association between stress and what we may best refer to as a state of 'distress' may be linked to commitment in many ways. A cause of stress may be associated with an employee being over-committed to his/her organization (Institute of Personnel and Development, 1995). For this type of employee, the organization will be dominant in their life. For many other employees, a working life that does not satisfy and affects one's self-esteem, basic needs or values, could be instrumental in producing feelings of distress. Commitment may be more likely if people perceive their environment as one that is capable of arousing their interest and is pleasurable. In contrast, 'distress' is likely if a person is aroused and displeased. Many jobs in organizations do not provide a high level of arousal, and some may provide too much.

Job satisfaction and commitment

Job satisfaction and organizational commitment have been found to be positively correlated across a number of studies (Bluedorn, 1982; Bateman and Strasser, 1984; Locke and Latham, 1990). Porter *et al.* (1974) argued that satisfaction, being highly correlated with the work environment and specific outcomes, develops more rapidly than organizational commitment, a more global construct. Nevertheless, employee satisfaction and employee commitment to the organization is linked. Seeking causation, Martin and Bennett (1996) state studies by Buchanan (1974) and Reichers (1985) suggest that job satisfaction is a cause of organizational commitment. Findings of Bateman and Strasser (1984) and Vandenberg and Lance (1992) support a reversed causal ordering, in which commitment is causally antecedent to satisfaction. The model is explained by means of a cognitive dissonance approach (Festinger, 1957), in which 'a cognitive outlook such as commitment is rationalized by subsequent attitudes of job satisfaction' (Bateman and Strasser, 1984). Williams and Hazer (1986) propose the relationship between commitment and satisfaction is reciprocal, but Curry *et al.* (1986) did not find a causal effect in either direction.

Although the majority of studies show a strong relationship between satisfaction and commitment, causality is not clear (Guest, 1992). However, regardless of the orientation of causality, a strong association between job satisfaction and employee commitment seems assured. Moreover, there now seems fair evidence to support the view that employee satisfaction leads to improved organizational performance. For example, a study by Sheffield University (Sheffield University, 1998) stated that a survey of 40 organizations involving 8000 employees found that improved profitability followed an increase in job satisfaction (and not the other way round).

Change strategies and commitment

Managers often turn to theory to manage change, for example, Lewin's (1951) change model, and Chin and Benne's (1976) change strategies. Importantly, change strategies aim to improve employee commitment. Various methods have been used, including those in Table 3.1.

Table 3.1 Change strategies and typologies

Activity	Type of intervention
Briefing groups	Normative re-educative/Empirical rational
Change champions as role models	Normative re-educative
Change agents	Empirical rational/normative re-educative
Quality circles	Empirical rational/normative re-educative
Training and development	Normative re-educative
Redundancy and replacement	Power coercive
Restructuring	Power coercive/empirical rational
Appraisal/performance review	Empirical rational/normative educative
New reward systems	Empirical rational

Research commissioned by the National Economic Development Office, citing companies such as ICI Paints, British Airways and H.J. Heinz, illustrate acceptance that a more 'open' style of management should be an integral part of introducing and promoting employee commitment. It is no coincidence that three-quarters of IBM's annual training programme for managers concentrates on people management (Bassett, 1986). Over several decades, companies have also attempted to persuade employees to be committed to the value of quality and customer service, mainly by the use of re-educative methods: examples include ICL's education programme in the early 1980s (Sparrow and Pettigrew, 1988a, 1988b), British Rail's 'Customer-care' and TQM programmes and Lucas TQM programmes (Storey, 1992a), and 'Team Building' Grampian Health Authority (Fullerton and Price, 1991).

Johns (1995) suggests 'organizations adopt ready-made solutions for fear of being left behind. This me-tooism leads inevitably to disillusionment, rejection and eventual death.' Armstrong (1996) also criticizes such programmes as 'largely ineffective if they are applied as top-down impositions on a compliant workforce and softened up by videos of the Chairman stating that our people are our greatest asset'. Ray (1986) suggests that senior management see change strategies as an addition to other forms of control that organizations have tried to implement in a direct attempt to enhance employee commitment toward improving productivity and financial performance. Pettigrew and Whipp (1991) note that, unfortunately, when senior management support conventional organizational values and goals, the action tends to encourage employees to believe that in stakeholder terms they are not a major priority. Legge (1995) states, 'change becomes problematic if the very instrumentality of the new espoused values act to negate moral dimensions'. Employee internalization of the values espoused through change strategies is only likely to result in increased commitment if employees perceive that potential leaders are not manipulating and/or bribing them to conform.

Employee involvement and commitment

Guest (1992) distinguishes five main forms of involvement:

1 Improving provision of information to employees, for example briefing groups.
2 Improving information from employees, for example from suggestion schemes and quality circles.

3 Changing the work systems through the development of autonomous working groups.
4 Changing incentives, for example, through employee share ownership schemes and performance-related pay.
5 Changing employee relationships, through more participative leadership and greater informality.

No relationship has been found between the use of employee involvement initiatives and company and plant performance, this is possibly to do with the number of confounding variables (Edwards, 1987; Marginson *et al.*, 1988). However, employees who actively engage in decision making throughout an organization tend to have higher job satisfaction, which increases commitment. The Sheffield University (1998) survey indicated that when techniques such as job enhancement, enrichment and employee involvement were employed, increased job satisfaction occurred. Moreover, the organizations showed that an increase in profitability occurred one year after the introduction of the techniques. Guest (1992) urges that 'conclusions must be tentative'. Further, there are issues of inadequate introduction and implementation of employee involvement schemes. Kelly and Kelly (1991) point to four reasons:

- Employees lack choice about participating in such initiatives.
- Employees lack trust in management.
- There is unequal status and outcomes.
- There is a lack of institutional support.

Marchington *et al.* (1994) found that employee attitudes to employee involvement initiatives are dependent, among others, upon experiences they have of employee involvement and work in general. They are also dependent on management's approach to employee relations, and the recent and projected corporate performance of the organization. They conclude that employee involvement initiatives are as much affected by the prevailing culture and environment as they are sources of cultural change. For instance, in a large-scale investigation of the influence of participative cultures on commitment, Miller (1988) found that the effect of participation on organization participants was strongly moderated by the overall culture of the organization. Guest is critical of attempts to change culture, he suggests:

Often techniques are introduced in a piecemeal way, more as the 'flavour of the month' than as part of a coherent strategy. (Guest, 1992, p. 128)

It is interesting to reflect that techniques such as job enhancement and employee involvement are usually instigated by senior management. Marchington's (1993) research verifies that employee experiences and perceptions about managerial leaders are core issues that require attention – possibly before (or instead of) additional employee involvement initiatives. For example, Marchington shares Walton's (1991) view that commitment is strongly related to trust. Senior management is chosen for particular attention. Trust is synonymous with commitment. Offering commitment indicates that the person is both willing and able to do what he or she has pledged. When one party views the other party as unwilling or unable to honour their commitments, then they do not trust the intentions and actions of the other side. They are in a state of 'lack of trust'. When there is suspicion based upon previous interactions between employees and their senior management then 'one-off' employee involvement initiatives are unlikely to be greeted with total commitment. Of course, the trust–commitment association will affect initiatives other than those relating to employee involvement. Indeed, the association is likely to affect the core relationship between employer and employee. Clearly, without a degree of trust, the leader–follower attribute will be subdued. It is interesting that 'trust' emerges as an essential aspect of leader–follower relations regardless of whether analysis focuses on leader attributes (as in Chapter 2) or follower commitment.

Communication and commitment

Communication is often cited by senior managers as the one important aspect of organizational life that they may never get totally right. It is therefore unsurprising that research by Storey (1992b) sampled 15 organizations and found that most were engaged in intensive and direct communication with employees as part of wide-ranging cultural, structural and personnel strategies. However, viewing communication as a universal panacea for organizational ills seems foolish. This may lead to unwarranted expectations in its introduction and qualified failure in its implementation (Hyman, 1982; Thompson, 1983).

Elements of the communication process are said to be associated with employee affective and/or continuous commitment. For example, the concept of instrumental communication refers to job-related information such as feedback and role clarity (Porter and Steers, 1973). Vance and Colella (1990) proposed that feedback was a direct determinant of commitment. Additionally, there is general agreement that instrumental communication has a negative impact on turnover (Cotton and Tuttle, 1986; Williams and Hazer, 1986). There is also evidence supporting the positive impact of instrumental communication on job satisfaction (Martin, 1979; Price and Mueller, 1981; Thompson and Terpening, 1983). That is, employees who are provided task-related information display greater job satisfaction and commitment than those who do not. A study of 48 US corporations by Nystrom (1990) found a strong positive relationship between vertical communication and commitment at all levels of management.

In an endeavour to improve commitment, organizations implement programmes designed to improve communication. However, research suggests that employee response to communication schemes of an educational nature is that of suspicion, especially when communication has been generally neglected in the past. For example, Marchington *et al.* (1994) note that none of the more educative communicative schemes which utilized team briefings and employee publications increased commitment or encouraged employees to work harder. Resistance to improved communication may also evolve from management themselves, it centres around several issues: lack of senior management support; organizational politics; fear of losing control; complaints that communication often resembles little more than a confusing collection of random information, and the amount of time and effort that such programmes require (Drennan, 1989b).

Walton and McKersie (1965) suggest that communication is not simply a rational educative approach related to job tasks. They broaden the definition, referring to communication as 'attitudinal restructuring'. Communication in this instance is the process by which an idea is transferred from a source to a receiver with the intention of changing his or her behaviour. However, the Confederation for British Industry, in its report on communication improvement schemes (CBI, 1976), states that it was unable to find any conclusive evidence that committed behaviour at work had actually changed or that teamwork functions had improved. In contrast, the second workplace 'Industrial Relations Survey' (CBI, 1981) found that the industrial climate, both with trade unions and the workforce as a whole, was more favourably assessed when management gave a lot of information to employees. The second survey also reported a high correlation between those employees regarding themselves as well informed and those reporting a high degree of job satisfaction.

A major survey conducted by the Institute of Directors in 1991 involving 115 medium and large companies in Britain categorically stated that there were improvements arising from management's giving extra attention to the need to communicate. These are identified in Table 3.2.

Table 3.2 Improvements attributed to communication initiatives

Activity	% (n = 115)
Improved morale/commitment	80
Fewer industrial disputes	68
Increased productivity	65
Better customer relations	47
Reduced employee turnover	46
Less time lost through absenteeism	41
Difficult to evaluate	8
No improvements	3

Source: Institute of Directors (1991)

The Institute of Directors' recorded outcomes are impressive; however, behavioural improvements are not necessarily a reaction to improved communication. They may occur because management provides, through a willingness to communicate with employees, an indication that the organization values employees. Could this be an essential characteristic of leadership, at least from the perspective of those who might follow? Marsh and Hussey (1979) suggest that it is the expressive nature of the communication rather than the factual content *per se* that employees value. Even the less than enthusiastic CBI (1976) report commented that, after an initial period of employee scepticism, they found that communication schemes were more likely to be accepted as the company 'taking the trouble' to improve communication. Such a reaction seems reminiscent of the Hawthorne lighting studies (Mayo, 1949).

The significance of that which is communicated can only be totally gained from understanding the substance of what is said. Simply, words need to match semantics. Meaning will be interpreted from the context, being 'the excess of meaning beyond the particular operational referent' (Cooper, 1986). Therefore, what potential leaders say will be interpreted by others 'within the context of what they say' and will be referenced against 'what they do'. Moreover, potential followers will be partially guided by what is not said but perceived by other senses. The disjunction between the sayer or doer and the said results in language (verbal or non-verbal) will have the power to generate meanings irrespective of the wishes of the sender. 'Text generates meanings with terrible liberality' (Sturrock, 1986); the context is as much a part of the communication itself. Hence, the importance of cohesion between what leaders communicate and what their actions might suggest.

- If the context is not synchronized with the words then the communication will be misinterpreted.
- If the words do not match the actions of the words then the communication may be misinterpreted.
- If the words do not relate to another's view of what the context should be, then the communication may not be effective.

While not denying the importance of communicating factual task-related information, what appears to be of equal importance is the process of communicating. Importantly, the process may contain indirect and perhaps conflicting messages that potential followers sense and interpret. Moreover, the outcome of employee perceptions may affect the level of commitment followers are willing to dedicate towards the goals of the organization and its leadership.

It is not just managers who sense the need to improve communication with employees. Potential followers sometimes attempt to improve communication with managers. For instance, Anderson and Matthew (1995) comment that employees in their study said that they 'communicated with their management to fulfil needs associated with (a) a satisfactory relationship (inclusion) and (b) closeness (affection)'. Findings of certain surveys suggest that communication involving senior management can bring about major improvements that can be measured in behavioural terms. Infante and Gorden (1993) found that employees who communicate with their superior senior management for pleasure report high satisfaction with those superiors. Simply, they are more inclined to view their management as leaders, and more inclined to follow their vision.

The search to predict human behaviour continues throughout the discipline of organizational behavioural theory. Unfortunately, no comprehensive answer exists as to what in human nature makes people behave the way they do. Moreover, when we talk of follower perceptions and values, we must consider internal psychological needs and motivations in order to gain a better understanding. The following sections attempt to assist.

Psychological energy

Schein (1980) offers some guidance to managers and students by suggesting that when considering human behaviour they should value a spirit of enquiry. The possibility of using the disparate disciplines of physics and psychology to inform understanding is intriguing, especially given difference in perceived objectivity sometimes associated with the two disciplines. The following brief text utilizes some basic explanations about 'energy' to help clarify what is meant by 'psychological energy' in behavioural terms. It was considered that such an interpretation held some answers as to why the term is often used when describing motivation and organizational commitment.

The term energy in relation to the study of physics is scientific in nature. Energy can exist in different forms: thermal, gravitational, nuclear, chemical etc. In human resource terms, we all possess personal energy in both physical and psychological terms. We must give credence to the difference between studying people compared with, for example, observing sub-atomic particles using the electron microscope. Nevertheless, many psychologists see psychology as modelling itself on the natural sciences. They counter critics of the discipline by suggesting that differences are only a matter of degree rather than kind.

Newton devised several laws about forces and motion. Put simply, an energy force is a push or pull of some kind. If you push or pull an object (which is free to move) it will begin to have motion. Organizational leaders require motion from potential followers, especially motion that is directed toward achieving specific goals. It is up to leaders to utilize their positional, expert and personal (or charismatic) power to energize potential followers. Indeed, the process of leadership might be measured by assessing a leader's ability to energize (push and pull) followers in a given direction. However, just as energy running through electricity pylons or gas mains can be misused or wasted – so too can psychological energy. The conditions under which individuals do and do not contribute their psychological energy to an enterprise are important. Energy wastage should be analysed, measured and checked. For example, common and observable signs of 'behavioural' energy wastage would include: politicking, manipulation and hidden agenda, rumour mongering, conflict rather than confrontation, goal displacement (unofficial goals), incongruent culture, employee complaints, absenteeism and lateness, blame stories etc.

Unfortunately, individual employees and not management processes are often blamed for 'energy wastage'. The inferred cause is often verbalized as the innate by-product of certain individuals. Moreover, signs of poor energy or energy wastage could be perceived by senior management as irrational manifestations of a negative organizational culture. However, further analysis may indicate poor commitment levels are the result of inadequate leadership. For instance, Harrison (1992) defines negative power as the power possessed by all employees, to withdraw energy, effort and commitment to the organization. Clearly, just as there are links between psychological energy and affective commitment, there are also links between negative power and alienative commitment. Management inability to understand and deal with negative power or non-committed energy is regarded as a major organizational weakness, and not one that should be associated with leadership.

Blumberg and Pringle (1982) suggest that employee performance is dependent upon an individual's capacity, opportunity and willingness to perform work tasks. Negative and positive energy relates to the willingness element. For example, a very capable (high capacity) employee working in an environment that offers many opportunities is still likely to perform unfavourably if their psychological energy (willingness to follow and perform) is low. Stated differently;

1.0 (Capacity) $\times$ 1.0 (Opportunity) $\times$ 0.1 (Willingness)

= 0.1 (Performance)

Conversely, a generally capable (medium capacity) employee working in an environment that offers some opportunities will perform more favourably if their psychological energy is high. For instance:

0.5 (Capacity) $\times$ 0.5 (Opportunity) $\times$ 1.0 (Willingness)

= 0.25 (Performance)

Most managers would agree that good energy usage and efficiency lies truly within their general responsibilities. As a measure, efficiency is equal to the useful energy output divided by total energy input. It is normal for management to monitor machinery efficiency by adopting the above rule. As for people, the basis of calculating productivity is by stating the human part of the equation as the number of employees engaged in the process. For example, units produced divided by the workforce 'head-count' gives an estimate of performance. Unfortunately, less attention is devoted to measuring the total psychological force input to the process. Leaders have a role to play. For example, it is up to senior management to ensure that sufficient and appropriate potential psychological energy is available. Knowing the extent of follower capacity is at least as important as knowing machine, manufacturing and/or production capacity.

Finally, if we reflect on the basic understanding of force and efficiency, we should acknowledge that psychological energy cannot be destroyed but simply moves or transforms itself from one kind to another. For example, if the organization restrains psychological energy, people may prefer to release energy outside the organization in other activities: the church, youth clubs, football, golf etc. Naturally, there is a need for social activity other than that provided by business organizations. However, often individuals cite the fact that due to the limitations of their job and inability of management to fully utilize their energy, they have to gain satisfaction (a home for their psychological energy and the source of regenerating energy) from external pursuits. A key leadership quality might therefore be seen as an acceptance by the leader to ensure that they behave in such a way that increases the chance of efficient and effective conversion *of* energy toward the good of the organization.

Speculation on the relationships and comparisons between laws of physics and psychology may provide insight. This section can be summarized as follows:

1 Psychological energy exists in all individuals.
2 Its amount varies with the 'state of mind' of the individual, and that state will be influenced by the individual's environment.
3 Psychological energy can leak from the organization or be wasted by the organization.
4 The amount of psychological energy in organizations is not fixed, nor is it limited. Therefore, improvements essential for the organization to move towards increased effectiveness are probable if they can distinguish and utilize appropriate levers.
5 The expression of psychological energy by an individual can never be permanently blocked but the individual may choose to re-direct it.

Importantly, good leaders appear to be able to bring out energy in followers. They do so by engaging with, and integrating the values and motivational needs of potential followers.

Follower values and attitudes

Chapter 2 described the strong influence of certain stakeholder values on management. Follower values and comparison with those of potential leaders may reveal important issues. Literature may assist.

Kassarjian and Sheffet (1982) define value as a general orientation of beliefs. They are normative standards that influence behaviour. They represent enduring beliefs that a specific type of conduct or end state is preferred (Jacob *et al.*, 1962).

Pennings (1970) defines work values as constellations of attitudes and opinions with which individuals evaluate their jobs and work environments. Herzberg *et al.* (1956) considered work values as representing motivational aspects, i.e. motivators and hygiene factors. Other authors see work values as representing Protestant work ethics, e.g. Furnham, 1984.

Value is the psychological aspect of thinking that relates to one's own principles and adopted standards that affect one's own judgement of what is valuable or important in life.

Values relate to what an individual would normally render important. Value from this standpoint is not simply useful and has estimable worth but is something that an individual puts a high value on obtaining. Borrowing terminology from the previous section, values are what people perceive as worthy of dedicating both physical and psychological energy.

Attitudes can be viewed as giving people a basis for expressing their values. For example, a manager who believes strongly in the work ethic will tend to voice attitudes towards specific individuals or work practices as a means of reflecting this value. A supervisor who wants a subordinate to work harder might put it this way:

Hard work has been the tradition of the company since its inception. It helped us get where we are today; everyone is expected to work hard.

Attitudes help to supply standards and frames of reference that allow people to organize and explain the world around them. No matter how accurate a person's view of reality is, attitudes towards people, events, and objects help the individual make sense out of what is going on. Importantly, attitudes are formed by means of reference to individual value systems, and they help employees adjust to their environment.

Kelly's (1955, p. 9) view of 'being' is that people act as scientists. People attempt to discover the reality of their environment and the truth of each situation by formulating theories, hypotheses and values. From this standpoint, followers' committed behaviour to an organization and its leaders results from individual assessment of their environment. Clearly, organizational groupings may share similar beliefs. Kelly's 'principle of commonality' confirms this notion. He suggests that constructs are often shared. There may be a natural and social overlap in construct systems 'to the extent that one person employs a construction of experience which is similar to that employed by another, his/her processes [and the work values that might arise – my interpretation] are psychologically similar to those of another person' (Kelly, 1955, p. 90). Commonality and sociality are promoted by direct pressures on us to see the world in the same way as others. This process can become ingrained into the culture of organizations. Moreover, the process may lead to organizations splitting into groups who share the same position on values of organizational life. Commonly, different value systems may separate employees at different levels within the organization.

In terms of values, organizations mean different things to different people who use them and work in them. For example, organizations may symbolize money or profit; order and stability; security and protection; as a means of obtaining status, prestige, self-esteem and self confidence, or power, authority and control; meaning, relevance and purpose etc. Likewise the goals of individual members or groups of members may be quite different from the collective purpose of the organized entity and hence a crucial organizational dilemma. Moreover, as mentioned in Chapter 2, power to define the collective purpose of the organization is not evenly distributed among its members. Managers at the top take the major decisions; other employees who have comparatively little influence are urged to comply. Therefore, some organizations attract the complaint that they dominate the liberty of the individual.

It may be worth remembering that organizations do not have goals. Only people have goals. Senior managers decide objectives and attempt to get others to agree with them by calling them 'organizational goals', but they are still the goals of people who determined them in the first place. None the less, owners urge employees adopting the role of a manager to be the agent of owners and steward of the organization. A senior manager will be ushered to estimate the worth of certain organizational aspects. In so doing, he or she is likely to behave in a way that reflects selected organizational goals and values. In this circumstance, personal values and organizational values may co-exist or be in conflict. If conflicting values exist, norms may provide management with informal guidelines on how to behave. Norms are unwritten rules of behaviour. They influence what we do, say, believe and even wear. The importance of certain values will be contained within organizational norms. Moreover, because they are often unwritten, and even unsaid, organizational norms can be difficult to reveal.

Employees may become quite skilled at showing behaviour that is seen as acceptable and conforms to the norms of the company. Clearly, conformity of behaviour may not reveal the true personal values of an individual, or the absence of conflict relating to incongruent and competing group values. It seems that many human problems of organization might be explained as conflict between individual human values and needs, and the constraints imposed on individuals in the interests of the organization's collective purpose. Fortunately for managers, employee attitudes, unlike deep-rooted values, can be changed, and sometimes it is in the best interests of potential leaders to try to do so.

Several authors consider values in general and work values specifically as important variables in explaining organizational commitment (Kidron, 1978; Putti *et al.*, 1989). According to Werkmeister (1967), commitment is a manifestation of the individual's own self, and reflects value standards that are basic to the individual's existence as a person. Kidron (1978) found a moderate relationship between work values and employee commitment. O'Reilly, Chatman, and Caldwell (1991) suggest that a measure of person-organizational fit based on shared values is significantly related to commitment. Consequently, the intensity of an employee's commitment may relate to the degree of cohesion between the individual employee's adopted theory-of-action in relation to an influential other's theory-of-action. To reiterate, one can suspect that if an individual perceives that influential 'others' consider their needs and values then it is likely that they will respond favourably. This notion would also suggest that congruent values are likely to result in committed behaviour. Conversely, values in disequilibrium may result in less committed behaviour – or simple compliance.

The late Princess of Wales said in 1995 'Everyone needs to be valued. If they are, they can give so much more back to society' (BBC, 1995). This is an interesting proposition, which seems to contain a good degree of face validity, especially in relation to the homeless of London. The Princess's use of language may seem more appropriate for organizations working in voluntary and charity sectors, and less appropriate for commercial organizations. Perhaps it is also inappropriate to view commercial organizations as a benevolent society. Most managers, after all, function as agents maintaining the financial interests of owners (principals). Consequently, it is not surprising that managers spend time encouraging and cajoling other employees to also act as agents to safeguard the interests of the principals.

If senior managers fail to act in accordance with owner wishes and values, the outcome may lead to what economists label the 'agency cost'. The agency cost is defined as the difference between what might have been earned if the owners (principals) had been the management, and what has been earned under the stewardship of management (agents) acting on behalf of the principals. Conventionally, principals turn to financial rewards to help motivate acceptable agent behaviour. Unfortunately, as discussed in Chapter 2, although managers may be convinced that management behaviour conducive to the wants of principals must be a prime concern, employees may not be so willing to act as agents. The result is divergence of interests and potential conflict. The principles of agency theory are 'alive and kicking' in most organizations but have been condemned by observers as 'managerialist' (Gomez-Mejia and Balkin, 1992). Armstrong (1999) refers to it as a 'dismal theory'. I would suggest that in capitalist economic society the relationship between principals (owners) and agents (managers) is a natural occurrence. However, agency theory does not transfer very well to the manager as 'principal' and worker as 'agent' relationship. Nevertheless, as firms come to rely more on the product of worker knowledge and attitudes as well as their labour, this problem is one requiring a solution.

It seems clear that managers as agents and owners as principals should not expect too much from people in any social setting if they are not valued at a level which they perceive to be the most appropriate. Consequently, it is up to leaders of organizations to ameliorate or limit divergence between the interests of owners and the interests of potential followers via rewards and incentives (Luthans, 2002). Ouchi (1981) and Pascale and Athos (1981) confirm that the best way to motivate people is to get their full commitment to the values of the organization. However, further analysis suggests that in addition to urging employees to accept the values of the organization, it is also possible that shared values and meanings may have a positive integrative effect (Janis, 1972; Shrivastava, 1985).

While considering the future of human resource management, Armstrong confirms this general principle but adds, 'the importance of shared values will become increasingly recognized. The emphasis will be on gaining commitment by using the hearts and minds approach to managing people' (Armstrong, 1991, p. 27). One can note the subtle philosophical change. For example, from the need to win the minds of employees by socializing them according to organizational priorities and needs, towards the acceptance that such a practice cannot be totally effective and thus senior management must develop methods to win the hearts of employees by promoting shared values.

The notion of 'mutuality' emphasizes identity and attachment between company and employee. Newman and Goswell (1995), chief executives of Mercury, support this notion and suggest that 'commitment will only take place if it is mutual. If the individual feels genuinely valued by the business, then they will take an immense pride in what they do.'

Successful leaders will ensure their actions relate to the implementation of shared values. Napoleon is said to have commented that 'leaders are merchants of hope, they succeed when they create senses of purpose, self-determination, impact, competence, and shared values'. However, the way in which potential followers perceive their values are integrated with those of the company may rest upon senior management's ability to balance the value-based role conflict of their responsibilities and ensure employee values are captured within their theory-of-action. Managers will have difficulty with this process – perhaps leaders do not.

Motivation

The term motivation comes from the Latin word *movere,* which simply means 'to move.' However, as suggested in the previous chapter, leaders want followers to do more than move. Willing and consistent behaviour toward the satisfaction of particular goals suggests more than movement.

What motivates people is itself a complex subject. Consequently, definitions abound and tend to favour a particular theory of motivation. Motivation has been referred to as a psychological process that gives behaviour some direction (Damachi *et al.,* 1983). Richie and Martin (1999) describe motivation as 'the drive behind the satisfaction of basic human needs and that such drives are specific to the individual'. Another definition suggests that motivation represents the forces that act on or within a person and can be viewed as 'that which causes the person to behave in a specific goal-orientated manner' (Hellriegel *et al.,* 1997). Similarly, Mitchell (1982) suggests motivation refers to those psychological processes that cause arousal, direction and persistence of voluntary actions that are goal-directed. Steers and Porter (1983) encompass many perspectives and approaches to motivation by stating 'when motivation is discussed, it is primarily concerned with what energizes human behaviour, what directs or channels such behaviour and how this behaviour is maintained and sustained'.

The importance of well-motivated employees is a growing concern because motivation affects the similarities and differences that exist in organization member behaviour. Importantly, motivated employees are central to high organizational performance. This is especially so for firms who operate in rapidly changing market environments where competition and the need for constant innovation and continuous improvements are intense. Of all the functions a manager and potential leader performs, motivating potential followers is arguably the most difficult. In 1994, Watson comments that 'motivation is the number one problem facing business today' – the problem is in danger of getting worse. Therefore, consideration of the interface between work motivation, senior management action, leadership and employee follower commitment is essential.

Psychologists often disagree about specific processes to which the term motivation refers. This is not surprising given that we cannot see a motive and it involves feelings. However, we may be willing to infer what motivation another person is exercising. To assist our understanding we are likely to use our own experiences, perceptions and judgement to help clarify the reasons for others' behaviour. However, it is possible that more than one motive is in operation at any one time by any one individual. Moreover, prime motivations may change. For example, research suggests that as an employee's income increases, money becomes less of a motivational factor (Kovach, 1987). Moreover, as an employee gets older, interesting work becomes more of a motivator. Clearly, we should accept the dynamic nature of the phenomenon. However, although individuals may differ as to the type, amplitude or intensity of the motivation, it is equally possible that groups of individuals will share a given motivation. The longevity of the motivation will probably relate to how long the motivational factor remains unsatisfied.

A working definition might suggest that motivation is an internal and individual process that guides, directs and/or drives behaviour toward the satisfaction of valued and perhaps prioritized needs or wants that can be enhanced or subdued by context. Such a definition recognizes that motivation is under the control of the individual but that personal experiences and perceived climatic factors may inherently affect or govern behaviour. From a managerial perspective 'motivation' may be referred to when trying to explain poor performance. However, when we say that a person is not motivated, what we are really stating is that a person is not motivated to do what we want them to do. They are motivated, but their motivation is directed at other things, for example, to save their energy for different pastimes and do as little work as possible.

Literature often seems to draw back from being overly positive, or negative, about the similarities and contrasts between motivation and commitment. Armstrong (1996) comments that 'Commitment is a wider concept than motivation and tends to be more stable over a period and less responsive to transitory aspects of an employee's job.' For example, it is possible that an employee could be highly committed to the organization while being dissatisfied with the job he or she performs. We can surmise therefore, that motivation and commitment have different time scales. However, this does not discount the notion that satisfied personal motivations within the workplace may substantially contribute to an individual's overall commitment. Agarwal (1997) makes a strong link between motivation and commitment by suggesting that 'most observers consider motivation to be concerned with an individual's expenditure of effort and energy and a sense of work commitment'. Moreover, Wallace (1997) asserts that the most important determinants for both continuance and affective commitment, is work motivation. He argues that management should therefore seek interventions that assist in motivating employees. Perhaps theory can help.

Motivational theory

Managers usually want a certain level of job performance from an individual and motivation is seen as one stage in a sequence of stages leading to that level of performance (Figure 3.1).

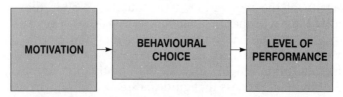

Figure 3.1 Stages from motivation to job performance level

There have been many attempts to gain a greater understanding as to why people decide to do 'the things they do' and 'adopt attitudes they adopt'. The former is often categorized as 'content' theories, and the latter 'process' theories. Theories have been subsequently used as a basis for managing. After reviewing the main theories of human motivation and their application to management, Schein (1980) concludes that all theories are right in some ways. The selection of theories that follow have been chosen on the basis that they have affected the theory or practice of managing in organizations. They are also important to understanding the source of follower psychological energy.

Needs (content) theories

Needs theory uses characteristics or attributes of the person to explain behaviour. There is likely to be an association between psychological energy and the satisfaction or dissatisfaction of needs, for example, the energy output to satisfy a need, the energy output to maintain satisfaction of a need, or the energy lost due to the lack of satisfaction related to a need. Needs/content theories include:

- *Murray's theory of human personality*: need for achievement; need for recognition; need for affiliation.
- *Maslow's hierarchy of needs*: physiological, safety, belonging-ness, esteem and self-actualization.
- *Alderfer's ERG theory*: need for existence, relatedness and growth.
- *McClelland's achievement motivation theory*: need for achievement, power and affiliation.
- *Herzberg's theory*: motivators and hygiene factors.

The idea of need is basic to Murray's explanations of human behaviour. Need is a hypothetical notion used to explain observable differences in behaviour among different people or the same person over time. In Murray's words:

> *Between what we can directly observe – the stimulus and the resulting action – a need is an invisible link, which may be imagined to have the properties that an understanding of the observed phenomena demands. (Murray, 1938, p. 73)*

Murray's need theory is based upon the premise that individuals will try to behave in a way that satisfies an activated need. Figure 3.2 lists the needs in his theory of human personality.

Theory should assist understanding. Murray's theory provides a list of needs, the priority of which may change. Indeed several

Need	Description
➤ Achievement	The need to attain perceived difficult goals
➤ Affiliation	The need to associate with others
➤ Acquisition	The need to gather belongings
➤ Aggression	The need to deride and blame others
➤ Autonomy	The need to be independent
➤ Blame-avoidance	The need to behave in a conventional manner
➤ Deference	The need to admire a person in authority
➤ Dominance	The need to control
➤ Exhibition	The need to draw attention to oneself
➤ Nurturance	The need to help others
➤ Order	The need to organize and arrange things
➤ Recognition	The need to receive credit for one's actions

Figure 3.2 Murray's theory of human personality (after Murray, 1938, pp. 80–3)

content theories are based on the assumption that man is a perpetually wanting animal dominated by unsatisfied needs. Maslow's (1943) Hierarchy of Needs illustrates an order of priority needs:

- *Level 1* – Biological/physiological/basic needs: air, thirst, hunger, sleep, warmth, sex.
- *Level 2* – Safety needs: protection, freedom from pain, security, order, law, stability.
- *Level 3* – Belongingness/social needs: love, friendships, work groups, family, affection.
- *Level 4* – Esteem needs/ego needs: self-respect; confidence, independence, achievement; respect from others, reputation, status, recognition, attention, importance, appreciation.
- *Level 5* – Self-actualization needs: to fulfil one's potential.

According to Maslow's theory, people have to satisfy various needs and that the priority given to needs will fluctuate. Maslow (1954) suggests that a need would only become a motivator if it were dissatisfied. Furthermore, attention would focus on the most basic need that is unsatisfied. Moreover, a person would not pursue the next higher order need in the hierarchy until their currently recognized need was substantially or completely satisfied. Clearly, when one is starving the need for esteem is far less relevant. Similarly, it is difficult (if not impossible) to expect someone to be motivated to achieve extensive sales targets if they are having problems in their marriage or if their house has just been repossessed.

In many organizations today, at least in the Western world, basic and safety needs of followers and leaders are normally satisfied, but the need for esteem remains. Esteem needs are based on a person's need to value themselves, for self-respect or self-esteem, and importantly to receive respect from others, especially influential others.

An essential criticism of Maslow's theory is that the theory is not always specific enough to let investigators develop testable hypothesis and to design studies that use the proper tests (Wahba and Bridwell, 1976). Furthermore, Maslow's theory creates an uncomfortable paradox for lecturers and students alike. The theory is widely accepted but there is little research evidence to support it. Two studies that tested the notion of progression did not find empirical support (Hall and Nougaim, 1972).

Similarly to Maslow's hierarchy of needs, a modified model by Alderfer (1972), describes three groups of basic needs applicable to the organizational setting. Existence, relatedness and growth need, commonly referred to as 'ERG' theory:

- *E*xistence needs: concern for survival – similar to Maslow's safety needs.
- *R*elatedness: concern for interpersonal relationships – similar to Maslow's social needs.
- *G*rowth: concern for personal development – similar to Maslow's esteem needs.

Complementary to Maslow, Alderfer perceives that an unsatisfied need is a motivator. Once a need is satisfied it is no longer a motivator. Two forms of movement are described. First, the satisfaction-progression movement is the same as developed by Maslow's theory. For example, satisfaction of a need leads on to a higher level of need. The second movement is frustration-regression. A person will move down the 'needs hierarchy' if the need required is frustrated. For instance, we might consider a situation where a potential follower may reach a level of growth needs but due to organizational influences is thwarted from satisfaction. Consequently, unsatisfied needs may lead to problem behaviour. For example, if an employee needs high recognition from his or her organizational context and does not receive it, or is prevented from doing so, then employee behaviour may become puzzling to managers. In this situation, employees may conform sufficiently to avoid disparagement, but they are unlikely to be

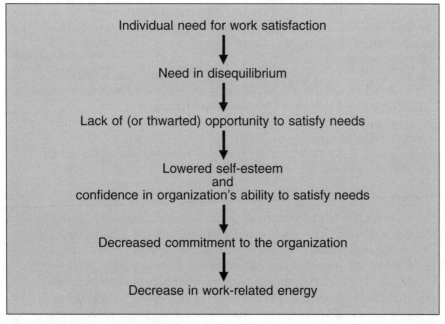

Figure 3.3 Needs in disequilibrium

enthusiastically following. Figure 3.3 illustrates the possible interconnection.

Alderfer's theory predicts that the individual in such circumstances will move down the hierarchy to relatedness needs. The individual may become locked into a 'deficiency cycle' at the bottom of the 'needs hierarchy'. In contrast, and by way of an incentive to leaders, potential followers can also become locked into the top of the hierarchy, the process is described by Alderfer as the 'enrichment cycle'. An individual who successfully satisfies growth satisfaction needs, wants them even more. Consequently, if leaders can provide room for satisfaction of growth needs, then employees will follow.

One can conclude that the satisfaction of needs helps increase psychological energy toward the satisfaction of the same need. Research suggests that the enrichment cycle has empirical support, especially in settings that offer challenge and satisfaction of personal achievement levels (Alderfer, 1972).

McClelland's achievement motivation theory

McClelland's achievement motivation theory is the product of an impressive research programme spanning some 40 years, although some criticism surrounds measurement methods (Entwistle, 1972). However, Atkinson (1981) and his colleagues have successfully rebutted the criticism, allowing some confidence in the research results. The essential nature of McClelland's theory focuses on three needs, each associated with different behaviour:

1 The need for achievement, defined as the need for success as perceived and measured by the individual.
2 The need for affiliation, defined as the need for friendly and warm relationships.
3 The need for power, defined as the need to control and/or influence others.

Achievement motivation theory seems very usable within Western society and Western organizational cultures because it stresses the need for achievement and perhaps the attainment of power through higher economic performance. People with a strong need for achievement take responsibility for the results of their behaviour. They want to succeed and set their own goals. They seek positions and situations that provide the opportunity to achieve. They look for and welcome feedback. They want to solve problems (McClelland, 1961). Not surprisingly, McClelland's research found that senior managers/directors/executives usually had higher needs for achievement scores than people in other occupations or levels of the organization. People who are highly motivated by achievement may have been socialized to accept the 'values of their organizational culture'. From experience, it is common for senior management self-assessment of their personality to reveal a high need for achievement (see Case Study 2, Chapter 2).

Could difference in hierarchical level provide insight as to why needs and values may often be viewed as incongruent in the workplace? Some employees at lower hierarchical levels may not have the same opportunity to satisfy their need for achievement. For instance, the work situation might not be sufficiently stimulating for some potential followers to satisfy higher order needs, especially those undertaking repetitious, uninteresting and generally monotonous work activities. Such people may also feel a lack of affiliation in terms of psychological separation from those who wish and/or are able to achieve. Secondly, employees who are not overly motivated by the value of 'achievement' in the organization may have a greater need for 'affiliation'. A strong need for affiliation will focus on 'establishing, maintaining and restoring positive affective relations with others' (Atkinson and Birch, 1978). These people desire close and warm relationships with those around them. Such people need the approval of others, especially those about whom they care or those they perceive as influential. Importantly, if a strong need for affiliation is thwarted, followership in these circumstances becomes inherently problematic. This is especially the case if managers are perceived as the influential others at the root of the frustration.

Miller, Catt and Carlson (1996) state: 'Employees who are treated with respect, encouraged to excel, and rewarded for their efforts are more likely to demonstrate motivated job performance.' Employees, however, may perceive a manager or group of managers as the cause of unfulfilled needs and consequent feelings of frustration. Clear signs of frustration might include behaviour signalling the importance of outside interests, general signs of boredom, resistance to change, blaming others, demanding more pay to compensate for frustration, or poor quality of work. Clusters of signs would clearly be better indicators of frustration.

Chapter 1 mentioned the influence of globalization and internationalization. Informed by the work of Hofstede (1980) on cultural difference, we might generally assume that employees in the Western world and Australasia care most strongly about achievement, esteem and self-actualization. Employees in South American countries, Greece and Japan may care more about security, while those in Scandinavian countries may be strongly motivated by social needs. Consequently, potential leaders might expect difference to occur as to preferences for satisfaction of certain needs – although some needs may not be so specific. For example, Trompenaars (1993) suggests that in terms of organizational behaviour, work relationships and rules, they are more or less universal. Such a finding might suggest that certain motivational dimensions that are key to work relationships may not vary across national divides. The importance of achievement to leaders and affiliation to followers may also prove to be international. As for understanding and improving specific work motivations, Herzberg's intrinsic satisfiers seem a fair point at which leaders might start.

Motivation and employee satisfaction

Herzberg (1966) produced factors that he stated were causes of satisfaction and dissatisfaction at work. He noticed that factors associated with satisfaction were quite different from factors associated with dissatisfaction. Removing dissatisfaction factors did not necessarily lead to satisfaction; conversely, increasing the satisfaction factors did not reduce levels of dissatisfaction. One group that 'if not satisfied' caused dissatisfaction was labelled 'hygiene factors'. Similar to Maslow's lower level needs, hygiene factors include working conditions, salary and relationships with other workers. The other group was labelled 'motivation factors' and is associated with satisfaction (see Figure 3.4). Motivation factors complement Maslow's esteem and self-actualizing higher order needs.

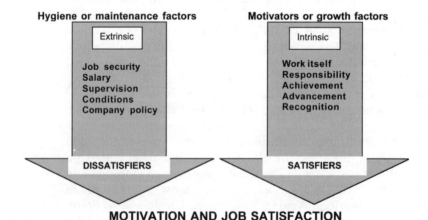

Figure 3.4 Herzberg's (1966) motivators and hygiene factors

Most people would acknowledge that the Herzberg categories exist in most organizations. Generally, the two-factor model identifies important drives for individuals working within organizations. However, confidence in the theory must relate to the methodology chosen by Herzberg.

Using an interview approach, Herzberg did his early research with samples of accountants and engineers. Each person was interviewed and asked to recall a past work event they found especially positive or especially negative (Herzberg *et al.*, 1959). Vroom questions the basic validity of retrospective interviews (Vroom, 1964). Simply, retrospective analysis relies upon the interpretation provided by the researcher. Herzberg has responded to critics suggesting that conventional methods of data collection also attract bias.

The original study has been replicated many times. Samples have covered a number of different nationalities. However, empirical research designed to test the motivator-hygiene theory has had mixed results. Some commentators state that work by researchers other than Herzberg and his team has not produced confirming evidence (House and Wigdor, 1967). Conversely, others have found that results have largely been consistent with Herzberg's original findings (Bockman, 1971; Filley *et al.*, 1976).

A common misinterpretation of Herzberg's theory is that pay is unimportant because it is not categorized as a motivation factor. Pay and salary is clearly important. Herzberg continues to argue the importance of pay – but as a hygiene not a motivation factor. Other observers comment that the theory has little appeal to manual workers whose primary motivation is pay. If indeed manual workers are highly motivated by pay, this finding may say more about the kinds of jobs held by manual workers, and as mentioned earlier, the view that such employees have less chance to operationalize growth factors.

The Herzberg categories are in constant use by trainers/tutors and lecturers in attempts to explain aspects of motivation. It is an attractive theory for management and students because it is easy to understand, it provides a common-sense guide to possible practical interventions and it is easy to remember. During research, I challenged different groups of senior managers/directors to criticize or add to the categories used by Herzberg. Derivatives were sometimes offered, but the framework was left intact. It was agreed that as a guideline to what motivates employees, the Herzberg categories appear to possess a fair degree of face validity. They implicitly offer management [and perhaps potential leaders] specific recommendations about how to improve employee motivation and commitment. For instance, managers wishing to manage by means of motivators must first improve hygiene factors so that the organizational context does not distract employees from experiencing motivational satisfiers.

Content theory provides categorization/dimensions useful to understanding work motivation. However, the weighting that managers or potential leaders might apply to each dimension is unclear. However, much of the organizational context is within the control of potential leaders, and employee perception of organizational context is often centred on how they behave. If managers can understand and work toward satisfying key needs of potential followers, then perhaps there is a better chance they will be perceived of as leaders. Moreover, if senior management can improve their understanding of employees' need structures in relation to their own organizational responsibilities, then it follows that they can improve their control of the circumstances that influence behaviour. Evans (1996) comments that 'if the individual needs of employees are satisfied then corporate needs of an organization will be equally satisfied'. He adds, 'it's as simple and as complicated as that'.

Expectancy (process) theory

Process theories focus on behavioural choice that can lead to desired rewards. Expectancy theory appears to borrow from 'needs theories' concerning individuals desire to satisfy a need. It also uses the behaviourist approach to human behaviour (Skinner, 1976) in that a certain action will result in a certain outcome. It concerns itself with probability considerations in relation to estimating the likelihood that a certain action/behaviour will result in a desired outcome. Vroom (1964) makes four assumptions relating to individuals and behaviour:

1 Forces in the environment and the individual interact to affect behaviour.
2 People choose a course of action.
3 People's choice is based upon preferences for a certain outcome.
4 The process of choice is rational.

Researchers generally agree that employees who do not have their expectations met are more likely to be less committed to their organization (Avner *et al.*, 1982; Caldwell and O'Reilly, 1983). Porter and Steers (1973) consider that met expectations are better understood by the discrepancy between what an employee encounters in terms of positive and negative outcomes and what was expected to be encountered. The provision and responsibility for positive and negative outcomes clearly lie with senior management. The practicalities of this issue are discussed further in Chapter 4.

The first notion of expectancy theory suggests that effort is the extent to which a person tries to perform at a given level of performance. The word 'try' is purposely used to assist appreciation that the outcome may not be totally within the control of the person. Behaviour is likely to consist of many contextual influences. Nevertheless, expectancy theory suggests that a person will work hard to meet a desired outcome thus formulating the *effort–performance* (E→P) relationship (Tosi and Carroll, 1982).

The second notion introduces the view that a person will relate *performance* to a desired *outcome* (P→O). Outcomes will vary, but Vroom lists instrumental rewards, for example pay as well as non-financial rewards such as praise from the boss.

The third idea in expectancy theory is that of valence. *Valence* (V) is the preference an individual has among available outcomes. An outcome an individual desires will have a positive valence. Outcomes that are unwanted receive a negative valence and if a person is indifferent to an outcome then valence is zero.

Expectancy theory says that people perceive a connection between effort or expended energy and a performance level. They also perceive a link between level of performance and a desired outcome. However, if indifferent to an outcome (valence zero), the individual will not be highly motivated even though they may believe they can achieve the outcome.

The general goal of organizational behaviour is to help the process of predicting and controlling human behaviour in the workplace. Hence, Vroom's theory is well accepted by organizational behaviour lecturers as a foundation for discussion. However, research literature shows mixed support (Heneman and Schwab, 1972; Shapiro and Wahba, 1974; Garland, 1984). Much criticism relates to the mechanical nature of the formulae offered within the theory. Moreover, it would appear that it presently falls short of recommending actions managers may take in the process of controlling or encouraging desired behaviour. However, the theory can serve as an analytical tool for understanding behaviour. An example may assist.

If an outcome is seen by a potential follower as positively valent, but he or she knows they cannot achieve it (expectancy zero), the theory predicts the person will not be highly motivated. To illustrate this, a potential follower may need recognition from their leader to be willing to follow. He or she may want the outcome of greater recognition (a high valence) but may believe that it will not occur (expectancy zero), and so he or she will not be highly motivated to follow. The physical and psychological effort a given individual would be willing to expend on the behalf of the organization would therefore not be optimized. Consequently, management behaviour that decreases (or does not have the propensity to increase) employee expectancy of a desired need (a positive valence), will not encourage high motivation and organizational commitment. Unfortunately, given differences in interests of various stakeholders and that many situations will occur that are outside the control of leaders, consistent satisfaction of all stakeholder expectancies is improbable – this is reality. None the less, from an employee and potential follower perspective, it may be more important for the leader to be perceived as trying to behave in accordance with follower expectancies. Failure by the leader may then be perceived by followers as simply beyond the leader's control.

Perception of a leader or follower is an important factor related to performance. Attribution theory (Heider, 1958) is a process by which we interpret the causes of behaviour in terms of perceived internal and external forces. Internal forces are those that generally relate to an individual's ability and skills. External forces are found in factors such as company policy, procedure and regulations as well as the manner and behaviour of superiors. External factors would also include luck, or environmental factors such as the influence of the weather. From an individual perspective, the theory suggests that if an individual attributes success in a task as a product of their own efforts (internal forces), then they are more likely to believe they can continue to influence their level of performance. Moreover, if individuals continuously attribute success to internal forces, they will be more satisfied with their job and will prefer a participatory style of management. Research suggests that such individuals are more likely to be found occupying management positions (Mitchell *et al.*, 1975). In contrast, individuals who perceive that external forces control outcomes are more likely to believe that they cannot influence performance and consequently will not be motivated to improve performance.

Potential leaders wishing to motivate employees might consider attributing and recognizing successful performance as being a product of internal forces. In theory, this process should assist individuals to change their locus of control and to reconsider outcomes as a product of their own efforts. Again, in theory, this would lead employees to attribute success as the outcome of their own efforts, to have greater work satisfaction, to be motivated to repeat the process, and thus provide improved work performance. However logical this notion is, it is not overly surprising that many managers would be reluctant to follow or to support the process. Even if management attributes success to an individual or group's internal forces, they might not wish to acknowledge it because of the economically rational fear of driving wages up. Perhaps the potential longer-term cost of poor performance caused by de-motivated or poorly committed employees is often ignored. Similar to difficulties of implementing many behavioural theories, such a response is probably due to the intangibility of theory. In this case, the intangibility of attribution theory as compared with the perceived tangibility of cost.

Exchange and equity theory

Classic exchange theory informs both leadership and follower-ship. Adams (1965) suggests that people come together because they can exchange items of value. If leaders provide more benefits than burdens for followers, then followers are likely to follow willingly. However, it is probable that followers may value certain items of exchange. For example, discussion suggests that it is more common today for employees to value higher order motivational needs in exchange for their knowledge and services. Consequently, a clear difference between managers and leaders may be that leaders understand which items are most valued and act accordingly.

Several studies support the positive impact of equity on job satisfaction (Price and Bluedorn, 1980; Bluedorn, 1982; Price and Mueller, 1986). A feeling of equity only occurs when each party perceives the inputs and outputs of the relationship are roughly equal. In comparing their own job inputs and outcomes with those of co-workers, employees perceive them to be fair when equity is high.

Huseman, Hatfield and Miles (1987) recognized three types of individuals who may have different preferences for equity. They categorize groups of individuals as 'entitleds', 'benevolents' and 'equity sensitives'. Entitleds are comfortable with their equity ratio. These individuals perceive that their equity ratio is higher than that of their comparison other. Benevolents are willing to accept that their equity ratio may be lower. In an individualistic and highly competitive economic environment, it seems likely that few people will neatly fit into this category. Equity sensitives perceive their equity ratio is lower than that of their comparison other and seek the means to adjust it.

Regarding comparison, the theory can also be interpreted in terms of the relationship of psychological contract between potential followers and leader. The psychological contract can only be in balance when employees perceive that their work needs are being satisfied, and the employer perceives that the workforce is providing the desired level of motivation and commitment to the business. Perceptions of positive inequity and negative inequity must be avoided in an attempt to achieve a workable balance. The aspect of equilibrium and the need for balance within the leader–follower relationship re-emerge.

From the 'equity sensitive' individual's point of view, he or she will attempt to reduce the conflict of disequilibrium. Altering the input–output relationship can do this. Weiss (1996) comments that individuals are motivated to reduce perceived inequities to make outcomes to inputs (O/I) ratios equal. For example, if an individual perceives that senior management value profitability while thwarting their need for recognition, then the individual may decide to reduce their input. In the condition of perceived negative equity, the employee may reduce their effort, productivity, or quality of work, thus bringing the perceived relationship into equilibrium. Unfortunately, the employee's action may be perceived by senior management as inequitable. Thus, the senior management–employee relationship may spiral downwards as parties attempt to achieve their perception of equity. By altering the input–output elements, the individual reduces tension and frustration. However, in the analogy it is possible that a reduction in tension will only be short-lived. Continuance may lead to what is commonly called the 'us and them' syndrome. From experience, this poor relationship state is very common, but it has no place in situations where potential leaders are wishing to encourage potential followers.

An alternative to reducing one's effort and thereby changing inputs is for an individual to attempt to change the output. In the contractual employee–employer relationship, this commonly takes the shape of employees asking for more pay. Nevertheless, if money is not the whole cause, perceived inequity will remain. The relationship may deteriorate until the next pay round 'once again' appeases the need for equity. An atmosphere of trust is unlikely to emerge.

Conceptually, there are similarities between cognitive dissonance and equity theory. Cognitive elements are defined as any knowledge, opinion or belief about oneself or one's environment. Festinger (1958) explains that when any two cognitive elements become inconsistent with each other it will lead to a psychologically uncomfortable state of cognitive dissonance. Aronson (1968) noted that it is the inconsistency between behaviour or attitudes and one's own self-concept that is dissonance-arousing. For example, it will be disturbing to an employee if he or she perceives they are good at their job but receive insufficient rewards. Similarly disturbing would be to expect consideration from management and not receive it.

Festinger (1958) suggests that in a situation in which the goals of the individual conflict with the goals of the firm, 'there is a tendency for the person to attempt to change one of them so that they fit together, thus reducing or eliminating dissonance.' Individuals generally adjust their aspirations downward when they do not accomplish their goals or satisfy their needs (Lewin *et al.*, 1944; Myers and Fort, 1963). It follows that in these circumstances the employee is likely to be de-motivated, and therefore demonstrate far less commitment to the company and probably none to its potential leaders. As an example, imagine a situation where an employee's intervention could save money or increase productivity. Perceiving inequitable treatment, they may be unlikely to take the initiative. Thus, faults and errors may creep into the work process. Clearly, mistakes, time delays or non-interventions by those who have the ability and opportunity to control process will cost money, thus reducing efficiency whilst increasing customer complaints and effecting organizational performance. Generally, the employee can withdraw a certain amount of effort before withdrawal of effort becomes too obvious. The employee is likely to operate within the rules. Consequently, in such situations employee behaviour will most likely resemble continuance rather than affective commitment. Further analysis might reveal a degree of alienative commitment.

Rewards and incentives

Tolman *et al.* (1946) suggests that individuals do not merely react in behaviourist terms to contingencies within their environment. All employees have the ability to anticipate, evaluate and choose a course of action that will satisfy some needs and values. Employees attempt to control their environment so that their work motivation needs and values receive the best chance that they will be satisfied. The individual can be conceived of as a rational goal-seeking entity which processes information and makes decisions in his or her own self-interest (Porter and Lawler, 1968; Campbell and Pritchard, 1976). Goal theory, sometimes called the theory of goal setting, is based on the premise that people's goals play an important part in determining behaviour. In organizations, people's goals may be the same as the goals of the organization. However, it would be an over-generalization to suggest that this is always the case. They maximize their own subjective expected utility (Edwards, 1954). Consequently, in terms of motivations, expectancy and performance, we expect individual behaviour to relate to outcomes that are perceived by the individual as the most desirable and probable (Vroom, 1964; Graen, 1969).

Researchers have found support for a relationship between commitment and rewards (Angle, 1983). All forms of commitment assume instrumental or calculative motivations based upon remuneration. While accepting that money is an incentive to all who have to work for a living, reliance on monetary reward is only likely to offset symptoms of organizational ill-health. Blinder (1990) comments that 'it appears that changing the way workers are treated may boost productivity more than changing the way they are paid'. Fletcher and Williams (1992) note the complex issues that are connected with motivation of people at work and acknowledge that there is little consistency of viewpoint on the motivating power of money. Moreover, their UK study found that there was a lack of thought and imagination tackling the issue of rewards and recognition.

Intrinsic and extrinsic non-financial motivations must be considered (Brief and Aldag, 1980; O'Reilly and Caldwell, 1980). Extrinsic motivation is related to tangible rewards and includes salary and fringe benefits. Non-financial extrinsic reward might include security, conditions of service, the employment contract and working conditions. Perhaps more important to the leader–follower relationship, intrinsic motivation relates to the need for esteem, for instance, psychological rewards such as a feeling of being appreciated, receiving positive reinforcement and recognition, being treated in a caring and considerate manner and being given the chance to use and achieve using one's own abilities. Chapter 4 adopts the assumption that intrinsic needs require particular leader attention and offers explanation and techniques as to how these needs might be addressed by leaders in organizations. Meanwhile, one reason why intrinsic factors might have been overlooked is that managers have a different view as to what motivates workers. It is intriguing to compare research appertaining to perceptions of management and workers as to the priority of what motivates workers (see Table 3.3).

Couger and Zawacki (1980) utilize common motivational factors to ascertain possible difference in worker/manager perspective. Clearly, their study suggests managers consider safety and instrumental security needs as key to worker motivation. Workers, however, appear to favour needs more commonly associated with a combination of security, emotional, social and esteem needs. In particular, the motivational factor 'recognition' is conspicuously weighted differently. A study by Kovach (1987) reveals a similar finding (see Table 3.4).

Tables 3.3 and 3.4 provide evidence of a disjunction between manager perception and workers' actual work need preferences.

Table 3.3 Motivation – worker and manager perspectives (Couger and Zawacki)

Worker's view of worker's motivation	Manager's view of worker motivation
1 Interesting work	1 Good salary
2 Recognition	2 Security
3 In the know	3 Personal development
4 Security	4 Working conditions
5 Good salary	5 Interesting work
6 Personal development	6 Empowerment (discretion)
7 Working conditions	7 Loyalty
8 Loyalty	8 Recognition
9 Social support	9 Social support
10 Empowerment (discretion)	10 In the know

Source: Couger and Zawacki (1980)

Table 3.4 Motivation – worker and manager perspectives (Kovach)

Worker's view of worker's motivation		Manager's view of worker motivation	
Recognition	First priority	Good salary	First priority
Good salary	Sixth priority	Recognition	Eighth priority

Source: After Kovach (1987)

Accepting that workers were telling the truth as to the intensity of what motivates them, difference lies with management inter-pretation of what motivates workers. Clearly, manager inter-pretations of worker motivation, at least in the Western world, is probably built on industrial/employee relations whereby trade union/company disputes focused on, or were settled by, pay bargaining. Constant attention to instrumental issues might have become the norm, and consequently managers concentrate on such issues.

Findings by Couger and Zawacki (1980) and Kovach (1987) may also infer that managers seek satisfaction from factors different to other employees. For management, pay and security, probably linked to a sense of achievement, are crucially important. Other

employees see interesting work and recognition as most important. Such a view is supportive of earlier analysis regarding
McClelland's theory. The variance in perspective could explain
why senior management might mistakenly adopt and maintain a
conventional theory-of-action. A consequence being the importance of motivational factors more closely related to emotional and
social worker needs might be overlooked. A further outcome
might be sub-optimization of potential employee commitment,
organizational performance and long-term competitive advantage.

De Bono (1973), in his book *Children Solve Problems,* suggests
that many years of formal education often affect our ability to
think. Conscious of the need to think laterally and imaginatively
in writing this book, I asked my young son what it is that we, his
parents, do that makes him try so hard at school. His reply was
simple, 'I try hard because you show you care about me and what
I do.' Is this analogy an illustration of 'moral glue'? We could
hypothesize that if potential leaders are considerate of the
workforce, it seems likely that employees will have confidence in
them and become more committed to the organization. My son's
commitment seems inherently associated with a motivational
need for being valued. This is a basic need and perhaps
supersedes all other motivational factors. It may also be important
to understanding the relationship between leadership and willing
followers.

Recognition

Figure 3.5 summarizes forms and levels of recognition.

Murray (1938) simply defined recognition as the need to receive
credit for actions. Herzberg (1966, 1968, 1974) sees recognition as
a motivator in contrast to a hygiene factor. Both assist our
understanding. However, findings suggest that recognition, as a
motivational factor requires additional thought.

In the sense of memory and consciousness, recognition means
realizing that a certain stimulus event is one you have seen or
heard before. For recognition, you need simply to match a
remembered stimulus against a present perception. Both are in the
consciousness of the individual (Zimbardo, 1988). An external
stimulus enters short-term memory and is processed to establish
meaning by reference to an internal stimulus. All of which helps
us to understand the facts as we perceive them and the semantics
or meaning of the stimulus.

Recognition can be seen in terms of recall and memory. It can
also be seen as a motivational need. However, in many ways the

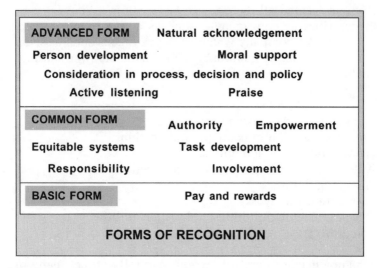

Figure 3.5 Forms of recognition

two are interconnected. Both involve external stimulus, short-term conscious processing and reference to long-term memories, thoughts and events. However, the need to be recognized rather than the memory process of recognition puts greater emphasis on motivation, values, beliefs, interests and needs.

The role of the manager in rewarding and recognizing perform-ance are two of the essential managerial practices identified by Yukl and Falbe (1990). Recognition from this point of view takes place when employees perform well. It is something that normally occurs after the event. Recognition is unlikely to be given to employees who do not perform well. This is an instrumental view of recognition. It is something that management can provide or withdraw at will.

Recognition or non-recognition of employees can also be explained by use of attribution theory. For instance, if managers perceive, believe, or explain good employee performance as attributable to external forces then they are unlikely to recognize employees or individual achievement. As a consequence, employ-ees who perceive success to be attributed to their own efforts and not external forces may be de-motivated by management reluc-tance to recognize their efforts.

Clearly, recognition is often seen as synonymous with pay. When senior managers (Institute of Directors, 1993–2002) were asked to describe non-financial rewards they invariably suggested the need for praise, especially 'a pat on the back'. Although interpretative parameters were unsurprising, nevertheless, descriptions seemed all too often to be 'shallow'. What Luthans (1995) describes as consumables such as a free lunch, manipulatives such as a company watch or car, or tokens such as share options were frequently mentioned. Non-financial rewards would also include the following (Kerr, 1975):

- Titles.
- Formal commendations and rewards.
- Favourable mention in company publications.
- Freedom concerning job duties.
- Private, informal recognition for a job well done.
- Challenging duties.
- Varied, interesting work.
- Important, meaningful duties and responsibilities.
- Having influence in setting goals and making decisions.

The senior management role would naturally attract many of the above items. Other employees however, may not be so gratified. Reward and recognition by means of the 'job itself' is less likely for employees who do not perceive they hold a job of their choosing that involves important, challenging, meaningful duties etc.

While Kerr's (1975) views about rewards and recognition by means of non-financial incentives provide classic reading, the essence and foundation of what it means to feel recognized within the organization is relatively untapped. Nevertheless, if employees are to feel recognized, it is important that managers discover the value of recognition, possibly from different perspectives.

The act of recognition is more than a list that managers can use as a reward for good performance. Although few would deny the importance of receiving money and benefits, recognition involves less tangible but none the less important artefacts. In principle, what I entitle the act of 'natural recognition' is simple. It involves thinking and asking questions about a certain issue, person or body. It also means asking questions in relation to their needs and values, and acting upon information in a way that is supportive. Parents show recognition by asking questions about their children's activities, their schooling and general development, their health etc. Children also expect parents to acknowledge their existence by talking to them (Schaffer, 1987; Donaldson, 1988). Such activities are all beyond financial support and providing a safe and healthy living environment. Recognition by the parent, being an influential figure within a child's world is both an essential developmental feature and a natural occurrence (Donaldson, 1988). Support, consideration, development and simple but continuous acknowledgement of one's existence might also describe natural recognition. Such aspects may include but go beyond social rewards such as friendly greetings, 'one off' compliments and formal acknowledgement of achievement. Importantly, natural recognition can occur before, during and after an individual performs well. During research, the following working definition proved useful: Recognition in the workplace involves the acquisition of financial and non-financial rewards, but in essence, feeling recognized relates to the value an individual places on the basic need to be acknowledged and considered by influential others within the organization.

It seems clear that each motivational factor is in some direct or indirect way under the control of senior management. Moreover, the factors are strongly influenced by senior management action. It is equally clear that leaders wishing to enthuse 'affective followership commitment' would go further than instrumental managerial strategies, and would include considered use of motivational factors such as recognition, praise, self-esteem etc. Importantly, the need for esteem is directly related to the motivational factor recognition.

A conclusion emanating from the Hawthorne Lighting experiment (Mayo, 1949) was that employee motivation had increased by making workers feel noticed or perhaps even special. One important aspect of the experiment relates to senior management involvement. Senior management had taken the trouble to explain the experiment to the employees involved in the study. Their actions would have communicated to employees that they were important, involved, recognized and considered. Goddard (1987) quotes evidence arising from cultural change recognition programmes within Western Electric, Western Airlines and many of the Fortune 500 companies in the USA. He reports that praise and recognition have shown to have beneficial effects on productivity.

Walton (1985, p. 79) states that 'managers have to choose between a strategy based on imposing control and a strategy based on eliciting commitment'. He argues that a commitment strategy is consistent with the continuous recognition of employees as an essential stakeholder in an organization, and it leads to higher levels of performance. Natural recognition, as described above, is likely to involve potential leader ability to recognize and integrate employee values and needs. It fits well with the motivational need for esteem, to have the esteem of influential others, to be regarded as useful and important. It involves employee need for contact with senior figures. Berne (1963) talks of 'recognition' hunger being the need for animate contact. It also involves a need to feel considered within the organization's communication process, and the need to feel recognized by means of organizational procedures, policies and practice. Ogilvie (1986) reports that there is a positive relationship between good human resource management (HRM) practices and commitment to the organization. People policy, procedures and practices link well with senior management responsibilities. Moreover, HRM policy is also associated with employee recognition, pay, personal development etc. I interpret HRM policy as the people management product of previous and potential leader decision and action. The use of recognition as an integral aspect of leadership for followership behaviour is the central theme of Chapter 4.

Towards encouraging employee commitment and followership

This chapter looked at commitment and motivation from a follower perspective. Theories tend to simplify human nature to arrive at practical recommendations. In practice, people are complex, have needs and values, some of which change with time and within the context of experience. Theory clearly captures aspects of human motivation that would affect human behaviour and committed 'energy' within the organization. There is something right in all theory. Thus, it would be a mistake for students to reject any out of hand.

From a manager perspective, experience suggests that most managers wish to improve their organization. They are interested in theoretical and conceptual frameworks, but only if they have practical implications for them and their company. This is particularly true of their wish to understand leadership, especially if such understanding leads to commitment that is more useful from followers.

Senior managers will be interested in sustaining and improving affective commitment because its focus is on future work effort and not simple employee/follower compliance associated with side-bets and a lack of employment alternatives. Research verifies that commitment is likely to be a product of leader actions. Clearly, there is a need for potential leaders to ensure their communications, for instance 'vision, mission and verbalized statements' compliment their behaviour. A requirement for shared values between leaders and potential followers is also reinforced.

Literature strongly supports the view that employee affective commitment is associated with employee satisfaction, and work satisfaction is linked to work motivational factors. Consequently, potential leaders would be wise to consider motivational issues during any activity that might affect follower commitment. Experience suggests that most activities involve employees, it would therefore be fair to state that managers should incorporate consideration for motivational issues as part of their daily leadership process.

Chapter 2 suggested organizational expectations relate to the wishes of the most influential members. In rational-economic terms, the values of senior management are likely to be more responsive to certain stakeholders. Shareholders will maintain the pressure for senior management to maintain economic values. None the less, the time and perhaps the willingness to adopt shared values may be emerging. Adam Smith (1759) provided an analysis of the interplay between the individual and society in the concept he named 'sympathy'. Sympathy can be seen as similar to the more modern notion of 'empathy'. He is well known for his book *Market Principles* but less well known for his *Theory of Moral Sentiment* He has been quoted as saying 'The choice is not between competition and co-operation, we must not read one book without the other. A partnership of both principles will be required.'

The findings of this chapter can be summarized thus:

1 Affective commitment is the form of energetic commitment that 'followers' most likely display; other forms may be exhibited by 'employees'. Moreover, affective commitment in a democratic society is a much more acceptable notion than resigned behavioural compliance.
2 Senior managers may need, or have demonstrated, a great sense of achievement. Affiliative working relationships may be more important to other employees.
3 Employee satisfaction is likely to be key to understanding what employees perceive affects their commitment to their organization.
4 Senior management leaders are involved in all aspects associated with follower satisfaction. Satisfaction, in terms of work values, motivations and the basic need for recognition may link potential leadership action to potential follower commitment.
5 Communication may be crucial to instilling confidence and reciprocal commitment from followers. The most significant communications relating to potential follower perceptions will be those that receive constant reinforcement over time.
6 For followers to follow leaders they must perceive and expect an equitable exchange.

Commitment is the phenomenon often quoted by successful managers as the substance that shows the difference between good organizations and the best. Importantly, employees who display affective commitment are more likely to be following organizational leaders. Analysis of literature, research and experiential reflection suggest that in order to encourage greater numbers of followers, a different and balanced leadership approach is required. Nevertheless, management will need convincing that a different approach will be successful. Chapter 4 may assist.

Case study 3: Anita Roddick

In 1976, the founder of The Body Shop, Anita Roddick, started making home-made natural products in a tiny store in Brighton, England. With a customer base of over 70 million, 1900 worldwide outlets and trading in over 25 countries, it is now estimated that the company sells a product somewhere in the world every half a second. The organization is famous for its skin, hair and health portfolio of 1000 products. In 1988, Anita Roddick was awarded an OBE. She is often referred to as a prime example of a strong and effective business leader.

The company's rapid expansion is in part attributable to its 'green and caring' branding and its association with social causes. In 1999 The Body Shop brand was voted the second most trusted brand in the United Kingdom (Consumer Association), and in 1998 a *Financial Times* survey commented that the company was the 27th most respected in the world. It was respected for its ecological approach, undaunted protection of the environment, concern for animal welfare and philosophical groundbreaking approach to management.

While creating a financially successful business, the company has also managed to gain recognition from the United Nations Environment Programme. In 1995 and 1997 the organization was judged to be 'a trailblazer' and was ranked highest in International and Environmental reports.

Behind the philosophy of the organization is the view that its business is primarily about human relationships, both inside and outside the organization. Crucial to this approach is the need for the organization to comply with social and human rights, animal and human welfare, worker safety and to be open and communicative with all stakeholders. Management principles include the need to work hard, to see work as natural, 'to labour where your love is', for caring and respect for all. Anita is also quoted as 'recognizing the bottom line should stay at the bottom'. Clearly, the philosophical and visionary balance as to finance and human needs of employees, customers, suppliers, society etc. is highlighted.

The company has not avoided criticism. Its business ethics have been a source of severe comment, and some observers would state that The Body Shop's marketed image has backfired. Discredit has focused on the alleged use of non-renewable petrochemicals, plastic packaging, synthetic colouring and fragrances, questions as to the amount of natural ingredients contained in products, and the organization's reluctance to encourage unionization. In contrast, the firm allows some disadvantaged people to work and gives away some profits to needy causes.

For The Body Shop, early success appears to be the outcome of a strategy to provide the right products at the right time for the right ends. However, this is a shallow view. Leadership seems to have been founded on the intuitive belief that vision and a willingness to work hard toward success should be balanced with consideration for human rights and be operationalized via solid and well-meaning relationships with stakeholders. In contrast, critics might add that the organization may have compromised its ideals when confronted with bottom-line pressures and opportunities.

Questions

1 Describe Anita Roddick's philosophy.
2 Who and/or what receives recognition from Anita Roddick?
3 Why might employees, suppliers and franchisers be committed to follow Anita Roddick's vision?

For discussion of the case see Appendix D.

Case study 4: Follower commitment?

A piece of unpublished research into leadership was conducted by the author within a large multinational organization over a period of three years. The role of the researcher was in an advisory capacity to a small team of internal administrators. The company required confidentiality. The company name could not be revealed, and some of the results were seen as being 'overly sensitive'. Two 'employee satisfaction' surveys from among over 6000 employees are described. Information arising from unstructured interviews is also provided.

The aim of the study from the researcher's viewpoint was to explore whether employee values and needs differed in relation to senior management goals and theory-of-action.

Company background

This major multinational organization reported similar pressures to many organizations. A changing external environment required the company to respond to increased customer expectations by improving product differentiation, extending its product portfolio, improving time to market etc. Again similar to many organizations based in the UK, the company needed to become more internationally focused because of price erosion and increased competition in its home market. Large redundancies had taken place. Labour reductions meant that the organization required a different structure and different work designs. People management changes were encompassing the need for devolved responsibility, right-sizing, business process re-engineering, the need for team building and autonomous project teams. They formally communicated the theme of empowerment, and the need for employee commitment while working towards a lean structure. Knowledge as proportional to sensory-motor skill was increasing. Much of what the organization sold relied upon people's creativity.

Both surveys focused upon employee satisfaction of various aspects of the organization, including organizational culture, immediate and senior management style, personal motivations and communication. Respondents represented all hierarchical levels within the organization. They were also located at various business locations. Although the company operates internationally, only UK divisions were surveyed.

General results

Employees perceived that the mission of the organization did not relate to their needs. Generally, the function of the mission was viewed as setting goals in terms of customer perceptions, and not employee perceptions. Employees also saw the mission as providing written proof that the organization was fulfilling its purpose in relation to investors. The statement mentioned the need for human resource strategies but only to move the business in the direction pressured by the external market situation.

Employees perceived the organization as hierarchical in structure. Senior management were viewed as having and using position power to override those below. It was generally accepted that decisions of a policy nature were the provinces of senior management. The employees believed that there was a high degree of formality associated with decision-making processes. Generally, the style of telling rather than selling was supported by both surveys. Employees indicated a generally autocratic management style, especially 'from the top', dominated the work environment. Most of those surveyed perceived that openness and trust was lacking in their individual situations. Each survey suggested that the climate of the company placed great emphasis on 'achievement of results'. Analysis and findings recorded that the organization was highly task orientated.

Specific results

In the first survey, 48% of respondents stated that they valued their job. A similar number perceived they received satisfaction from their job. However, 68% considered that their pay was unsatisfactory.

Only 16% thought that working conditions were unsatisfactory. Although, 19% suggested that the organization did not give sufficient consideration for employee health and safety.

Employees were asked about the training and development offered to them. Only 36% believed that training and development was satisfactory.

The most challenging finding was that only 13% thought the company valued employees.

The second survey was completed one year later. The following results were obtained.

To the question 'Does the company value its employees?' 53% said 'No', 11% said 'Yes', and 36% were neutral.

To the question 'Are you satisfied with your immediate manager?' 65% said 'Yes', 12% said 'No', and 23% were neutral.

To the question 'Are you satisfied with your physical working conditions?' 42% said 'Yes', 16% said 'No', and 42% were neutral.

To the question 'Are you satisfied with your job training?' 46% said 'Yes', 25% said 'No', and 29% were neutral.

To the question 'Are you satisfied with the personal development the company offers to you?' 32% said 'Yes', 31% said 'No', and 37% were neutral.

To the question 'Are you satisfied with your career development opportunities?' 32% said 'Yes', 34% said 'No', and 34% were neutral.

To the question 'Are you satisfied with the pay you get in terms of the job you do?' only 7% said 'Yes', 63% said 'No', and 30% were neutral.

Qualitative inquiry

During research, several interviews were conducted with a cross-section of employees. The following quotes represent employee views as to how people are managed.

'The senior decision makers are task focused'

'There is a clash between the policy mission statement and actual practice – [it is an] idealistic statement which is not supported by key managerial action'

'My manager works on the basis that he is my manager so he has to exert authority over me'

'I am committed to my team and team leader but I am not committed to the organization'

'. . . very few managers inspire a shared vision'

'Most decisions that have a significant impact on the business come from senior management'

'Subordinates are expected to be self-motivated and competent – this is under the influence of leadership that only uses authority to get things done'

'. . . senior management are unapproachable – them and us scenarios'

'What we have is management by intimidation'

'Management do not listen or act on ideas from the workforce'

'Generally, management do not want to know about employee-related problems'

As for communication, the majority of employees believed that the grapevine system was more informative than management. They also voiced poor interdepartmental and inter-site communications. The general view was that there were 'information sponges at middle management level'. Discussion with middle management revealed that the wants of below are not compatible with the wishes of above. Middle management cannot pass information relating to the needs of those below them in an upward direction or vice versa because priorities are different.

Questions

1 Why are the potential followers dissatisfied?
2 What advice might you offer senior management if they were interested in improving the willing commitment of followers?

For discussion of the case see Appendix D.

References

Abelson, R.P. (1976) Script Processing in Attitude Formation and Decision-making, in J.S. Carrol and J.W. Payne (eds), *Cognition and Social Behaviour*, Hillsdale, NJ: Erlbaum, pp. 33–45.

Adams, J.S. (1965) Inequity in Social Exchange, in L. Berkowitz (ed.), *Advances in Experimental Social Psychology*, New York: Academic Press, pp. 276–99.

Agarwal, A. (1997) Your Key to Success in the Competitive Marketplace? Unlocking Employee Potential, *Industrial Engineering*, 22 (8), p. 35.

Alderfer, C.P. (1972). *Existence, Relatedness, and Growth: Human Needs in Organizational Settings*, New York: Free Press.

Allen, N.J. and Meyer, J.P. (1990) The Measurement and Antecedents of Affective, Continuance and Normative Commitment to the Organization, *Journal of Occupational Psychology*, 63 (1), pp. 1–18.

Anderson, C.M. and Matthew, M.M. (1995) Why Employees Speak to Coworkers and Bosses: Motives, Gender, and Organizational Satisfaction, *Journal of Business Communication*, 32 (3), pp. 249–60.

Angle, H. (1983) Organizational Commitment: Individual and Organizational Influences, *Sociology of Work and Occupations*, 10, 123–46.

Angle, H.L. and Lawson, M.B. (1993) Changes in Affective and Continuance Commitment in Times of Relocation, *Journal of Business Research*, No. 26, 587–95.

Angle, H.L. and Perry, J.L. (1981) An Empirical Assessment of Organizational Commitment and Organizational Effectiveness, *Administrative Science Quarterly*, 26, 1–14.

Arkin, A. (1996) Take It or Leave It, Reporting on the Guardian Employee Survey, *People Management*, 2 (21), 53.

Armstrong, G. (1996) Employers Urged to Bridge Credibility Gap, conference address by the Institute of Development's Director General, IPD, p. 7.

Armstrong, M. (1991) *A Handbook of Personnel Management Practice*, 4th edn, London: Kogan Page.

Armstrong, M. (1996) *A Handbook of Personnel Management Practice*, 6th edn, London: Kogan Page, pp. 321–5.

Armstrong, M. (1999) *A Handbook of Human Resource Management Practice*, 7th edn, London: Kogan Page, p. 177.

Aronson, E. (1968) *Dissonance Theory: Progress and Problems*, in R. Abelson, E. Aronson, W. McGuire, T. Newcombe, M. Rosenberg and P. Tannenbaum (eds), *Theories of Cognitive Consistency: A Source-book*, Chicago: Rand–McNally.

Atkinson, J.W. (1981). Studying Personality in the Context of an Advanced Motivational Psychology, *American Psychologist*, 36, pp. 117–28.

Atkinson, J.W. and Birch, D. (1978) *An Introduction to Motivation*, 2nd edn, New York: Van Nostrand, p. 82.

Avner, B.K., Guastello, S.J. and Aderman, M. (1982) The Effects of a Realistic Job Preview on Expectancy and Voluntary Versus Involuntary Turnover, *Journal of Psychology*, 111, pp. 101–7.

Bassett, P. (1986) *Strike Free*, London: Macmillan.

Bateman, T.S. and Strasser, S. (1984) Organizational Commitment: Individual and Organizational Influences, *Academy of Management Journal*, No.27, pp.95–112.

BBC (1995) Report of a speech by Diana, Princess of Wales, BBC Daytime News, 6 December.

Becker, H.S. (1960) Notes on the Concept of Commitment, *American Journal of Sociology*, 66, pp. 289–96.

Becker, T.E., Billings, R.S., Eveleth, D.M. and Gilbert, N.L. (1996) Foci and Bases of Employee Commitment: Implications for Job Performance, *Academy of Management Journal*, 39 (2), p. 464.

Bern, D.J. and Allen, A. (1974) On Predicting Some of the People Some of the Time: The Search for Cross-situational Consistencies in Behavior, *Psychological Review*, No. 81, pp. 506–20.

Berne, E. (1963) *The Structure and Dynamics of Organizations and Groups*, New York: Grove Press.

Blinder, A. (1990) *Paying for Productivity*, Washington, DC: Brooking Institute.

Bluedorn, A.C. (1979) Structure, Environment and Satisfaction: Toward a Causal Model of Turnover from Military Organizations, *Journal of Political and Military Sociology*, No. 7, pp. 181–207.

Bluedorn, A.C. (1982) A Unified Model of Turnover from Organizations, *Human Relations*, No. 35, pp. 135–53.

Blumberg, M. and Pringle, C.D. (1982) The Missing Opportunity in Organizational Research: Some Implications for a Theory of Work Performance, *Academy of Management Review*, 7 (4), pp. 78–83.

Bockman, V.M. (1971) The Herzberg Controversy, *Personnel Psychology*, 24, pp. 155–89.

Brief, A.P. and Aldag, R.J. (1980) Antecedents of Organizational Commitment Among Nurses, *Sociology of Work and Occupations*, No. 7, pp. 210–21.

Brooke, P.P, Jr. and Price, J.L. (1989) The Determinants of Employee Absenteeism: An Empirical Test of a Causal Model, *Journal of Occupational Psychology*, 62 (1), pp. 1–19.

Buchanan, B. (1974) Building Organizational Commitment: the Socialization of Work Organizations, *Administrative Science Quarterly*, No. 22, pp. 533–46.

Caldwell, D.F. and O'Reilly, C.A. (1983) The Impact of Accurate Information on Job-choice and Turnover Decision, Proceedings of the 43rd Annual Meeting of the Academy of Management, in R.D. Iveron and P. Roy (1994) A Causal Model of Behavioural Commitment: Evidence from a Study of Australian Blue-collar Workers, *Journal of Management*, 20 (1), p. 15.

Campbell, J.P. and Pritchard, R.D. (1976) *Motivation Theory in Industrial and Organizational Psychology*, in M.D. Dunnette (ed.), *Handbook of Industrial and Organizational Psychology*, Chicago: Rand–McNally.

Cantor, N. and Mischel, W. (1979) Prototypes of Person Perception, in E.L. Berkowitz (ed.), *Advances in Experimental Social Psychology*, 12, pp. 30–52.

Carsten, J.M. and Spector, P.E. (1987) Unemployment, Job Satisfaction, and Employee Turnover: A meta-analytical Test of the Muchinsky Model, *Journal of Applied Psychology*. No. 72, pp. 374–81.

CBI (1976) Priorities for In-Company Communication, London: *Confederation of British Industry Report* (Prepared by M. Brandon and M. Arnott).

CBI (1981) Workplace Industrial Relations Survey, *Confederation of British Industry* (Second Report).

Chin, R. and Benne, K. (1976) *General Strategies for Effecting Changes in Human Systems,* in W.G. Bennis, K.D. Benne, R. Chin and K.E. Corey (eds), *The Planning of Change*, New York: Holt, Rinehart and Winston.

Cohen, A. and Lowenberg, G. (1990) A Reexamination of the Sidebet Theory as Applied to Organizational Commitment: A Meta-analysis, *Human Relations*, 43 (10), pp. 1015–50.

Cooper, D.J. (1993–2002). Discussion documents: The Institute of Directors, Diploma in Directorship.

Cooper, R. (1986) Organization/Disorganization, *Social Science Information*, 25 (2), pp. 299–335.

Coopey, J. and Hartley, J. (1991) Reconsidering the Case for Organizational Commitment, *Human Resource Management Journal*, 3 (Spring), pp. 18–32.

Cotton, J.L. and Tuttle, J.M. (1986) Employee Turnover: A Meta-analysis and Review with Implications for Research, *Academy of Management Review*, No. 11, pp. 55–70.

Couger, J.D. and Zawacki, R.A. (1980) *Motivating and Managing Computer Personnel: The 1986 Study,* New York: John Wiley and Sons.

Cox, C.J. and Cooper, C.L. (1985) The Irrelevance of American Organizational Sciences to the UK and Europe, *Journal of General Management*, Winter, pp. 29–30.

Curry, J.P., Wakefield, D.S., Price, J.L. and Mueller, C.W. (1986) On the Causal Ordering of Job Satisfaction and Organizational Commitment, *Academy of Management Journal*, No. 29, pp. 847–68.

Daley, D. (1988) Profile of the Uninvolved Worker: An Examination of Employee Attitudes Toward Management Practices, *International Journal of Public Administration*, 11 (1), pp. 65–90.

Damachi, N., Shell, R.I. and Souder, H.R. (1983) Using Behavioural and Influence Factors to Motivate the Technical Worker, *Industrial Engineering*, August, pp. 58–62.

De Bono, E. (1973) *Children Solve Problems*, Harmondsworth: Penguin Education.

De Cotiis, T.A. and Summers, T.P. (1987) A Path Analysis of a Model of the Antecedents and Consequences of Organizational Commitment, *Human Relations*, 40 (7), pp. 445–70.

Demos, D. (1995) The Time Squeeze, *The Demos Quarterly*, June. Also in Aikin, O. (1995) Be Aware of the Risks, *People Management,*1 (13), pp. 25–8.

Denton, D.K. (1987) Getting Employee Commitment. *Management Solutions*, 32 (10), p. 17.

Donaldson, M. (1988) *Children's Minds*, Fontana Press, pp. 76–85.

Drennan, D. (1989a) Are You Getting Through? *Management Today*, March.

Drennan, D. (1989b) How to Get Your Employees Committed, *Management Today*, October, pp. 121–9.

Edwards, P.K. (1987) *Managing the Factory: A Survey of General Managers*, Oxford: Basil Blackwell.

Edwards, W. (1954) The Theory of Decision Making, *Psychological Bulletin*, No. 51, pp. 380–417.

Entwistle, D.R. (1972). To Dispel Fantasies about Fantasy-Based Measures for Achievement Motivation, *Psychological Bulletin*, 77, pp. 377–91.

Evans, D. (1996) Rewards and Recognition, *Management Training*, November/December, p. 32.

Farrell, D. and Rusbult, C.E. (1981) Exchange Variables as Predictors of Job Satisfaction, Job Commitment, and Turnover: The Impact of Rewards, Costs, Alternatives, and Investments, *Organizational Behavior and Human Performance*, No. 28, pp. 78–95.

Festinger, L. (1957) *A Theory of Cognitive Dissonance*, Stanford, CA: Stanford University Press.

Festinger, L. (1958) *The Motivating Effect of Cognitive Dissonance in Assessment of Human Motives* (ed. Gardner Lindzey), New York: Holt.

Filley, A.C., House, R.J. and Kerr, S. (1976) *Managerial Process and Organizational Behavior*, 2nd edn, Glenview, IL: Scott Foresman.

Fletcher, A. and Williams, H. (1992) The Route to Performance Management, *Personnel Management*, October, pp. 12–13.

Fullerton, H. and Price, C. (1991) Cultural Change in the NHS, *Personnel Management*, 3 (23), pp. 50–3.

Furnham, A. (1984) Work Values and Beliefs in Britain, *Journal of Occupational Behavior*, 5, pp. 281–91.

Garland, H. (1984). Relation of Effort-Performance Expectancy to Performance in Goal-Setting Experiments, *Journal of Applied Psychology*, 69, pp. 79–84.

Goddard, R.W. (1987) 'Well Done!' (employees' need for praise and recognition), *Management World*, 16 (6), p. 14.

Gomez-Mejia, L.R. and Balkin, D.B. (1992) *Compensation, Organizational Strategy, and Firm Performance*, Mason, OH: South-Western Publishing.

Graen, G. (1969) Instrumentality Theory of Work Motivation: Some Experimental Results and Suggested Modifications, *Journal of Applied Psychology Monograph*, No. 53, pp. 1–25.

Guest, D.E. (1987) Human Resource Management and Industrial Relations, *Journal of Management Studies*, No. 24, pp. 503–21.

Guest, D.E. (1991) Personnel Management: The End of Orthodoxy, *British Journal of Industrial Relations*, 29 (2), pp. 149–6.

Guest, D.E. (1992) Employee Commitment and Control, in J.F. Hartley and G.M. Stephenson (eds), *Employment Relations*, Oxford: Blackwell, pp. 111–35.

Hackett, R.D., Bycio, P. and Hausdorf, P.A. (1994) Further Assessments of Meyer and Allen's (1991) Three Component Model of Organizational Commitment, *Journal of Applied Psychology*, No. 79, pp. 15–23.

Halaby, C.N. (1986) Worker Attachment and Workplace Authority, *American Sociological Review*, No. 51, pp. 634–49.

Halaby, C.N. and Weakliem, D. (1989) Worker Control and Attachment to the Firm, *American Journal of Sociology*, No. 95, pp. 549–91.

Hall, D.T., Schneider, B. and Nygren, H.T. (1970) Personal Factors in Organizational Identification, *Administrative Science Quarterly*, No. 15, pp. 176–90.

Hall, T. and Nougaim, N. (1972) Examination of Maslow's Need Hierarchy, in E.E. Lawler and J.L. Suttle, A Causal Correlation Test of the Need Hierarchy Concept, *Organizational Behaviour and Human Performance*, 7, pp. 265–87.

Harrison, R. (1992) Employee Development, *Institute of Personnel and Development Publications*,. 1 (3), pp. 116–19.

Heider, F. (1958) *The Psychology of Interpersonal Relations*, New York: John Wiley.

Hellriegel, D., Slocum, J.W. and Woodman, R.W. (1997) *Organizational Behavior*, The Instructors Resource Guide, St Paul, MN: West Publishing, pp. 117–41.

Heneman, H.G. and Schwab, D.P. (1972). Evaluations of Research on Expectancy Theory Predictions of Employee Performance, *Psychological Bulletin*, 78, pp. 1–9.

Herzberg, F., Mausman, B. and Synderman, B. (1956) *The Motivation to Work*, 2nd edn, New York: Wiley.

Herzberg, F. (1966) *Work and the Nature of Man*, Cleveland: World Publishing Company.

Herzberg, F. (1974) *Work and the Nature of Man,* London: Granada Publishing.

Herzberg, F. (1968) One More Time: How do you Motivate Employees? *Harvard Business Review*, 46, pp. 54–62.

Herzberg, F., Mauser, B. and Snyderman, B. (1959) *The Motivation to Work,* 2nd edn. New York: John Wiley.

Hofstede, G. (1980) *Culture's Consequences: International Differences in Work-Related Values*, London: Sage.

Hollenbeck, J. and Klein, H. (1987) Goal Commitment and the Goal Setting Process: Problems, Prospects, and Proposals for Future Research, *Journal of Applied Psychology*, No. 72, pp. 212–20.

House, R.J. and Wigdor, L.A. (1967) Herzberg's Dual-Factor Theory of Job Satisfaction and Motivation: A Review of the Evidence and a Criticism, *Personnel Psychology*, 20, pp. 369–89.

Huseman, R., Hatfield, J. and Miles, E. (1987) A New Perspective on Equity Theory: The Equity Sensitivity Construct, *Academy of Management Review*, No. 12, pp. 222–34.

Hrebiniak, L.G. and Alutto, J.A. (1973) Personal Role-related Factors in the Development of Organizational Commitment, *Administrative Science Quarterly*, No. 17, pp. 555–72.

Hyman, J. (1982) Where Communication Schemes Fall Short of Intention, *Personnel Management*, March, pp. 30–3.

Illes, P., Forster, A. and Tinline, G. (1996) The Changing Relationship between Work Commitment, Personal Flexibility and Employability: An Evaluation of Field Experiment in Executive Development, *Journal of Managerial Psychology*, 11 (8), p. 18.

Iles, P., Mabey, C. and Robertson, I. (1990) HRM Practices and Employee Commitment, *British Journal of Management,* No. 1, pp. 147–57.

Infante, D.A. and Gorden, W.I. (1993) How Employees See the Boss: Test of Argumentative and Affirming Model of Supervisors' Communicative Behavior, *Western Journal of Speech Communication*, No. 56, pp. 294–304.

Institute of Directors (1991) *Communications at Work: The Challenge and the Response. A Survey of Communication within Britain's Medium-sized and Larger Companies*, London: Institute of Directors (IoD) and Bolton Dickinson Associates.

Institute of Directors (IoD) (1993–2002) *Diploma in Directorship Programme, The University of Salford*, unpublished discussions with directors.

Institute of Personnel and Development (1995) Occupational Stress – Ignore It at Your Peril, *People Management*, 1 (9), p. 37.

Institute of Personnel and Development (1996) The Birkbeck College Harris Research Centre Report on Employee Loyalty, *People Management,* 2 (22), p. 7.

Jacob, P., Flink, J. and Schuchman, H. (1962) Values and Their Function in Decision Making, *American Behavioural Scientist*, 5 (Suppl. 9), pp. 6–38.

Jacobson, R. (2000) *Leading for a Change: How to Master the Five Challenges Faced by Every Leader*, Oxford: Butterworth–Heinemann, pp. 58–9.

James, R.L. and Jones, A.P. (1974) Organizational Climate: A Review of Theory and Research, *Psychological Bulletin*, No. 81, pp. 1096–112.

Janis, I. (1972) *Victims of Groupthink*, Boston, MA: Houghton Mifflin.

Johns, T. (1995) Don't be Afraid of the Moral Maze, *People Management*, 1 (21), p. 32.

Kassarjian, H.H. and Sheffet, M.J. (1982) *Personality and Consumer Behaviour: An Update*, in H.H. Kassarjian and T.S. Robertson (eds), *Perspectives in Consumer Behaviour*, Glenview, IL: Scott Foresman, p. 36.

Keisler, C.A. (1971) *The Psychology of Commitment: Experiments Linking Behaviour to Belief*, New York: Academic Press.

Keisler, C.A. and Sakumura, J. (1966) A Test of a Model of Commitment, *Journal of Personality and Social Psychology*, No. 3, pp. 34–59.

Kelly, G.A. (1955a) *The Psychology of Personal Constructs*, Vols 1 and 2, New York: W. W. Norton, p. 9.

Kelly, G.A. (1955b) *The Psychology of Personal Constructs*, Vols 1 and 2, New York: W.W. Norton, p. 90.

Kelly, J.E. and Kelly, C. (1991) Them and Us: Social Psychology and the New Industrial Relations, *Human Relations*, 1 (29), pp. 25–48.

Kerr, S. (1975) On the Folly of Rewarding 'A', While Hoping for 'B', *Academy of Management Journal*, December, pp. 769–83.

Kidron, A. (1978) Work Values and Organizational Commitment, *Academy of Management Journal*, 21, pp. 119–28.

Kirschenbaum, A. and Weisberg, J. (1990) Predicting Worker Turnover: An Assessment of Intent on Actual Separations, *Human Relations*, No. 43, pp. 829–47.

Klenke-Hamel, K.E. and Mathieu, J.E. (1990) Role Strains, Tension, and Job Satisfaction Influences on Employees' Propensity to Leave: A Multi-sample Replication and Extension, *Human Relations*, No. 43, pp. 791–807.

Kovach, K.A. (1987) What Motivates Employees? Workers and Managers Give Different Answers, *Business Horizons*, No. 30, pp. 58–65.

Krackhardt, D. and Porter, L.W. (1985) When Friends Leave: A Structural Analysis of the Relationship between Turnover and

Stayer's Attitudes, *Administrative Science Quarterly*, No. 30, pp. 242–61.

Legge, K. (1989) *Human Resource Management: A Critical Analysis*, in J. Storey (ed.), *New Perspectives in Human Resource Management*, London: Routledge.

Legge, K. (1995) *Human Resource Management: Rhetoric and Realities*, London: Macmillan.

Lewin, K. (1951) *Field Theory in Social Science*, New York: Harper.

Lewin, K., Dembo, T., Festinger, L. and Sears, P. (1944) *Level of Aspiration,* in J.M. Hunt (ed.), *Personality and the Behaviour Disorders*, New York: Ronald.

Locke, E.A. and Latham, A.A. (1990) *Theory of Goal Setting and Task Performance*, Englewood Cliffs, N.J: Prentice Hall, pp. 249–50.

Locke, E.A., Shaw, K.N., Saari, L.M. and Latham, G.P. (1981) Goal Setting and Task Performance: 1969–1980, *Psychological Bulletin*, No. 90, pp. 125–52.

Luthans, F. (1995) *Organizational Behaviour*, 7th edn, New York: McGraw–Hill, p. 210.

Luthans, F. (2002) *Organizational Behaviour*, 9th edn, McGraw–Hill.

McCall, J. (1996) quoted by Arkin, A., 'Take it or Leave it', reporting on the *Guardian* Employee Survey, *People Management*, 2 (21), p. 53.

McClelland, D.C. (1961) *The Achieving Society*, Princetown, NJ: D. Van Nostrand.

McEwan, N., Carmichael, C., Short, D. and Steel, A. (1988) Organizational Change – a Strategic Approach, *Long Range Planning*, 6 (21), pp. 71–8.

McGee, G.W. and Ford, R.C. (1987) Two (or more?) Dimensions of Organizational Commitment: Re-examination of the Affective and Continuance Commitment Scales, *Journal of Applied Psychology*, 72, pp. 638–41.

Mangham, L.L. (1979) *The Politics of Organizational Change*, London: Associated Business Press.

Marchington, M. (1993) Close to the Customer: Employee Relations in Food Retailing, in D. Gowler, K. Legge and C. Clegg (eds), *Case Studies in Organizational Behaviour and Human Resource Management*, London: Paul Chapman, pp. 134–43.

Marchington, M., Wilkinson, A., Ackers, P. and Goodman, J. (1994) Understanding the Meaning of Participation: Views from the Workplace, *Human Relations*, 8 (47), pp. 867–94.

Marginson, P., Edwards, P.K., Martin, R., Purcell, J. and Sisson, K. (1988) *Beyond the Workplace: Managing Industrial Relations in Multi-Plant Enterprises*, Oxford: Blackwell.

Marsh, A. and Hussey, R. (1979) Survey of Company Reports, Croydon: *Company Secretary's Review.*

Martin, T.N. (1979) A Contextual Model of Employee Turnover Intentions, *Academy of Management Journal,* No. 22, pp. 313–24.

Martin, C.L. and Bennett, N. (1996) The Role of Justice Judgements in Explaining the Relationship Between Job Satisfaction and Organizational Commitment, *Group and Organization Management,* 21 (1), p. 84.

Martin, P. and Nicholls, J. (1987) Creating a Committed Workforce, *Institute of Personnel Management Journal,* pp. 26–38.

Maslow, A.H. (1943) A Theory of Human Motivation, *Psychological Review,* July, pp. 370–96.

Maslow, A.H. (1954) *Motivation and Personality,* New York: Harper.

Mathieu, J.E. and Zajac, D.M. (1990) A Review and Meta-analysis of the Antecedents, Correlates, and Consequences of Organizational Commitment, *Psychological Bulletin,* No. 108, pp. 171–94.

Mayo, E. (1949) *Hawthorne and the Western Electric Company: The Social Problems of an Industrial Civilization,* London: Routledge.

Meyer, J.P and Allen, N.J. (1984) Testing the 'Side-bet Theory' of Organizational Commitment: Some Methodological Considerations, *Journal of Applied Psychology.* No. 69, pp. 372–8.

Meyer, J.P. and Allen, N.J. (1991) A Three Component Conceptualization of Organizational Commitment, *Human Resource Management Review,* No. 1, pp. 61–89.

Meyer, J.P., Allen, N.J. and Gellatly, I. (1990) Affective and Continuance Commitment to the Organization: Evaluation of Measures and Analysis of Concurrent and Time Lagged Relations, *Journal of Applied Psychology,* No. 75, pp. 710–20.

Meyer, J.P., Paunomen, S.V., Gellatly, I.R., Goffin, R.D. and Jackson, D.N. (1989) Organizational Commitment and Job Performance: It's the Nature of the Commitment that Counts, *Journal of Applied Psychology,* No. 74, pp. 153–6.

Michaels, R.E., Cron, W.L., Dubinsky, A.J. and Joachimsthaler, E.A. (1988) Influence of Formalization on the Organizational Commitment and Work Alienation of Salespeople and Industrial Buyers, *Journal of Marketing Research,* 4 (25), pp. 376–83.

Miller, K.I. (1988) Cultural and Role-based Predictors of Organizational Participation and Allocation Preferences, *Communication Research,* 6 (15), pp. 699–725.

Miller, J. and Labovitz, S. (1973) Individual Reactions to Organizational Conflict and Change, *The Sociological Quarterly,* No. 14, pp. 556–75.

Miller, D.S., Catt, S.E. and Carlson, J.R. (1996) *Fundamentals of Management: A Framework for Excellence.* St Paul, MN: West Publishing, p. 321.

Mintzberg, H. (1983) *Power In and Around the Organization,* Englewood Cliffs, NJ: Prentice-Hall.

Mitchell, T.R. (1982) 'Motivation: New Directions for Theory, Research and Practice', *Academy of Management Review,* 7, pp. 80–8.

Mitchell, T.R., Smyser, C.N. and Weed, S.E. (1975) 'Locus of Control: Supervision and Work Satisfaction', *Academy of Management Journal,* September, pp. 623–31.

Mobley, W.H. (1982) *Employee Turnover: Causes, Consequences, and Control,* Reading, MA: Addison–Wesley.

Morris, J.H. and Sherman, J.D. (1981) Generalizability of an Organizational Commitment Model, *Academy of Management Journal,* 34, pp. 487–516.

Mottaz, C.J. (1989) An Analysis of the Relationships between Attitudinal Commitment and Behavioral Commitment, *The Sociological Quarterly,* No. 30, pp. 143–58.

Mowday, R.T., Steers, R.M. and Porter, L.W. (1982) *Employee-Organization Linkages: The Psychology of Commitment, Absenteeism and Turnover,* New York: Academic Press.

Mullins, L.J. (1996) *Management and Organizational Behaviour,* 4th edn, Pitman Publishing, pp. 716–22.

Murray, H.A. (1938) *Exploration in Personality,* New York: John Wiley and Sons, p. 73.

Myers, J.L. and Fort, J.G. (1963) A Sequential Analysis of Gambling Behaviour, *Journal of General Psychology,* No. 69, pp. 299–309.

Newman, K. and Goswell, R. (1995) The Pioneers Who Put People First, *People Management,* 1 (16), pp. 20–1.

Norman, W.T. (1963) Toward an Adequate Taxonomy of Person Attributes: Replicated Factor Structure in Peer Nomination Personality Ratings, *Journal of Abnormal and Social Psychology,* No. 66, pp. 574–83.

Nystrom, P.C. (1990) Vertical Exchanges and Organizational Commitments of American Business Managers, *Group and Organization Studies,* 15 (3), p. 296.

Ogbonna, E. and Wilkinson, B. (1988) Corporate Strategy and Corporate Culture: the Management of Change in the UK Supermarket Industry, *Personnel Review,* No. 17, pp. 10–14.

Ogbonna, E. and Wilkinson, B. (1990) Corporate Strategy and Corporate Culture: the View from the Checkout, *Personnel Review,* No. 19, pp. 9–15.

Ogilvie, J.R. (1986) The Role of Human Resource Management Practices in Predicting Organizational Commitment, *Group and Organization Studies,* 11 (4), p. 335.

O'Reilly, C.A. and Caldwell, D.F. (1980) Job Choice: The Impact of Intrinsic and Extrinsic Factors on Subsequent Satisfaction and Commitment, *Journal of Applied Psychology*, No. 65, p. 562.

O'Reilly, C.A. and Chatman, J. (1989) Organizational Commitment and Psychological Attachment: The Effects of Compliance, Identification, and Internalization on Prosocial Behavior, *Journal of Applied Psychology*, No. 71, pp. 492–9.

O'Reilly, C., Chatman, J. and Caldwell, D.F. (1991) People and Organizational Culture: A Profile Comparison Approach to Assessing Person-Organization Fit, *Academy of Management Journal*, No. 24, pp. 512–26.

Ouchi, W.G. (1981) *Theory Z*, Reading, MA: Addison-Wesley.

Oxford Encyclopaedic English Dictionary (1991), Oxford: Oxford University Press.

Pascale, R.T. and Athos, A.G. (1981) *The Art of Japanese Management*, New York: Simon and Schuster.

Payne, R.L. and Pugh, D.S. (1976) *Organizational Structure and Climate*, in M.D. Dunnette (ed.), *Handbook of Industrial and Organizational Psychology*, Chicago: Rand McNally.

Pennings, I.M. (1970) Work Value Systems of White-collar Workers, *Administrative Science Quarterly*, No. 15, pp. 397–405.

Peters, T. and Waterman, R.H. (1982) *In Search of Excellence, Lessons from America's Best Run Companies*, New York: Harper and Row.

Pettigrew, A. and Whipp, R. (1991) *Managing Change for Competitive Success*, Oxford: Blackwell.

Porter, L.W. and Lawler, E.E. (1968) *Managerial Attitudes and Performance*, Homewood, IL: Irwin–Dorsey.

Porter, L. and Steers, R.M. (1973) Organizational, Work and Personal Factors in Employee Turnover and Absenteeism, *Psychological Bulletin*, No. 80, pp. 151–76.

Porter, L., Steers, R., Mowday, R. and Boulian, P. (1974) Organizational Commitment, Job Satisfaction and Turnover among Psychiatric Technicians, *Journal of Applied Psychology*, 59, pp. 603–9.

Price, J.L. and Bluedorn, A.C. (1980). Test of a Causal Model of Organizational Turnover, in D. Dunkerly and G. Salaman (eds), *International Yearbook of Organizational Studies*, London: Routledge and Kegan Paul, pp. 217–36.

Price, J.L. and Mueller, C.W. (1981) *Professional Turnover: The Case of Nurses*, New York: SP Medical and Scientific.

Price, J.L. and Mueller, C.W. (1986) *Absenteeism and Turnover of Hospital Employees*, Greenwich, CT: JAI.

Putti, J.M., Aryee, S. and Ling, T.K. (1989) Work Values and Organizational Commitment: A Study in the Asian Context, *Human Relations*, 42, pp. 275–88.

Randall, D. (1987) Commitment and the Organization: The Organization Man Revisited, *Academy of Management Review*, No. 12, pp. 460–71.

Randall, D. (1990) The Consequences of Organizational Commitment: Methodological Investigation, *Journal of Organizational Behavior*, No. 11, pp. 361–78.

Ray, C.A. (1986) Corporate Culture: the Last Frontier of Control?, *Journal of Management Studies*, 3 (23), pp. 287–97.

Reed, M. (1985) *Redirections in Organizational Analysis*, London: Tavistock, pp. 20–36.

Reichers, A. (1985) A Review and Reconceptualization of Organizational Commitment, *Academy of Management Review*, No. 10, pp. 465–76.

Richie, S. and Martin, P. *Motivation Management,* Gower.

Ritzer, G. and Trice, H.M. (1969) An Empirical Study of Howard Becker's Side-bet Theory, *Social Forces*, No. 47, pp. 475–9.

Rusbult, C.E. (1980) Commitment and Satisfaction in Romantic Associations: A Test of the Investment Model, *Journal of Experimental Psychology*, No. 16, pp. 172–4.

Rusbult, C.E. and Farrell, D. (1983) A Longitudinal Test of the Investment Model: The Impact on Job Satisfaction, Job Commitment, and Turnover of Variations in Rewards, Costs, Alternatives, and Investments, *Journal of Applied Psychology*, No. 68, pp. 429–38.

Salancik, G.R. (1977) Commitment and Control of Organizational Behaviour and Beliefs, in B.M. Saw and G.R. Salancik (eds), *New Directions in Organizational Behaviour*, Chicago: St Clair Press, pp. 420–53.

Salancik, G.R. (1982) Commitment is Too Easy!, in M.L. Tushman and W.L. Moore (eds), *Readings in the Management of Innovation*, London: Pitman.

Salancik, G.R. and Pfeffer, J.A. (1978) A Social Information Processing Approach to Job Attitudes and Task Design, *Administrative Science Quarterly*, No. 23, pp. 224–53.

Schaffer, R. (1987) *Mothering: The Developing Child*, London: Fontana Press.

Schein, E.H. (1980) *Organizational Psychology,* 3rd edn, Englewood Cliffs, NJ: Prentice–Hall.

Shapiro, H.J. and Wahba, M.A. (1974) Expectancy Theory as a Predictor of Work Behaviour and Attitudes: A Reevaluation of Empirical Evidence, *Decision Sciences*, 5, pp. 481–506.

Sheffield University (1998) 'A link between improved profitability and increased job satisfaction has been found', BBC Radio 4 *Today* programme, 4 October.

Shore, J.M. and Barksdale, K. (1991) A Longitudinal Assessment of the Antecedents of Effective Commitment and Continuance Commitment, *Academy of Science Conference*.

Shore, L.M. and Barksdale, K. (1995) Managerial Perceptions of Employee Commitment to the Organization, *Academy of Management Journal*, 38 (6), p. 3.

Shrivastava, P. (1985) Integrating Strategy Formulation with Organizational Culture, *Journal of Business Strategy*, No. 5, pp. 103–11.

Skinner, B.F. (1976) *About Behaviourism*, New York: Vintage.

Smith, A. (1759) *A Theory of Moral Sentiments*, London Press.

Sparrow, P.R. and Pettigrew, A. (1988a) Strategic Human Resource Management in the Computer Supply Industry, *Journal of Occupational Psychology*, 1 (61), pp. 25–42.

Sparrow, P.R. and Pettigrew, A. (1988b) Contrasting HRM Responses in the Changing World of Computing, *Personnel Management*, 2 (20), pp. 40–5.

Steel, R.P. and Ovalle, N.K. (1984) A Review and Meta-analysis of Research on the Relationship between Behavioral Intentions and Employee Turnover, *Journal of Applied Psychology*, No. 69, pp. 673–86.

Steers, R.M. and Porter, L.W. (1983) *Motivation and Work Behaviour*, New York: McGraw–Hill.

Steers, R.M. and Rhodes, S.R. (1978) Major Influences on Employee Attendance: A Process Model, *Journal of Applied Psychology*, No. 63, pp. 391–407.

Storey, J. (1992a) *Developments in the Management of Human Resources*, Oxford: Blackwell.

Storey, J. (1992b) HRM in Action: The Truth is Out at Last, *Personnel Management*, 4 (24), pp. 28–31.

Sturrock, J. (1986) *Structuralism*, London: Paladin.

Thompson, F. (1983) The Seven Deadly Sins of Briefing Groups, *Personnel Management*, February, pp. 32–5.

Thompson, K.R. and Terpening, W.D. (1983) Job-type Variations and Antecedents to Intention to Leave: A Content Approach to Turnover, *Human Relations*, No. 36, pp. 655–82.

Tichy, N.M. (1983) *Managing Strategic Change*, New York: John Wiley.

Tolman, E.C., Ritchie, B.F. and Kalish, D. (1946) Studies in Spatial Learning: II. Place Learning versus Response Learning, *Journal of Experimental Psychology*, 36, pp. 221–9.

Tosi, H.L. and Carroll, S.J. (1982) *Management*, New York: John Wiley and Sons.

Trompenaars, F. (1993) *Riding the Waves of Culture*, London: Nicholas Brealey.

Vance, R.J. and Colella, A. (1990) Effects of Two Types of Feedback on Goal Acceptance and Personal Goals, *Journal of Applied Psychology*, No. 75, pp. 68–76.

Vandenberg, R.J. and Lance, C.E. (1992) Examining the Causal Order of Job Satisfaction and Organizational Commitment, *Journal of Management*, March, pp. 153–67.

Vroom,V.H. (1964) *Work and Motivation*, New York: John Wiley, p. 129. Vroom,V.H. (1966) Organizational Choice: A Study of Pre- and Post-Decision Processes, *Organizational Behaviour and Human Performance*, No. 1.

Vroom, V.H. and Jago, A.G. (1988) *The New Leadership: Managing Participation in Organizations*, Englewood Cliffs, NJ: Prentice–Hall, ch. 6.

Wahba, M.A. and Bridwell, L. (1976) Maslow Reconsidered: A Review of Research on the Need Hierarchy Theory, *Organizational Behaviour and Human Performance*, 15, pp. 212–40.

Wallace, J.E. (1997) Becker's Side-bet Theory of Commitment Revisited: Is it Time for a Moratorium or a Resurrection? *Human Relations*, 50 (6), p. 727.

Walton, R.E. (1985a) From Control to Commitment in the Workplace, *Harvard Business Review*, March–April, pp. 76–84.

Walton, R. (1991) From Control to Commitment in the Workplace, in R.M. Steers and L.W. Porter (eds), *Motivation and Work Behaviour*, New York: McGraw–Hill.

Walton, R. and McKersie, R. (1965) *A Behavioural Theory of Labor Negotiations*, New York: McGraw–Hill.

Watson, T. (1994) Linking Employee Motivation and Satisfaction to the Bottom Line, *Chartered Management Accountants (CIMA) Journal*, 68.

Weiss, J.W. (1996) *Organizational Behavior and Change*, St Paul, MN: West Publishing, pp. 91–2.

Werkmeister, W. (1967) *Man and His Values*, Lincoln, NB: University of Nebraska Press.

Williams, L.J. and Anderson, S.E. (1991) Job Satisfaction and Organizational Commitment as Predictors of Organizational Citizenship and In-role Behaviors, *Journal of Management*, 3 (17), pp. 601–17.

Williams, L.J. and Hazer, J.T. (1986) Antecedents and Consequences of Satisfaction and Commitment in Turnover Models: A Re-analysis Using Latest Variables Structure Methods, *Journal of Applied Psychology*, No. 71, pp. 219–31.

Yukl, G. and Falbe, C. (1990) Influence, Tactics, and Objectives in Upward, Downward, and Lateral Influence Attempts, *Journal of Applied Psychology*, April, pp. 132–40.

Zimbardo, P.G. (1988) *Psychology and Life*, Harper Collins, p. 317.

4

Leadership for follower commitment recognition strategy

Introduction

This chapter adopts a functional approach and offers several challenges to potential leaders and followers. It is functional because the text supports and exploits selected techniques and processes that can be developed and learned. In essence, the whole chapter combines to form a leadership for follower commitment 'recognition strategy' for use by senior management. Readers may wish to refer to the diagram in Appendix A.

A need for practical measures to enhance follower perception of leaders

The theory and concepts elaborated in earlier chapters provide characteristics and behaviours useful for the development of leader qualities. However, in total, they provide many differing perspectives; some provide contrasts and others conflicting views. Readers may construe that only 'super-men' and 'super-women' can fulfil the many leader-related conclusions emanating from both literature and analysis. Nevertheless, director/managers continue to request workable methods and solutions that have the quality of improving the manager–worker relationship within their business (Institute of Directors, 1993–2002). Simple suggestions to potential leaders such as 'smile and give employees praise', 'treat employees better', 'move towards democratic management', 'involve people', 'change your management style' or 'make people your most valued asset' are unlikely to be successful. Recommendations to potential leaders of organizations also need to take into account certain fundamental aspects.

1 Recommendations must assist organizational learning.
2 They must add value to the importance of profitability and productivity.
3 Any suggested process or redefined process must work within a recognized business framework.
4 Day to day decision-making activities should not become cumbersome.
5 Any framework should be seen as overlaying normal and conventional senior management decision making processes.
6 Some means of feedback would be essential for review and control purposes.

The sections that follow work within the above parameters; they move from the need for leaders and followers to acknowledge responsibilities and differing perceptions, through to offering explanations as to the need for behavioural change. Importantly, the text provides techniques and process that can assist implementation of a follower recognition strategy.

Follower and leader responsibilities

Some research clearly suggests that followers affect leaders as much as leaders affect followers (Greene, 1975). This chapter adopts the view that leaders must initiate changes. However, followers hold responsibility to behave appropriately and respond positively to leaders' efforts to improve the relationship. If they do not, then they must not be surprised that leaders behave managerially and initiate structure, process and procedure to help ensure appropriate employee behaviour and at least adequate organizational performance.

Readers and potential followers may wish to note that what is not expected of a leader is to be chronically concerned about only making decisions and behaving in a way that is conducive to employees. This would be naïve and would not recognize the hard business decisions management sometimes have to take as agents of owners and on behalf of the organization. Moreover, organizations do not always develop and flourish, especially during economic recessions. Consequently, followers need to accept that organizations will probably go through periods of growth, retrenchment or decline.

Organizational success depends on many factors, some of which are beyond the control of senior management. None the less, it has been too easy for managers to adopt the view that their subordinates have an obligation to follow. If followers fail to respond, managers feel entitled to adopt or perhaps sustain a conventional theory-of-action. Today, such a response is not useful, and may not even be excusable. Potential leaders must accept responsibility to adopt behaviour and act in a way that is likely to attract follower trust. Cirilli (1998) comments that trust is an essential ingredient for effective work. It is the highest form of motivation. However, trust is also a reciprocal process. Followers as well as leaders must be willing to work toward a climate of trust. A climate of trust is worth having. For example, from a potential follower perspective it provides greater opportunities for work satisfaction. From a potential leader viewpoint, if trust has been attained, followers may still sometimes assert disapproval, but they are more likely to be acceptant of a potential adverse situation. Moreover, leaders would expect followers to work enthusiastically to ameliorate negative behavioural implications. Importantly, when trust exists, short-term leader actions should not affect medium- to long-term relationships.

Trust between leader and followers will not be an overnight occurrence; more likely, it is a product of a lengthy and painstaking period of adjustment. Potential leaders should appreciate the time lag involved between interventions aimed at improving leader–follower relations and a sufficient mass of follower trust. Moreover, experience suggests that expectations of total trust or followership are idealistic and perhaps utopian. Some employees, perhaps due to behavioural deficiencies or deep-seated sensitivities may never respond. However, working toward establishing a critical mass of followers will bear dividends.

Perception and the self-concept

Theories provide valuable information as to the leader–follower relationship. However, it is worthwhile considering that it is leader and follower perception that is critical to the relationship. This is not to suggest that knowledge of motivation and commitment, employee values, managerial/leader style, theory-of-action etc. are irrelevant. Simply, that the dynamics and outcome of the leader–follower relationship rest on perceptions held by the different parties. So what is perception?

Perception is formed and/or maintained in organizations via individual senses. We use our senses to search for cues in our environment that help provide meaning. Information is stored in our memory and is used as reference for future behaviour. We each have our own set of unique characteristics and experience by which information is received, analysed, collated, filtered, used, parked or disregarded. In many ways, perception is the root of individual and organizational behaviour because it concerns how we make use of information and then make judgements about other people, situations and causes of situations.

Some perceptions may have received so many confirmations that behaviour related to them becomes almost automatic. However, if information is received that challenges our perception of a situation, we all have the ability to reconstruct or replace perceptions with more accurate ones that reflect new experiences. The extra good news for aspiring leaders is that small appropriate changes can affect many potential followers' perceptions at the same time. Chapter 3 briefly mentioned the connection between a need for recognition and self-esteem. The change process offered in this chapter is designed to appeal to followers' concept of self and to enhance opportunities for improved self-esteem.

Rogers (1951, 1959) asserts that there are two primary sources of self-concept. One is 'self' as formed by experiences; the other is evaluation of self by others. Each person develops a self-concept based on the sum total of others' perceptions of oneself combined with our own perception of self (Mead, 1934). James (1892) split the 'self-concept' into what he called the 'I' and the 'Me'. The 'I' is the self as subject and represents the basic capacity of all individuals for awareness, or as Descartes put it, 'I think therefore I am'. Simply, while the 'Me' reflects social influence on us, the 'I' ensures our individuality. The social or organizational effect on the 'Me' of our self-concept is the major focus of this book. Significant people in our world form this source, for example parents, teachers, spouse, owners, managers etc. The individual extracts and gains confirmation about values from all of them.

> *Whatever a man's position may be, he is bound to take a view of human life in general that will make his/her own activity seem important and good. (Tolstoy, 1899)*

It is possible to regard all human action as individuals striving to enlarge and enrich their self-concept, in particular to make it more like their self-ideal. People can consume satisfaction from all kinds of activities, and an organization, regardless of sector, is a major source of such activities. Therefore, the organizational environment, within which owners and senior manager perspectives have a relatively strong influence, will become part of an individual's self-concept.

Moreover, self-esteem can only be obtained via interaction within a social setting. An individual will contribute energy to an enterprise if they think it likely that by so doing there will be some increase in their valuation of themselves. However, psychological energy can only thrive within conducive organizational environments. The context of the organizational environment should therefore enable positive responses.

> *Motives and actions very often originate not from within but from the situation in which the individuals find themselves. (Mannheim, 1940, p. 249)*

Motivational aspects inform the self-concept, and if satisfied raise an individual's self-esteem. For the senior manager–employee relationship, both extrinsic and intrinsic motivational outcomes intertwine making this relationship potentially crucial to performance. Although managers do not directly deliver intrinsic outcomes, they can find ways for employees to experience intrinsic outcomes. Perhaps leaders do this particularly well.

People will always have needs. Therefore understanding employee needs and motivation are important aspects of the leader–follower relationship. Figure 4.1 provides a pictorial representation of essential linkages to follower perception and motivation.

An important factor within the motivational process that emanated from discussion in Chapter 3 was that of natural

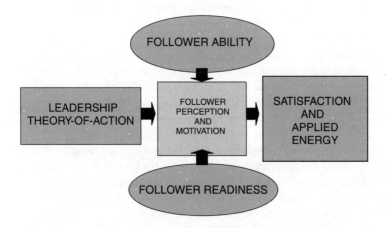

Figure 4.1 Key linkages with follower perception and motivation

recognition. It has been argued that receiving natural as well as contrived recognition is likely to lead to the intrinsic reward of a greater feeling of affiliation with the organization. Moreover, greater affinity with the company is related to organizational commitment levels.

We all have a desire for recognition, attention, importance and appreciation. Satisfaction of the need leads to greater self-esteem, self-confidence, personal worth, strength and capability. Thwarting the need produces feelings of inferiority, of weakness and of helplessness. Consequently, if we do not feel recognized or considered by those who hold influence within the social framework of organizations, it is improbable that we can behave with greater self-esteem. Additionally, if we do not possess sufficient self-esteem we are unlikely to be able to raise our energies and achieve the goal-directed aspects required by our ego needs. This line of discussion would lead us to confirm that it is social acceptance or acknowledgement of our social worth that satisfies our need for recognition. Without social acceptance, follower commitment is likely to be subdued or misdirected.

We may individually see the world around us differently. However, from an organizational perspective, different groups of interested parties may share similar perceptions. Indeed, the use of the term followership implies a collective of individuals. Groups of employees will share similar views as to why the organization and/or senior managers adopt certain priorities, values and principles by which priority objectives and decisions are made. However, a shared understanding does not necessarily mean acceptance. Importantly, acceptance and willing followership are intertwined – the latter struggles to exist without the former.

The psychological contract between potential leaders and followers encompasses both the expectations of management, which emanate from their role and behavioural approach, and expectations and perceptions of individual employees related to their motivational needs, values, self-concept and self-ideal. The feelings aroused by breaches of this contract are usually very intense. If the organization's attitude to the employee does not match how employees see themselves, then potential followers may not be able or willing to contribute sufficient psychological energy to the enterprise. Pessimistically, Argyris (1964) suggests that work has become meaningless. He argues that what is missing in most conditions of work is not money or social need but personal meaning or relevance. People clearly want a lot more than money for work. However, if individuals do not, or cannot enhance their self-esteem at work then they may use the money they earn as a substitute for valuing themselves; it may simply provide a surrogate sense of worth. Hence, it is natural for employees to ask for more money to compensate for the unfulfilling nature of their work, rather than to ask for changes in the nature of work or the context within which they conduct their duties.

From a potential follower perspective, the above conditions define the prospect of psychological success. Gaining psychological success will, in turn, determine whether an individual or group 'commit' the appropriate level of psychological energy to the activity, which again in turn is likely to have an impact on organizational performance. For potential leaders, the aim should therefore be to 'work with' employees' self-concept using the natural source of activities available within the organization. However, much would appear to depend on the assumptions and perceptions managers as influential others hold about employees, and whether potential leaders and followers are willing to work towards improved relations.

Managers are left with three choices. First, they can choose to ignore the implications of motivation, potential follower values, self-concept, self-ideal, self-esteem etc. In some ways this solves the immediate problem. Nevertheless, if follower commitment is desired, leaders must find a means of enabling it. Payment alone is unlikely to motivate all individuals at the desired intensity. Secondly, management may choose to educate employees as to the value of organizational goals. This conventional and obvious response is designed to elicit employee commitment to management perception of priority goals. However, Chapter 2 warned of the dangers of rational-economic approaches and the difficulties that may arise if senior management assumes unitary goals exist. Finally, potential leaders could attempt to integrate both organizational values and goals with those relating to employee self-concept and self-ideal, thus providing for follower self-esteem. Conceptually, successful integration will generate affective commitment. If managers accept this argument, then gaining a desired level of follower commitment should not be an insurmountable task. Indeed managers may be making the task more difficult for themselves by not paying adequate attention to this phenomenon.

This book has identified several overriding issues that appear to restrict development of a leader–follower relationship within organizations. First, senior management over-reliance on organizational aspects such as finance. Due to continual reinforcement, dominance of this aspect of business might become second nature to most interested parties. However, it is likely that automatic acceptance of its prominent position prevents consideration of important information that might challenge perceptions. Different weighting of financial against other imperatives is required. Certainly, a need for balance is overdue. This essential is considered in sections that follow, entitled:

- Leadership and follower commitment: links with the balanced scorecard
- Finance may not be so economically rational!
- Why have a recognition strategy?

Second, is the view of many potential follower employees that their needs are not adequately addressed or satisfied within the work environment. Thus, a possible improvement to their self-esteem and the development of affective commitment to their organization is restricted. Practical measures and techniques are considered in sections below entitled:

- Leader recognition of followers: human resource (HR) strategy, policies and procedures.
- Recognition involves asking questions.
- Merging human behavioural questions.
- Systems to integrate recognition: The product life cycle and business review process.
- Leader recognition of followers: The role of employee training, development and coaching.
- Recognition strategy: implementation.
- Leadership and follower commitment: integration with the EFQM Excellence Model.

Third, although managers wish for committed employees, their actions may inevitably be preventing potential followers from perceiving them as leaders. The good news for managers who may wish to be seen as leaders of their organization is that perceptions can be adjusted and behaviour can be changed. Clarification is provided below within sections entitled:

- Behaviour modification.
- Lessons for potential leaders.

Leadership and follower commitment: links with the balanced scorecard

Chapter 2 briefly mentioned the notion of balanced scorecards. The idea emerged from a sponsored one-year multi-company study by Kaplan and Norton (1996a, 1996b). Their research was motivated by a belief that existing performance measurement approaches relied too heavily on financial measures. Kaplan and Norton's (1993) original ideas about the development of a balanced scorecard simply suggest that whatever the strategic goals of the organization, benefits will occur if many measurement dimensions are monitored and not simply financial measures.

Generally, it seems acceptable to suggest that one of the hallmarks of leading-edge organizations has been the successful adoption and application of performance measurement. The process informs leaders as to organizational effectiveness and efficiency of its processes, assists decision and generally helps them 'manage' their organization. The balanced scorecard notion provides a structured methodology for using performance measures, to prioritize resources and via the monitoring process help shape and re-shape direction. It also assists integration and translation from organizational strategic objectives into a series of performance indicators among the four chosen perspectives: customers, financials, business processes, and learning and growth.

Measurement is clearly crucial, and identifying several areas for measurement in addition to financial is admirable and more likely to capture the reality of the organization's context – including various stakeholders. However, as Nils-Goran *et al.* (1999) point out, 'It is not enough for someone to put together a collection of measures in a single scorecard. The discussion concerning the scorecard is what determines whether it will have any effect.' Discussion would include the dimensions the organization feels are worthy of inclusion. Importantly, discussion should also include the weighting or importance of each dimension. The balanced scorecard is not explicit about the need to encourage people or for managers to behave in a way that encourages followership. However, the Kaplan and Norton model captures the need for leaders to 'think out of the box'.

Leaders have to investigate and contemplate people-related measures, and to consider financial aspects as simply one category of measurement and not a goal in itself. To this end, the balanced scorecard seems very cohesive with my own analysis in Chapter 2. This is interesting given that my discipline is occupational psychology and my research started from a totally different perspective – that of understanding the psychological forces that influence potential followers.

Running counter to potential leaders accepting this view is the outer influence of the business situation and what traditional economists suggest is a single business motivation, that of profit maximization. Mannheim (1940) posits that business people change their motives as they assume different roles on the way up the business ladder. Having had to come to terms with the profit motive once in order to achieve, they will not wish to reverse their thinking and 'jump through the hoop' again. Moreover, it is one thing to suggest that potential leaders think more about dimensions other than finance. It is quite another to ask management to reconsider their conventional theory-of-action in relation to potential followers. Nevertheless, the incentive for potential leaders and the organizations principal owners is clear. The application of a recognition strategy should lead to greater potential follower satisfaction. Higher levels of follower job satisfaction should lead to improved follower self-esteem and increased levels of affective commitment, and follower affective commitment results in individual and organizational performance improvements.

The following extract may assist potential leaders of organizations to think differently about the prominence of financial imperatives. Thinking differently may allow sufficient room to consider the needs of potential followers and help adjust perceptions vital to the development of the leader–follower relationship.

Finance may not be so economically rational!

Man has conventionally turned to evidence from the physical sciences, as for technological improvement. Physical substances act as we rationally feel they ought. Finance is commonly defined as 'management of revenue, science of revenue' or more simply 'the management of money'. Science is defined as 'systematic and formulated knowledge'. Moreover, it is concerned with exact knowledge based upon universal truths and general laws that are repeatable and which experiment can demonstrate. Science is the subject therefore that refines the laws that govern changes and conditions by using objective information and associated decision making. Common-sense thinking may consider the application of science as a precise way of completing any task and assessing outcomes against rules that govern completion.

Various rules operate within the finance and accounting discipline, some of which are imposed by regulatory bodies and some that could be viewed as extensions to 'rules of nature'. The basic and most obvious rule is that of mathematics. Mathematics is often described as the purest science. Moreover, it might be argued that as the mechanics of accountancy and finance is totally dependent upon 'numbers' then the mathematics of science becomes a direct association. By using both simple and complex equations and formulas, the science of mathematics might be viewed as part of the science of accountancy and finance. Given this logic, it is easy to see why 'finance' is viewed as so rational and important in most organizations. Nevertheless, we should bear in mind that the financial numbers are based on qualitative interpretations and assumptions.

Along with other social sciences such as economics and politics, Glautier and Underdown (1991) describe finance as a social science. It seems that despite the unfortunate and stereotyped 'number crunching images' that accountants are often mistakenly ascribed, accountants often need to display a fair degree of flair, understanding and experience. Sometimes accounting methods are politically motivated, and in consequence, they may say more about the decision maker than the numbers concerned with the decision – not a totally rational means to an end.

Adaptation of data relies on the accountant's skill rather than rules of nature, mathematics or any other science. Moreover, financial activity involves far more than simply preparing financial statements. Data can be produced in many different ways. The skill and art of finance is to understand user requirements and to provide purposeful information that relates to requirements. Importantly, the interpretation upon which the manager decides is often a matter of personal intuitive judgement rather than any scientifically proven theory.

When we move away from the process of recording transaction towards a science that helps in the decision-making process, finance can be seen as an interdisciplinary science involving economics, behavioural science and sociological science. Perhaps this interrelationship supports the conclusion that finance is a science but perhaps not the pure science that many managers perceive it to be. For example, strategic decision is based on assumptions. Moreover, a senior manager's worth is judged by the accuracy of assumptions, some of which cannot be informed by past data. The decision-maker's competency should relate to his or her ability to assess a situation or perceived opportunity. It should require skills and knowledge relating to all organizational resources – including prediction as to the effects of a decision on potential followers. The Dearing Report (1988) observed that there is 'a need for a forum to deal with new issues relating to organizational performance and reporting, people issues being one of them, however – as yet there is no conceptual framework'.

To summarize, if finance is more of a social science than a pure science, then economic rational decision-making processes are not as 'purely rational' as managers would wish to believe. None the less, many managers seem totally to subscribe to financially-related building blocks and derivatives to conduct the process of management. However, as argued in Chapter 2, the process inherently involves people, their perceptions and assumptions. Chapter 3 also commented that the process of leadership involves managing in order to encourage affective commitment. Moreover, given the impact of globalization and the knowledge economy, affective follower commitment might be seen as the essence of wealth maximization in the future. However, in order for the organization to benefit, leaders and followers may need to modify their behaviour.

Behaviour modification

The author has applied the above argument in business settings. The reason for doing so was not to deride the importance of financial controls or the need for efficient cost and cash management, but to open dialogue as to the merits of employing techniques that encourage followership commitment. The writer's intervention was aimed at behaviour modification in terms of managerial action. The incentive to senior management was that employee behaviour might also be positively modified. Similarly, for a recognition strategy to be successful, several behavioural modifications may be required:

1 Potential followers need to behave appropriately as a response to attempts by potential leaders to improve manager–employee relations.
2 Potential leaders may have to challenge their current theory-of-action with a view to adopting behaviour more conducive to the encouragement of followers.
3 Potential leaders will need to establish and implement interventions that promote behavioural change from their managers as well as their employees.

If you want to know why someone did something, do not ask. Analyse the person's immediate environment until you find the reward or punishment. (Schwartz and Lacey, 1982, p. 15)

Much of the content of this book has focused on why leadership for follower commitment appears so difficult to establish and sustain in organizations, especially those firms most closely tied to a highly charged, competitive and commercial environment. Analysis in Chapter 3 considered current use of rewards in organizations and suggested rewards that may have been overlooked or underused. Rewards and incentives are the most obvious and probably best available vehicle to potential leaders who wish for behavioural changes – some background information may assist.

Followers of classical conditioning (Pavlov, 1927) view the association between stimuli and responses as the basic units on which a science of psychology is built. For instance, what is termed stimulus–response psychology conveys the idea that what is learned can be observed by a change in behaviour brought about by a stimulus. Watson (1930) suggested that a science of behaviour would consist of documenting and explaining the relationship between stimuli and responses. Thorndyke (1911) suggests that complex behaviour called intelligent or creative (the essence of the knowledge economy) could really be reduced to learning a number of simple stimulus–response associations or connections. For instance, instrumental conditioning (Thorndyke, 1911) offers that learning is the process formed by individuals making associations between stimuli and responses. An instrumental contingency is arranged between a response and a reinforcer. For instance, senior management might receive promotion or an increase in salary which is contingent on the organization performing well. Equally, employees may obtain a bonus contingent on high productivity.

Critics of the behaviourist approach suggest human behaviour is complex and not easily explained by the notion of association. Nevertheless, behaviourists offer the idea that all employees behave through stimulus and reward. At higher organizational levels, rewards are greater and perhaps the risks of failure are greater. Measurement of success will be based on goals and targets related to organizational profitability. Consequently, we can visualize senior management being rewarded by owners or higher influential stakeholders when management have improved profitability. Senior management behaviour will therefore focus on repeating this outcome. Moreover, to avoid the criticism of owners, senior management will behave in a way that lessens the probability of comments from owners (or other influential bodies) that would otherwise lower their self-concept/self-esteem. For the manager, criticism (negative reinforcement) would prevent the satisfaction of primary needs – perhaps those of achievement and power. Hence, it is not surprising that a conventional theory-of-action is adopted and maintained.

In an attempt to control the human resource, managers may hope that employees will respond to conditioning in a way that ensures the required behaviour assists organizational performance. In terms of instrumental conditioning, it will be hoped that employees learn to commit themselves to the organization in order to receive valued rewards. If senior managers adopt a conventional theory-of-action then instrumental rewards are likely to be offered. Previous findings suggest such behaviour may not be conducive to optimal levels of affective commitment.

If aspiring leaders discover their adopted theory-of-action is negatively associated with follower commitment, then changing and actively sustaining a recognition strategy should result in extinction of existing employee perception. This would give potential leaders the opportunity to promote commitment from followers. However, recognizing that strong feelings of inequity can develop over time seems important (Cosier and Dalton, 1983). Past inequities may have a cumulative effect. None the less, changing behaviour seems feasible if past inequity ceases. Extinction is a notion borrowed from behaviourist theory. It is a procedure in which over time reinforcement no longer follows a response – simply, the former contingency is no longer in effect. Leaders can apply positive reinforcement via supportive interventions that increase the frequency or strength of desirable behaviour.

Zimbardo states that to assist conditioning one must use both extinction and positive reinforcement (Zimbardo, 1985). This process should be continued over time so that extinction of the desired behaviour is less likely to occur. What would this look like? Positive reinforcement could occur if senior management develop process by which employee needs receive attention. For example, if employee need for training and development was actively considered; if senior management gave continuous consideration to the structure of employees jobs; if aspiring leaders change employment policies, practices and procedures to encourage employee commitment etc. Continuous reinforcement would shape desired behaviour and prevent its extinction.

The process of 'shaping' involves changing behaviour in small steps that successfully approximate the desired performance – or a behavioural outcome. By carefully combining reinforcement for the 'correct' response, a potential leader could shape the desired 'high level' follower reaction. Behaviourists agree that shaping could gradually increase employee commitment. However, such action infers over-clinical and manipulative means. None the less, where does good people-management start and manipulation finish? It could be argued that the very nature of people management has always been manipulative. Nevertheless, there is a philosophical difference between pure manipulation for the sake of one's own wants, and manipulation for the sake of improving relationships. As parents, we use conditioning on our children: for example, 'Do as you are told and I will get you some sweets' – positive reinforcement. Chastising is used as a negative reinforcement. Likewise, in schools and other educational establishments we use rewards and punishment to achieve a desired outcome; for example, the positive reinforcement of an award of 'distinction'. Accepting the need to adopt ethical behaviour towards others, perhaps we should not be too squeamish about considering conditioning as a means of assisting desired behaviour.

What is suggested is that by considering people as potential followers and as assets of the organization, attempts at conditioning could be successful. Success from this standpoint would be defined in terms of followers perceiving that their needs and values are expressed as part of the function of the business, and owners benefiting from the increased effectiveness of their investment. In this sense, shaping can be seen as a means to an important and mutually beneficial outcome.

A word of caution, before potential leaders attempt to shape follower behaviour they should assess their own behaviour in terms of compatibility with the desired behavioural outcome and adjust as necessary.

Why have a recognition strategy?

Natural treatment of people may not be overly natural in work environments. For instance, many writers focus on the need for organizations to manage change (Drucker, 1985; Kanter, 1989; Kanter *et al.*, 1992; Egan, 1994), however fewer texts consider the need to manage continuity. None the less, managing for strategic competitive advantage seems as much to do with the need for internal integration and sustaining employee commitment as it is to do with understanding market trends, customer demands and financial implications. Simply, too much concentration on external adaptation at the expense of internal integration is unlikely to lead to an optimum level of employee commitment.

It has been argued that followership is a process that results from a positive comparison of personal values with one's perception of leader values. It relies on potential follower perception that their values and needs are integrated within leader principles, priorities, strategy, tactics, decisions and general behaviour. Congruence is likely to result in committed behaviour. Conversely, disequilibrium may result in less committed behaviour – or simple compliance.

Leader recognition of followers: human resource (HR) strategy, policies and procedures

An interesting way to judge the philosophy, priorities and values of the organization, and its senior management theory-of-action is to review the development and operation of human resource strategy, policies and procedures. This documentation is the written product of senior management decision about human resources. It is also interesting because it is possible for potential leaders to demonstrate acknowledgement and recognition of potential followers in all three aspects.

Strategy is a process whereby the medium- to long-term aims of the organization are set by the organization. It is essentially a process by which senior management decides where the organization is, where the organization wants or needs to be, and how it intends to achieve its new, preferred or best position. Strategic plans and projections usually cover a medium- or long-term three- to five-year period and normally start with an external focus that includes market analysis and competitor intelligence. It is also common for the organizational mission, strategy and objectives to be informed and driven by internal and external environmental analysis based on assessment of internal strengths and weaknesses, and external assessment of opportunities and threats.

To enable a recognition strategy, leaders of organizations would ensure they assess current and planned employee skills, knowledge, attitudes, motivation and commitment to the company. Moreover, internal analysis would record employee willingness to be flexible and responsive, their acceptance of the need to be held responsible and accountable, their enthusiasm to use their competencies for the betterment of the organization etc. Information would be used as the initial 'behavioural' benchmark. Gap analysis can then help in indicating the difference between current and desired behaviour. The result of this process would help inform policy and procedural changes.

Secondly, a recognition strategy would require a clearly defined and expressed business strategy that acknowledges and internalizes the importance of human resources as an essential source of added value that leads to competitive advantage. Vision and mission statements are the most obvious vehicles. The following extract might provide assurance to potential followers that the company intends to integrate their needs:

The Company
Mission, Values and Guiding Principles

Our mission is built upon the belief in the value of our employees, our customers, our owners, and our suppliers. The business exists as a team of people. We value the effort and contribution made by each of our employees.

For our business to prevail, we must produce profit at a level to attract capital that will provide for our long-term growth and prosperity. Planning for deliberate growth will mean new opportunities for employees. Dedication to continuous improvement must be recognized. This will result in more satisfied employees, customers, expanding markets, new jobs, and will ensure company longevity.

Third, a follower recognition strategy would need to be integrated and supportive of the overall corporate strategy, integration will be a product of designing and developing human resource policies and procedures that reinforce and sustain the philosophy of recognition. These policies and procedures provide signals to potential followers because they hold detailed information and guidelines to managers as to the implementation of strategy and the way managers should act toward human resources. HR policies can be implicit or explicit. Implicit policies might be found in new organizations or in business environments that do not wish to be restrained by the potential inflexibility of an explicit set of HR policies. None the less, policies and procedures might typically include the following:

Policies	*Procedures*
Career management	Appraisal
Employee development	Disciplinary
Employee relations	Grievances
Equal opportunities	Promotion
Health and Safety	Recruitment
Pay	Redundancy
Resourcing	Selection
Training	Transfer

Policies provide a general framework for implementing HR strategies while procedures suggest systematic managerial guidelines. Kochan and Dyer (1993) assert that policies must be designed and managed in such a way that 'the first instinct in good times and bad should be to build and protect the firm's investment in human resources, rather than indiscriminately add and cut people in knee-jerk responses to short-term fluctuations in business conditions'.

There is a direct link between operation of HR procedure and follower perception of managerial theory-in-use. For example, their contents openly display leadership values and priorities and convey information to potential followers. They act as a framework by which employees receive continuous information as to their worth to the organization and provide structure by which people and groups can assess how much the organization wishes to recognize employee contributions. Measuring employee satisfaction as to human resource policies and procedures is likely to provide essential information for potential organizational leaders regarding the readiness of employees to follow. Method is described later in this chapter.

Additional to HR policies and procedures, senior management may also instigate campaigns to win the 'hearts and minds' of potential followers, and as a consequence increase commitment. For example, earlier chapters discussed quality, communication, involvement and empowerment programmes. Campaigns seem to come and go, leaving potential followers thinking that 'another one will come along – if they wait long enough.' It is definitely not suggested that aspiring leaders use this chapter as a theme for another campaign. In contrast, the need for recognition must be an ongoing philosophical and strategic process, hence the need to integrate within the company strategy, policies, procedures and the decision making framework.

Finally, human resource policies and procedures need to be cohesive with a potential leader's actual theory-in-use. Conflicting messages between policies and actual managerial behaviour will result in suspicion and a general lack of trust. In contrast, it would follow that the use of human resource policies and procedures that continue to relay 'recognition' of employees help sustain positive follower perceptions. Consistent and continued use may also assist medium- to longer-term cultural change.

Recognition involves asking questions

Analysis suggests that the impact of managers/potential leaders upon employee feelings is probably underestimated. It is also likely that leaders are able to act in ways that followers at least perceive their feelings are acknowledged, counted and considered. The act of recognition can be used as a conduit between leader and potential follower. Clearly, aspiring leaders wishing to integrate actions supportive of the need for recognition of followers will require simple process. Chapter 3 asserted that parents show recognition by asking questions about their children. It is not suggested that managers should adopt a parental role or behave in a parental manner. However, questioning is a natural process by which recognition for another can be shown. Consequently, questions can be used to good effect.

Revans (1992) suggests action learning means 'doing better tomorrow by asking how well the job is being done today', a process seen as a fundamental element of learning. However, from a human resource behavioural rather than human resource cost standpoint, in comparative terms, questions asked by senior figures within most organizations often appear to ignore the human element. Case study 2 in Chapter 2 provides evidence that senior management considerations tend to dwell on imperatives closely linked to objective measures of organizational performance. For instance, questions heavily weighted towards enquiry and improvements of aspects such as:

- Strategic goals and objectives centred on finance and its derivative key performance measures.
- Marketability relating to actual sales value achieved against forecast.
- The performance of the product or service.
- Availability of the product or service.
- Manufacture, in terms of a conforming product at an economic cost.
- Profitability and measurement of actual costs/revenue in terms of forecasted figures.
- Credit control and liquidity etc.

While concerns about such areas are admirable, the focus conveys a conventional unbalanced theory-in-action. Arie De Geus (in Pickard, 1998) offers the hypothesis that decision making is a learning process; in making really difficult decisions, we are not applying knowledge, but having to find new solutions. Concentrating on the above aspects may inhibit learning. Fortunately, questions can be added. This is especially important if by asking more questions the quality of decisions can be improved.

Merging human behavioural questions

Essentially, questions other than those related to rational-economic issues should encapsulate motivation and needs theory as well as good people-management. For example:

Employee status	Interpersonal relationships
Working conditions	Employee competence
Job design	Responsibility
Security	HR policy and practice
Self-respect and esteem	Communication and feedback

Formal recognition	Natural recognition
Career aspirations	Psychological contract
Organizational culture	Organizational climate
Employee benefits	Employee relations
Employee involvement	Health and safety
Welfare	Training and development

The list above is not exhaustive. Nevertheless, continuous senior management consideration of the above aspects would provide for employees the view that they are recognized and valued by the organization. Clearly, such questions can be asked as part of regular senior management team forums. The Chief Executive Officer or Managing Director may wish to ensure discussion is equally divided between task and behavioural issues. This approach may also be integrated within common business review and risk management systems.

Systems to integrate recognition: the product life cycle and business review process

Management decisions involve the enactment of strategic plans that directly affect employee commitment. Consequently, in a 'leadership for follower commitment recognition strategy' there needs to be a match between the organization's philosophy, strategy, human resource policies, procedures and practices. This can be achieved by using management systems and processes.

Ideas, like products, organizations and people, go through a life cycle of four phases: birth, growth, maturity and death. From a market viewpoint, the concept of a product life cycle is not new. Academics and professional management consider the idea to be a useful representation of the life of a service or good. Every business whether it is predominantly a supplier of a good or service uses the idea of life cycles. The idea gives the user a graphical illustration of where the organization, its product, product portfolio or services are within their life.

Many organizations turn to product life cycle management to help manage their business. Its attraction is that by managing the process it is felt that the organization is attempting to manage and control the circumstances affecting the business rather than circumstances controlling the company. Product life cycle management techniques are commonly used on projects important to the company that involve major investment, as for time, money and employee effort.

An organization will stage business or project reviews of its operations in relation to a good or service or portfolio of products, several business ventures, or project groups. In essence, management wish to perceive the effect each activity of the business has upon the total business. To help understanding the following key deliverables might be considered within each review:

- An outline of marketing and the product plan.
- An outline of systems requirements.
- An outline business case.
- A forecasted investment appraisal.
- Risk analysis.
- Forecasted profit and loss statements.

The important aspect to stress is that analysis is continuous throughout the business review process. At each business review meeting the decision-making group should discuss and consider important aspects related to the project or business. However, having taken part in many such reviews it can be stated that the elements conventionally discussed are related to the risk and probability of preferred aspects. These elements seem generally well fixed on criteria related to expected turnover, costs, equipment utilization and projected profits. Such measures are often transferred and debated within an organization's risk management process, for example:

1 What is the risk of slow payment or default by customers?
2 What is the risk that inflation will erode profit margins?
3 What is the risk of sales being substantially lower than forecast?
4 Are the material and resource costs accurate?
5 What is the risk of changes to labour cost per annum?
6 What is the risk or change to material/component costs per annum?
7 What is the risk that the project/company will not generate sufficient cash flow? etc.

The above questions simply encapsulate what the company perceives are the essential success factors. Unfortunately, processes and aspects relating to human resources are significant by their absence. Thus, they are systems that normally help sustain employee perception that the organization does not 'recognize' their worth. A conventional management theory-of-action is in operation. Clearly, risk does not end with forecasts and estimates of material costs, sales volume, price and logistical information relating to fixed asset utilization.

It is comparatively simple to forecast costs of materials and to estimate the sensitivity of a fall in turnover or erosion of price. It is more difficult to estimate the likelihood that by adopting a strategy of a new product range within say six months what the effect will be on the organizational commitment level of potential followers. Nevertheless, risk exists in relation to human assets/ resources as well as materials and financial assets/resources and should not be conveniently ignored.

Risk is becoming an issue of growing significance as markets become increasingly competitive, pressurized and quality conscious. Information critical to the success of a company, product or project needs to be available in ever-reducing time scales to enable decision makers to decide in the most effective way. For instance, market intelligence, costs of finance, manufacturing capacity etc. However, as corporate knowledge becomes more important, an essential organizational aspect will be its ability to utilize the knowledge of its workforce; if it cannot, its business and competitive risk increases. The more business comes to rely on employee knowledge, the more sensitive people issues will become to the attainment of business objectives.

Issue: Risk Assessment: Business Review Process   Date: X/X/0X

WHAT IS THE RISK?	Risk factor (0–10)*	Impact factor (1–3)	Weighted risk impact (1–10)
Of commitment falling at the shopfloor level?	5	2	10
Of commitment falling at any other level?	1	3	3
That employees do not possess appropriate competencies?	0	3	0
That interpersonal relationships will suffer?	3	2	6
To health and safety?	0	3	0
Of changing labour costs?	1	1	1
Of Research and Development overspend?	2	3	6
Of foreign exchange fluctuations affecting revenues?	1	1	1
If sales were substantially lower than forecast?	8	2	16
Of changes to material/component costs?	1	1	1

*Risk factor: Low = 0–3; Medium = 4–7; High = 8–10.

Figure 4.2 Risk analysis

The risk analysis process illustrated in Figure 4.2 is used to introduce a simple, systematic and effective way of ensuring that the management of vital elements that contribute risk have been considered as each stage in a company or project/product life cycle. It incorporates the need:

● To clarify and agree the most significant risk factors.
● To formulate appropriate questions.

- To evaluate the risk: for example, how likely is it to happen?
- To evaluate the impact of risk: for example, what would be the effect if it did happen?

Judgemental risk factors are normally numerical and can be divided into low, medium and high risk. For example, common assigned risk factor values are:

Low	0–3
Medium	4–7
High	8–10

The number and nature of questions are theoretically unlimited. However, in operating a recognition strategy, a management wishing to incorporate followers needs would balance task and people/process related concerns. Such balance would be integral to a corporation's ongoing consideration of risk, be part of the business and project review process, and would form an essential element within the company risk register.

In the example in Figure 4.2, management view the most important factors requiring interventions to limit exposure to be those of lower than forecast sales and shopfloor commitment levels. Importantly, inclusion of questions related to employee needs systematically captures the motivational element 'recognition' – seen as an essential element to the establishment and maintenance of the leader-follower relationship.

The choice as to which human resource factors should be considered will be situation specific and rely on management understanding. Likewise, risk assessment of each question will rely on senior management skill to interpret employee behavioural implications of their decision.

The affect on follower commitment will also rely, if deemed necessary, on the choice of suitable interventions deemed necessary to assist implementation. Consequently, also included within a risk register and project planning process would be the need to identify existing controls, key actions, responsibility for actions and a timing element. This would ensure that a written process signalling theory-of-action translates into an actual theory-in-use. Cohesion between a senior manager theory-in-action and actual theory-of-use will signal to potential followers that their needs are not only considered but are acted on.

Monitoring the effect of decisions on people as well as their commitment to the organization would help sustain people perception as to whether the organization is considerate of their needs. The process would also provide senior management with vital information as to current and potential commitment levels.

Additional to the systems mentioned, the firm may wish to assess levels of employee satisfaction and commitment. Appendix C illustrates item statements from a satisfaction survey used by the author during field research. When combined with a commitment survey similar to the Organizational Commitment Questionnaire in Appendix B, enquiry can provide valuable information by which potential leaders can benchmark and then periodically review employee satisfaction and commitment.

Leader recognition of followers: the role of employee training, development and coaching

It has been argued that HR strategy, policy and procedure must be aligned and be supportive of a recognition process. Additionally, previous sections assert that building questions relating to people and their needs within strategic and tactical decision would be a clear demonstration by management of their consideration of the workforce. However, employees often view senior managers as being distant. This appears especially so in medium and large organizations. Moreover, such a notion would not be conducive to building a leader–follower relationship. Furthermore, senior management might conventionally focus on strategic and not operational issues, and there is always a question of senior people not having sufficient time to dedicate to concerns of employees. Consequently, lower level managers and supervisors are normally given responsibility to motivate staff. While managers at all levels hold responsibility for developing commitment, this tactic completely misses the importance of the link between senior managers and all employees. The solution is for potential leaders to accept that they have no alternative but to develop and utilize methods to encourage followers by using skills that assist in bridging the gap, at least from the perspective of employees.

Strebler (1997) reports and comments on the DfEE commissioned study that set out to consider the need to 'Change the role of the senior manager'. Eighteen leading employers interviewed in the study identified interpersonal skills as one of the most important gaps. DfEE findings also suggest that greater spans of command in flatter organizations have been accompanied by a shift in emphasis from management to leadership skills. Strebler states that senior managers who have been socialized in a command and control culture, where macho management has made them successful in the past, are finding the change for the need to employ softer skills difficult. However, any manager who wishes to promote followers amongst subordinate employees can employ basic people-related skills. Some of the more obvious that can be developed as a 'tool-kit' of skills include training, appraising and coaching. Regardless, of organizational level, effective use of all three can enhance the leader–follower relationship.

Training

Training and developing people improves their commitment to management and to the organization itself. It is interesting therefore that given the connection, cutting training budgets is often the first reaction of firms when performance outcomes appear threatened. Such a response could only occur if senior management theory-of-action was focused on short-term financial imperatives. Clearly, everyone would accept the need for organizations to survive in difficult periods. However, management should accept that cutting resources allocated for training and development not only affects the opportunity of employees to apply newly found knowledge and skills for the betterment of the organization, but equally affects employee motivation and commitment to their organization. The converse is also true. Training and development is as much about employees feeling appreciated and considered by their management as it is a chance to develop themselves. Consequently, it is an important element of recognition. Therefore, it can be used by management to show consideration and help enhance commitment. Additionally, human resource development does not have to cost too much. This is especially the case for in-house development initiatives.

Training of potential followers can assist the development of skills, provide knowledge to help manage change, improve communication and help develop a positive and progressive culture. Senior managers might therefore take an active interest in the formulation of training plans. They could also develop trainer skills and take part in training – perhaps making guest appearances during training events. A decision to use training specialists should result in an increase in knowledge. However, if managers, and senior managers in particular, take an active role, it seems likely that the training outcomes will also include a willingness to implement new found knowledge and an increase in follower commitment. Simply, taking part in training potential followers helps develop the interface between leaders and followers; it is an opportunity no senior manager should miss.

Appraising

Performance review/appraisals are concerned with two parties getting together to engage in dialogue about performance and development. The process involves agreed assessment, an open exchange of views, feedback, positive reinforcement, an assessment of manager support, a discussion as to future support and agreement as to future work and personal development plans. The process is not something done to an individual – it is something that the potential leader and potential follower carry out together. From the perspective of the employee/follower, appraisals/performance reviews might provide an opportunity to state their views. In practice, and from experience, the process also helps the employee to confirm their perceptions as to management objectives, intentions and priority values. Clearly, a fundamental communication device that informs employee perceptions as to the governing theory-of-action of their manager and of the organization. Equally, the process can provide manager/leaders with awareness as to employee perception of managerial values and priorities that would otherwise not be overly transparent.

It is unfortunate that many employee appraisals appear to result in worse manager–employee relationships. Cynically, some observers comment that it takes one year for the appraised to 'get over' the effects of the previous appraisal. However, if managers can develop adequate skills and be willing to question their theory-of-action, it is probable that the process can provide meaningful dialogue and perhaps positively change perceptions of both parties. Improvements are instigated via feedback. Feedback can therefore be viewed as an element of follower recognition.

Goal theory mentioned in Chapter 3 suggests that people will strive to achieve in order to satisfy goals and emotional needs. Goals direct performance, but performance can only be maintained via accurate and timely feedback. The law of effect is a basic principle of learning that states learning is controlled by its consequences. If follows that without knowledge of consequences then learning cannot take place. Reviewing and feeding back information to people as to performance is vital to a process of continual improvement. Additionally, according to attribution theory, feedback would be essential for people to assess how much their success is related to their own individual efforts and how much relates to external factors.

Feedback to senior managers is often filtered. It is not surprising therefore that potential leaders may receive very little honest comment as to how their actions might affect others. No one wants to tell the boss that things are going wrong, even less if subordinates perceive that it is the boss and his or her behaviour and decisions that are making things go wrong. Who wants to risk the possibility of the boss taking exception to opinions – despite their well-meaning and constructive nature?

Review processes such as the 360-degree appraisal/perform-ance review can assist in providing important information as to people issues to leaders. However, 360 schemes are limited to a few individuals who have contact with the appraised leader. Indeed, in medium to large enterprises, most employees are disconnected from contact with managerial leadership by locality and/or job responsibilities. Consequently, if shopfloor employees feel that the psychological contract between employees and employer is broken, what can they do?

Although most employees may feel able to explain their frustrations in terms of their needs not being satisfied, they will be equally aware of the consequences of a possible negative response from management. It is only when senior management is receptive to potential follower perception can change be initiated.

Contact is both a form of recognition and an element of a recognition strategy. Consequently, leaders need to find ways of ensuring adequate contact with potential followers. It has been argued that human resource strategy, policies and procedures carry important and explicit communicative messages to potential followers. However, because followership is mostly to do with perceptions, contact does not have to be a daily occurrence, nor does it have to be systematically overt. 'Grapevine' contact with employee perception may be the most vital form of leader contact. For example, a leader message contained within leader behaviour does not have to be seen to be acknowledged. Secondly, priorities contained within leader decisions do not have to be experienced to know they exist. Finally, concern for followers can be perceived without it being openly communicated to any one individual. Indeed, effective leaders seem particularly gifted at providing meaning via symbolic gesture. From experience, a well-meaning management response to an employee in difficulty spreads through the organization like 'wild fire'. 'Walking the floor' and 'back to the floor' activities also assist contact with potential followers.

One successful notion operated by a 'blue-chip' multinational organization was to offer all employees the chance to e-mail the managing director with problems and frustrations, ideas, personal and/or group views etc. The initiative opened up direct com-munication where previous direct contact had either not existed or the communication had become filtered so much that the original message became blurred. Initially, employees were suspicious that 'the boss' was not actually the one returning their e-mail – then they were amazed that communication could be so candid. The managing director's reputation as someone who recognized the importance of employee opinion grew 'almost overnight'. The MD was equally impressed with the quality of contact.

Coaching

Coaching is a process that develops staff at the same time as getting the job done. It systematically increases competence by giving planned tasks, with counselling and control provided by the manager. The manager enables learning opportunities and assists reflection of planned experiences. Manager skills related to the process of coaching include searching questions, discussion, encouragement, demonstrating understanding, providing information, and giving and receiving feedback. Readers will note the similarity between coaching and the need of followers for recognition. Clearly, for the senior manager, the coaching process requires interpersonal skill development, dedicated time and a willingness to incorporate the process on a regular basis. Often, managers are apathetic and argue the importance of other more pressing priorities and a lack of immediate results. However, such views help sustain a conventional theory-of-action and are typical of managers – but perhaps atypical of leaders. Potential leaders should acknowledge that the importance of coaching must start and be driven by senior management at the top of the organization.

Recognition strategy: implementation

It is unlikely that spasmodic attention to employee recognition will result in long-term commitment by employees to the company. Long-term goals require constant and continuous attention, consequently the writer does not recommend implementation of the recognition strategy via a standard organizational development (OD) approach. What is suggested is an ongoing and more contingent process:

- Determine current follower commitment and satisfaction.
- Decide which human-related aspects encompass sensitivity.
- Ensure that human resource-related aspects are an essential feature of decision making.
- Consider decision implementation in terms of probable implications for activating or potential deactivation of committed follower behaviour.
- Monitor effectiveness of the decision-making process. This will include risk analysis and probability estimates.
- Monitor effectiveness of interventions designed to offset or improve follower commitment.

Potential leaders should expect lags to occur between interventions and outcomes. They also need to be able to differentiate between special and common cause variation regarding follower behaviour. Follower commitment is, by nature, a long-term perception. Consequently, leaders may be wise to subdue 'knee-jerk' reactions to short-term people problems. Shorter-term restraint from leaders is likely to lead to longer-term understanding of follower perceptions and the affects of perceptions. Advice to potential leaders:

- Employ sensory methods to assist verification of follower perceptions and continuously assess new information against current and past information as to follower satisfaction and commitment levels.
- Seek out common causes before instigating action.
- Accept that oscillations and delays with regard to feedback from leader interventions will occur.
- Avoid short-term 'quick-fire' interventions.
- Learn from the process, do not simply acknowledge it!

Leadership and follower commitment: integration with the EFQM excellence model

It is not my intention to describe the European Foundation for Quality Management Model (EFQM) model, but rather simply to refer readers to the model and add explanation as to links between key aspects of this book, a recognition strategy and the EFQM framework. Generally, a recognition strategy can form an element of the EFQM process. Equally, it can stand-alone.

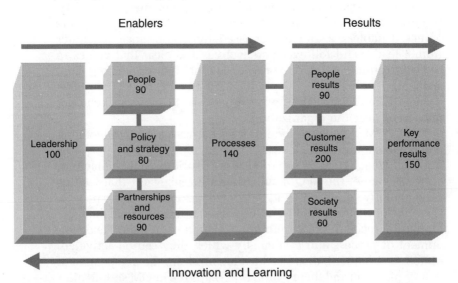

Figure 4.3 The EFQM Excellence Model
© EFQM. The EFQM Excellence Model is a registered trademark. Reproduced with permission of the European Foundation for Quality Management

The EFQM was formed in 1988 by the presidents of 14 European companies as they realized that global competition was threatening Europe's market position. Its mission was to promote and assist European managers to understand and apply total quality principles. The model (see Figure 4.3) has been widely used by organizations worldwide.

The intention of the EFQM model is to provide a non-prescriptive and diagnostic framework that organizations wishing to define and work toward organizational excellence can adopt as part of their decision making framework. It purports to be a model for incorporating all other management initiatives. Contained within the EFQM model are several aspects that might be directly influenced by issues discussed earlier in this book, for example, leadership, decision making, organizational values, leader behaviour and employee motivation. As a consequence, what follows is my interpretation of how analysis, ideas and recommendations contained within the previous text might be used to good effect within the EFQM framework by leaders of organizations. It may also assist in informing the continuous development of the EFQM model.

Within the EFQM model, leadership is defined as 'How leaders develop and facilitate the achievement of the mission and vision, develop values required for long-term success and implement these via appropriate actions and behaviours. Leaders are personally involved in ensuring that the organization's management system is developed and implemented.' Certainly, the process of leadership relies heavily on adopting appropriate values. Chapters 2 and 3 discussed the importance of values from a leader and follower perspective. It is clear that values in disequilibrium will prevent excellent performance. Consequently, leaders need to understand the values of all stakeholders regardless of the power advantage any one stakeholder may have over the organization.

The EFQM excellence model urges active leader involvement, and talks of appropriate leadership behaviour. Unfortunately, it is not clear what would be regarded as appropriate leader behaviour, although one of the EFQM sub-criteria does suggest that leaders need to motivate, support and recognize the organization's people. Clearly, the writer would wish for greater prominence of the need for natural recognition, promotion of shared values and the development of process and systems by which they can be activated. Moreover, Chapter 2 discussed leadership from the perspective of theory-of-action and theory-of-use. Perhaps the EFQM should offer 'enabler' guidance to organizations as to the importance of theory-of-action and theory-of-use, at least from the perspective of behaviour appropriate to potential employee followers. Awareness of what I call a conventional theory-of-action may also provide potential leaders with an opportunity for reflection.

The scoring system of the model suggests 90 points should be allocated to people results, 60 points to society results and 200 points to customer results. From the perspective of improving the leader–follower relationship, this weighting seems inappropriate. If it is accepted that the interface between employees and their organizational leaders is crucial to organizational performance, then elevating customer perceptions and performance measures above those of employees may only serve to reinforce the importance of markets, customers and profit. Simply, while monitoring of all key performance results are important, distinguishing customers as 'more' and people [potential followers] as 'less' important might be damaging to the employee manager relationship. It inadvertently puts barriers in the way of potential followers recognizing potential leaders. Perhaps equal weighting in terms of key result areas may be more appropriate.

The EFQM model goes out of its way to indicate the need to monitor both qualitative and quantitative measures. Questions similar to those mentioned earlier and incorporating people/follower needs might form an integral part of the decision making process and be contained within the leadership 'enablers' section of the model. The same questions could be used as part of the people 'results' element operationalized within project and business planning review processes, performance review/appraisal processes and management development plans.

Importantly, the model draws management attention to the importance of stakeholder perceptions as well as key performance measures. It has been argued that follower perception is vital to follower commitment. I would suggest that while reviewing results, leaders should analyse any disjunction between their own and follower perceptions. From a 'recognition strategy' perspective, understanding and operationalizing the needs of potential followers will be key to success.

Finally, the importance of learning 'runs through' the EFQM model. Continuous improvement and eventually excellence can only be gained through learning. The EFQM model offers the need to review results as the means to continuous learning. Results provide a benchmark by which leaders might strive to improve their organization. The issue of leader learning is discussed in Chapter 5.

Lessons for potential leaders

Most employees reluctantly accept that business risks inherently involve personal/job risk. What appears unacceptable to employees is their perception that they are not considered as an integral element of the business. Using the words 'human resources', employees often report being treated as an exploitable 'resource' but not necessarily in a 'human' manner. Indeed, the title human resource has unfortunate connotations that remind people that their status is similar to that of financial and physical resources. However, managers can show recognition for people in almost everything they say and do. Human resource management, development and planning processes that emerge from senior management provide information to potential followers as to the extent the organization values their contribution. Employee satisfaction with Human Resource Policy will continue to be a strong indicator of the link between employee/follower commitment and senior management/leadership action. The establishment of appropriate human resource policies would be the natural outcome of consideration of employee needs and cohesion between organizational and individual values.

Senior management can shape and change the jobs people do, they can enhance and enrich jobs, give people more responsibility, empower them and provide for greater achievement in the job task. All Herzberg's motivational factors are in some way under the jurisdiction of senior management. Importantly, senior management shaping and implementation interconnect with employee commitment. The general message is clear, management, regardless of level, should consider potential impact on follower commitment when designing jobs, restructuring, communicating and rewarding employees, during strategic and project decision making, when conducting appraisals, when planning and implementing training and development activities etc.

The significant problems we face today cannot be solved at the same level of thinking we were at when we created them. (Albert Einstein)

Leaders perhaps understand that the human need for recognition is continuous. In principle, the essential aspect that senior management may wish to integrate has been termed applying 'natural recognition'. It involves thinking and asking questions that relate to potential follower needs and values, making decisions conducive to that philosophy, and behaving and acting upon information in a way that is supportive of the philosophy. Techniques have been offered that help instigate a continuous 'recognition' process.

Employees are now better educated and litigious. The extent to which employees feel an obligation to any one employer is decreasing. Leaders must be far more sensitive to the needs and rights of their employees. Those who fail will have considerable difficulty getting anything accomplished. Consequently, to be a leader, a manager must persist tirelessly to develop relationships with potential followers and be committed to work with them to develop a meaningful sense of acknowlegement, confidence and trust. Leaders are not leaders unless followers recognize them as leaders. The need for behavioural change is acknowledged. Consequently, in the light of research, analysis, discussion and findings, Figure 4.4 summarizes behavioural recommendations that senior management could apply if they wish their employees to view them as leaders rather than managers. They form the essentials of a 'leadership for followership commitment recognition strategy'.

Figure 4.4 is all about applying consideration and recognition. When viewed holistically and implemented, the recommendations will develop the relationship between senior managers and employees towards that of 'leaders' and 'followers'. The relationship would be characterized by mutual trust, continuous covert and overt communication, and respect for ideas and needs.

Comment and articles in respected journals such as the Chartered Institute of Personnel and Development's *People Management* constantly remind organizations of the importance of

---

- Review managerial theory-of-action
- Consider psychological contracts as well as contracts of employment
- Monitor employee/follower behavioural signals
- Develop an understanding of employee environmental pressures, motivation and commitment
- Consider employee needs and develop a 'shared value' approach
- Rationally consider people process as well as task needs
- Integrate recognition of potential followers as part of business strategy, strategic decision, process and systems
- Work with and develop formal and informal rewards, but concentrate on applying natural recognition
- Enthuse by means of consideration
- Support learning and development
- Work to ensure two-way continuous commitment

Figure 4.4 Recommendations for leaders who wish to attract willing followers

people. However, change is slow and progress often erratic. Employees are expected to invest their physical and mental capital, their skills, time, knowledge and dedication to the firm. However, just as managers see their business as a process of risk and return, so do potential followers. From their perspective, a good return for their risk is in the hands of potential leaders. Conventional financial return will always prove inadequate in situations where higher order needs require satisfaction. Psychological returns will have greater influence in the foreseen future.

The task of management is to ensure the right people are in the right job with the right competencies at the right time. The role of the leader also includes responsibility for providing a context within which employees can have and maintain the right attitude. This chapter has suggested that potential leaders can make vast improvements if their actions encompass, internalize and operationalize consideration for employee needs through a strategy and process of recognition. The linkages are complex. None the less, genuine concern for followers not manipulation should be successful.

Case study 5: Student case study

Treating the whole of Chapter 4 as a working case study, imagine you are a consultant advising an organization as to the merits of employing the ideas and techniques contained in the chapter.

Questions

1 You have discovered that senior managers in an organization known to you convey and/or display scientific management and economic-rational thinking. How might you convince them that in order to benefit from increased commitment they should work with your ideas?
2 Provide explanation as to the theoretical linkage between potential follower needs, motivation, recognition, work satisfaction and performance.
3 Briefly explain the importance of integrating a recognition strategy as part of known management processes.
4 Why are concepts such as knowledge management/exploitation, and individual and organizational learning so important to continued competitive advantage?
5 How would you go about evaluating the potential change in organizational commitment of followers over a 12-month period?

For discussion of the case see Appendix D.

References

Argyris, C. (1964) *Integrating the Individual and the Organization*, New York: John Wiley.

Argyris, C. and Schön, D. (1974) *Theory and Practice: Increasing Professional Effectiveness*, San Francisco: Jossey-Bass.

Cirilli, N. (1998) Recognition: Managers Don't Give It . . . Because They Just Don't Get It, *Industrial Management*, 40 (4), p. 28.

Cosier, R.A. and Dalton, D.R. (1983). Equity Theory and Time: A Reformulation, *Academy of Management Review*, 8, pp. 311–19.

Dearing Report (1988) *The Making of Accounting Standards*, London: HMSO.

Drucker, P.F. (1985). *Innovation and Entrepreneurship*, London: Pan.

Egan, G. (1994) Cultivate your Culture, *Management Today* (April), pp. 29–42.

European Foundation for Quality Management (EFQM) (1993). *Total Quality Management: The European Model for Self-Assessment. Guidelines for Identifying and Addressing Total Quality Issues,* Eindhoven: EFQM.

Glautier, M.W.E. and Underdown, B. (1991) *Accounting Theory and Practice*, 4th edn, London: Pitman.

Greene, C.N. (1975) The Reciprocal Nature of Influence between Leader and Subordinate, *Journal of Applied Psychology*, 60, pp. 187–93.

Institute of Directors, University of Salford (1993–2002), Discussions with Directors attending the Diploma in Directorship, unpublished work.

James, W. (1892) *Psychology: the Briefer Course,* New York: Harper Torch Books.

Kanter, R.M. (1989) *When Giants Learn to Dance*, New York: Simon and Schuster.

Kanter, R.M., Stein, B.A. and Jick, T.D. (1992) *The Challenge of Organizational Change*, New York: Free Press.

Kaplan, R. and Norton, D. (1993) Putting the Balanced Scorecard to Work, *Harvard Business Review*, September–October, pp. 134–47.

Kaplan, R. and Norton, D. (1996a) The Balanced Scorecard: Translating Strategy into Action, Boston, MA: *Harvard Business School Press*.

Kaplan, R. and Norton, D. (1996b) Using the Balanced Scorecard as a Strategic Management System, *Harvard Business Review*, January–February.

Kochan, T.A and Dyer, L. (1993) HRM: An American View, in J. Storey, *Human Resource Management: A Critical Text*, London: Routledge.

Mannheim, K. (1940) *Man and Society in an Age of Reconstruction*, New York: Harcourt, p. 249.

Mead, G.H. (1934) *Mind, Self, and Society*, Chicago: University of Chicago Press, p. 135.

Nils-Goran, O., Roy, J. and Wetter, M. (1999) *Performance Drivers – A Practical Guide to Using the Balanced Scorecard*, New York: John Wiley.

Pavlov, I.P. (1927) *Conditional Reflexes*, London: Oxford University Press.

Pickard, J. (1998) Natural Lore: An Interview with Arie de Geus, *People Management*, 4 (20), pp. 41–3.

Revans, R. (1992) *Action Learning*, Quote from Lecture to the Edge Hill College of Further Education, Ormskirk, Liverpool.

Rogers, C.R. (1951) *Client-Centred Therapy*, New York: Houghton.

Rogers, C.R. (1959) A Theory of Therapy, Personality and Interpersonal Relationships as Developed in the Client-Centred Framework, in S. Koch. (ed.), *Psychology: A Study of a Science*, Vol. 3, pp. 184–256.

Schwartz, B. and Lacey, H. (1982) *Behaviourism, Science and Human Nature*, New York: Norton.

Strebler, M. (1997) Soft Skills and Hard Questions. Report on the DfEE commissioned study 'Changing Roles for Senior Managers', *People Management*, 3 (11), pp. 20–4.

Thorndyke, E.L. (1911) *Animal Intelligence*, New York: Macmillan.

Tolstoy, L. (1899/1966) *Resurrection*, Harmondsworth: Penguin

Watson, J.B. (1930) *Behaviourist*, New York: Norton.

Zimbardo, P.G. (1985) *Psychology and Life*, New York: Harper-Collins, pp. 260–84.

5

Leadership, learning and follower commitment

Introduction

The intention of this short concluding chapter is not to regurgitate theory and critique contained elsewhere in this book. While holding licence to comment on the usefulness of theory, this chapter attempts to provide terms of reference for readers so that they may debate and then make up their own minds as to the relevance of theory. The chapter also offers consolidation of the need for follower recognition by leaders, and suggests that successful progress involves organizational learning.

Reviewing theory

A theory is a supposition or system of ideas that purports to explain something. This book records a wealth of theoretical material. Readers may have been willing to accept some theories, found some interesting but not necessarily practical, and perhaps rejected others 'out of hand'. For readers who may wish to reflect a little as to the validity of theory, Thomas and Tymon (1982) provide useful guidelines.

First, theory should contain scientific rigour. It should be possible for a theory to be generalized. Any researcher should be able to repeat the original research, perhaps in different organizational settings, and reach the same theoretical conclusion.

Unfortunately, most of the areas discussed, for example motivation, commitment, leader values and follower perceptions, are a product of people's minds. Silverman and Shulman (1970) suggest that doing experimental work with humans is like doing chemistry with dirty test tubes. In experiments with humans, the contaminants are the needs, motives, values and expectations of the people participating in the research wherever it is conducted. Such contaminants are the very focus of this book.

Second, we might expect that any theory should have the capability to be applied and implemented by manipulation of the independent variable contained in the theory. For instance, when carrying out experiments, psychologists have to agree about what they are doing when they manipulate an independent variable, and predict the effect on the dependent variable. They have to agree terms, definitions and measurements. Objectivity in this sense can therefore be defined as the consensus between researchers. Unfortunately, researchers most frequently disagree rather than agree terms, definitions and/or measurement. As evidenced within the text of Chapters 2 and 3, this is especially so in the social sciences, and would include well-known theory such as Herzberg's two factor model and Maslow's hierarchy of needs.

Experimental research designs generally try to control their subject matter by identifying and then manipulating the causes of what they observe; however, human behaviour involves complex connections and interconnections of causal relationships. For example, employee commitment is a part of human behaviour, and behaviour is multi-faceted and multi-causal. In multi-causal models, the several causal factors may be independent or be interrelated. When trying to disentangle problems of causality, many associations or correlations can be found, but of themselves, these correlations are not proof of causality.

It seems appropriate to differentiate between associations or 'mere correlates' and actual causes. The reason associations are not given the status of 'causes' is because each association's place in a complex network of causality may not be known. However, striving for evidence of causality is not always appropriate. First, research time is a finite resource. Second, sufficient proof is unlikely to be gained. Third, there are some areas of research that should not wait until proof emerges; practical interim solutions seem feasible given that strong associations are supported. The main reason for avoiding a search for causality is the view that association patterns can give a strong hint about causality, and perhaps suggest an effective intervention method though the cause remains unknown in absolute terms. While I applaud scholarly disagreement because it helps refine theory, too much academic challenge for subjects that may never be able to provide sufficient evidence (let alone proof) does not necessarily assist managers who are looking for reasoned guidelines to help them manage today. This leads to Thomas and Tymon's third aspect.

Theories should focus on problems that managers (and potential leaders and followers) have to deal with, even if they are not obvious or are hard to measure. Unfortunately, the focus of many researchers has been to look at problems that hold interest for other scholars. Despite exceptions, theory can tend to remain theoretical, leaving managers and students excited but a little bemused as to how to operationalize within the workplace. Nevertheless, this book has highlighted particular works that have received, and continue to receive a good following from academics, students and managers. The works of McGregor, Kotter, Herzberg and Mowday *et al.* are prime examples. These approaches have a logic that makes them easy to understand. Theory such as Great Man, trait, style, goal-theory etc. provide insight and structure by which reflection and further conceptualization can take place. I have found theory and conceptual offerings such as scientific-management principles, rational-economics and Argyris's work, when clustered together with the concept of follower motivation and commitment, particularly influential. Process theory such as that offered by Vroom might appear comparatively complex, and consequently may prove difficult to translate into organizational practice, but expectancy and equity theory offer common sense face validity, especially for those who have worked in industry.

A clear weakness of most current leadership theory is its over-emphasis on the qualities and characteristics of the leader, and not the needs of followers. As mentioned at the start of this book, leaders cannot be leaders without followers. Therefore, students and managers must look to what followers need in order to willingly follow.

Theory should offer the manager, leader or potential follower an insight into experiences that are not readily available today. For example, Chapter 2 described conventional management practice that might have become so ingrained in organizational life that managers fail to realize that there may be a better way of encouraging follower commitment. Simply, the experiences of adopting a different theory-of-action may never enter the working life of most managers – or employees.

Finally, theory should be available to managers to deal with problems as they arise. Importantly, theory should not arrive too late to add value. This is a common concern of Directors (Institute of Directors, 1993–2002). Often they use the word academic in a disparaging way – 'It's only academic.' The semantics of its use suggest that theory is often unusable, too complicated, or it arrives too late to be of use. The need to enthuse and exploit follower knowledge, skill and application is an issue for today – and for tomorrow. Equally, the need for leadership that understands people behaviour, needs and emotions is now seen as essential to organizational success.

Perhaps the clear importance of 'natural recognition' might be seen in theoretical terms – a leadership for follower commitment 'Theory of Recognition'. Such a claim may be justified if readers accept that regardless of the area of investigation, i.e. leadership theory, human resource management, training and development, employee motivation, commitment, communication, leader skills etc., the theme of 'recognition' has continuously assisted explanation as to linkages between potential leaders and followers. Importantly, recognition of someone is vital to the development of a trusting relationship. Without trust, a relationship of mutual commitment cannot exist. Regardless of whether readers might wish to acknowledge theoretical credentials, the author suggests that recognition has been established as a means by which followership can be encouraged.

Leadership and learning

The learning organization is an inspirational concept that has been invented but not innovated (Senge, 1990, 1991). It constitutes a view of what might be possible (Pedler, 1991). Gonsalves (1997) comments that 'the learning organization is an ideal, a vision'. Easterby-Smith (1996) comments that it is an abstract conception, and that organizations or parts of organizations can achieve in varying degrees. In contrast, Williams (1997) states that the theory is flawed and that a deeper appreciation is needed.

It is unclear whether a learning organization is one that is skilled at creating, acquiring and transferring knowledge, or is one that uses the process of learning at the individual, group and system level (Easterby-Smith, 1996). Overell (1996) offers that 'all organizations are learning organizations, but it depends on what they learn'. Bernard Sullivan as general manager of Rover in 1996 stated that 'for Rover the learning organization was really the unlearning organization'. He states that 'the ultimate challenge is to do things differently . . . systems by themselves will not enable change, but marginal changes in the attitudes of people sometimes bring leaps forward'.

It is generally accepted that a feature of a learning organization is that it is structured in such a way that adopted systems can promote continuous learning. Harrison (1992) posits that continuous learning is reliant on three factors. First, everyday experience should be carefully examined, because everyday experience affects learning. Second, the organization should be viewed and managed as a continuous learning system. Third, there must be a conscious decision to develop an organizational environment that will promote and sustain desired kinds of organizational learning. The influence of underlying principles contained within the concept of organizational learning, such as those offered by Harrison, is clearly evident in Chapter 4.

Williams' (1997) observation that the theory of the learning organization is flawed may be correct. However, the writer's experience strongly suggests that the theory is only flawed if organizational values are left unchallenged. Kolb *et al.* (1974) says that learning should be an explicit organizational objective, 'pursued as consciously and deliberately as profit or productivity'. He stresses that the organization must 'promote a climate which sees the value of such an approach . . . developed in the organization' – clearly a role for the senior manager leader.

Williams (1997) states that traditional Marxist tendencies still exist. The basic oppressive relationship between management and employee remains. Whether the general workforce shares the Williams view is unclear. Nevertheless, it is reasonable to accept that many employees may perceive the relationship with senior management as fundamentally not supportive. Such learning may be held deep in what Gonsalves (1997) terms the 'organizational memory'.

The process of learning is obviously in the hands of senior management. Pedler *et al.* (1986) hold that the leader has an important role to play in making learning part of organizational life, to the point that learning itself becomes ingrained and integrated within the organizational culture. Kets de Vries (1996) asserts that senior management leadership needs to change their attitudes and become organizational detectives. He writes, 'I want them to learn how to look beyond the obvious to find deeper meaning of certain actions'. However, organizational maps, images and managerial action will have to be challenged before a vital attitudinal change can take place.

Leaders recognize the importance of symbols as a means of encouraging followers. Symbols are representations of what is going on in the real world surrounding us and language provides the most potent symbols. The symbols management use are firmly based upon the decisions they make. Importantly, leadership decisions form a major part of employee perception of organization values in relation to his/her 'self'. The whole process works towards a leader–follower relationship by which learning can be stimulated or subdued at all levels. Potential benefits to the organization and its leadership are clear. Knowledge and learning could permeate the organization's culture at all levels, employees will be more willing to learn and offer their knowledge to the organization and followers are more likely to view managers as leaders – and vice versa.

An important aspect of the learning organization is that the company must consciously transform itself (Pedler *et al.*, 1995). Thus, the concepts of transformational leadership and the learning organization complement each other. By using the word 'consciously', Pedler *et al.* intend that learning organizations transform themselves with 'a sense of awareness and intentionality, rather than reacting to change by being buffeted by an ever-increasing turbulent external environment'. A conventional theory-of-action may prevent self-awareness. Consequently, intention may not exist. None the less, the notion that organizational leaders can respond or pre-empt environmental changes by being conscious or self-aware is derived from the idea of viewing the organization as a living organism. Rather than a mechanical entity formed to generate a good financial return, as an organism, the organization can think and learn. The product is still an efficient and effective organization, but the means to the ends is refreshingly different.

The difference between transactional and transforming leadership (Tichy and Devanna, 1986; Bass, 1990; Armstrong, 1996) was discussed in Chapter 2. Atkinson (1988) states that progression to the level of senior management is usually determined by transactional type managers. Past performance as a middle or lower level manager has been more closely related to doing things right rather than doing the right things. It should not be surprising therefore that performance measures, sticking to budget and applying the organization's personnel procedures and practices have become a way of life. However, while urging managers to aspire to be leaders, the charismatic figure of Sir John Harvey Jones comments that 'if all that I had achieved in life was meeting budget then I have achieved nothing'.

Managing by way of quantitative targets focused upon profitability, productivity or budgets can be viewed as having rational but simplistic characteristics, at least as for the leadership of people. Leadership requires a different form of thinking and learning. Earlier chapters argued that for managers to be perceived as leaders they need to become self-aware as to the impact of their actions on others. This development process may require some managers to remove personal 'blind spots' that prevent learning.

Argyris (1976) introduces two kinds of learning to explain the above potentially destructive phenomenon, single and double-loop learning. In single-loop learning, the individual tries out various strategies for achieving a goal. Those strategies that succeed are stored in a repertoire of actions – others are discarded. Managerial strategies that gain short-term action can be witnessed more easily as being effective. Therefore, managers perceive such strategies as having a greater impact. By implication, strategies that in the longer term might prove most beneficial will become less frequently adopted. For example, discipline and negative feedback may have an immediate effect, while attitude change strategies may not be perceived or 'witnessed' at all. Consequently, it is likely that long-term people-related strategies are relegated to a level of 'rhetoric' but disregarded in use. How many readers recall company conferences and seminars whereby the importance of people featured as 'the key to unlock competitive advantage'? Moreover, how many readers when returning to the workplace have faced a totally different context? That sinking feeling is usually made worse by someone, perhaps their immediate line manager, commenting that he or she 'has heard it all before' and 'don't hold your breath waiting for change'. From experience, strategic decision normally excludes behavioural issues – so how can things change?

Learning organizations are those that incorporate double loop learning. Keuning (1998) offers that a 'learning organization' is one that operates according to the double-loop learning model. Double-loop learning is made possible by encouraging individuals, especially those who have a greater ability to change the direction of the organization, to challenge deeply rooted but perhaps inappropriate organizational norms and routines.

There are rewards related to the adoption of double-loop learning. Kim (1993) comments that 'learning with double-loop creates important opportunities for improvements in that it provides a framework to open up a totally new direction for solutions'. Nevertheless, until values, beliefs and relationships are conducive for the implementation of learning organization techniques, it is unlikely that the techniques will result in improved performance.

Most senior management 'espouse' theories that could be viewed as liberal and participative, and which may include a substantive measure of person-orientation. Therefore, the issue of how to encourage willing followership does not seem attributable to high level managerial ignorance of such factors. The brainstorm listing by directors in Chapter 2 (see page 32) illustrating the characteristics of a good leader seems to verify this finding. However, there may be a mismatch between intentions and practice. To explore this phenomenon in relation to essential aspects of decision-making criteria, I conducted a short piece of research with directors. During a workshop, aspects of human resource strategy were discussed. Particular attention was given to the importance of affective and normative commitment, the need to treat people as an asset and the utilization of the resultant 'commitment' to gain competitive advantage. There was general verbalized agreement of the major importance of this approach. However, when directors were asked to illustrate how boardroom strategic decision making integrates human resource behavioural and psychological issues, all struggled to provide sufficient supportive evidence. One could conclude therefore that espoused reasoning does not necessarily relate to director action.

The author suggests that while senior management may understand the effect of employee attitudes upon job performance, they are less knowledgeable about what within the organization maintains undesirable employee behaviour. Continuous learning that gives senior management behavioural data that they can analyse, reflect upon and utilize is therefore an essential requirement. Without it, learning related to emotional or psychological maturity is limited. In total contrast, if managers are to be perceived as leaders by followers they need to understand, reflect, learn and strategically, tactically and operationally integrate the competency of emotional intelligence. The explanation, description, techniques and processes offered in Chapter 4 are set to improve information by which learning by action can develop.

Pointing the way forward

Chapter 1 introduced the concept of knowledge management. The inference contained within the text suggested that to be successful within competitive markets, business must fully utilize employee knowledge. The term 'learning capital' is also used to describe an essential resource, if not the only organizational resource, that can create competitive advantage and which is identifiably human. Organizations are becoming more reliant on the knowledge, skills and application or willingness of their human resource and have a need to learn at the individual and team level as well as the organizational level. It is here that the organization must develop the capacity to compete more effectively. As opposed to managing for control and stability, leaders may need to accept a perpetual state of learning. Rogers (1978) suggests that learning will take place if there is 'acceptance and trust of the learner and educator'. The learner should perceive empathy that illustrates a genuine concern for the learner. In terms of the potential leader and follower relationship, the role of learner and educator should be dynamic.

Although Taylorist principles are unlikely to become extinct, now more than ever there are chances to encourage enriched relationships between employee and employer. In order for this to take place, it has been argued that followers and leaders need opportunities to satisfy their motivational needs in order to enhance their self-esteem and improve their psychological well-being. In many ways, the importance of esteem has become a baseline requirement. Unfortunately, many organizations appear to operate at high levels of psychological naivety. Consequently, there needs to be widespread acceptance and a working appreciation of its central importance. Some managers treat subordinates in ways that depreciate their creativity, intelligence and abilities. This is exactly what organizations and leaders must not do. Senior management is required to question what doing the right thing means, and continually learn from the experience. It is therefore both a quality and much needed skill of a leader.

Cirilli entitles his 1998 article 'Recognition: Managers Don't Give It . . . Because They Just Don't Get It'. The title has a clever double meaning. Recognition as defined in this book is a function of senior management's acknowledgement of the importance of the workforce. It is the vehicle by which senior management might communicate shared values to the workforce. In essence, it is also an expression of the role taken by senior management as part of the organization's psychological contract with the employee. Crucially, it is an expression of senior management commitment to the workforce that can affect employee commitment to the company. Like the substance of most relationships,

Figure 5.1 Theory of action: leader review

recognition must be a reciprocal process. However, recognition is something that can only be instigated by management.

The findings of all chapters assert that the process of leadership for follower commitment should begin with a review of the current theory-of-action adopted by senior management. To this end, Figure 5.1 provides key questions for the senior management team.

The framework in Chapter 4 (illustrated in appendix A) is founded on the need for a recognition strategy to be simple to operate, robust, adaptive, easy to control, generally comprehensive and easy to communicate. Moreover, the mechanics and techniques offered are based on known managerial techniques and practice. Thus, the chance of rejection by senior management is minimized. In action learning terms, it represents the writer's call on programmed learning, that which is known, to assist the development of a system capable of encouraging questions to explore what is comparatively unknown. It should be stated that successful implementation is dependent in no small measure upon senior management acceptance that the need for recognition of employees is a direct responsibility of senior management.

Conclusion

What senior managers do, prioritize and act upon strongly influences employee commitment. It is essential to the establishment of improved leader–follower relationships. However, senior management often interprets working on strategic necessities as involving the need to understand and predict customer needs and market changes. In comparative terms, they often ignore the environmental analysis of the organization's internal context. People are the internal context; more indirectly, they also strongly influence the external context. Most, if not all, senior management would immediately agree with this common-sense view. Internalizing this view is clearly more difficult.

The need of followers for what has been labelled 'natural recognition' emerges as an essential motivational factor that encourages followership. This is not an unexpected conclusion. Recognition is the one factor that appears to bind leadership action to potential follower perception of how well the organization reciprocates their commitment.

The text suggests that if employee needs are incongruent with priorities displayed by senior management, then employee commitment cannot be optimized. Nevertheless, there seems 'room enough' for any organization, in whatever sector, market or industry, to appreciate both the needs of the organization and employee needs – it might even be imperative. As organizations come to rely more on employee knowledge, then employee commitment will steadily become more of a priority. Simply, if employees do not commit knowledge and other competencies to the organization, then gaining competitive advantage may be elusive. Thus, wealth generation cannot be maximized. Ignoring this situation is not rational.

Followers need leaders. It is a natural occurrence for groups of individuals to 'seek out' a leader. More importantly, from an organizational perspective, leaders need followers. However, only leaders that continuously satisfy the needs of followers will remain leaders – although they may remain managers. Interestingly, such a philosophy echoes the words of Nelson Mandela (2002): he simply states: 'A true leader puts the interests of others above their own.' Unfortunately, this is a tall order in competitive business environments, but, hopefully, not insurmountable.

Finally, evidence to support the view that senior managers are willing to adopt a true balanced approach is scarce. Nevertheless, the importance of gaining follower commitment in organizations is identified by reference to affective commitment. Most senior managers acknowledge the essential dimensions of this form of commitment. However, it is strongly suggested that leadership cannot survive without an appreciation that commitment is a reciprocal process. Simply, leaders should not expect willing and committed followership for the betterment of the organization if committed and willing leadership for the betterment of employee needs does not occur. Moreover, the relationship must be continuous not spasmodic. While cultural change and attitudinal development programmes aimed at improving employee attitudes and commitment are useful, they are unlikely to have a lasting effect if they are not part of a continuous process of recognition.

In many ways, findings suggest that followers are more likely to follow leaders if leaders can adopt and put into action the philosophy, explanation and managerial practice outlined in this book. However, change will not occur overnight and evidence as to success may be elusive – at least in the short term.

References

Armstrong, M. (1996) *Personnel Management Practice*, 6th edn, London: Kogan Page.
Argyris, C. (1976) *Increasing Leadership Effectiveness*, New York: John Wiley and Sons.
Argyris, C. and Schön, D. (1974) *Theory and Practice: Increasing Professional Effectiveness*, San Francisco: Jossey–Bass.

Atkinson,J. (1988) Recent Changes in the Internal Labour Market Structure of the UK, in W. Buitelaar (ed.), *Technology and Work: Labour Studies in England, Germany, and the Netherlands,* Aldershot: Avebury, pp. 133–49.

Bass, B.M. (1990) *Handbook of Leadership,* New York: Free Press. See also Bass, B.M (1990) Bass and Stogdill's *Handbook of Leadership Theory, Research, and Managerial Implications,* 3rd edn, New York: Free Press.

Cirilli, N. (1998) Recognition: Managers Don't Give It . . . Because They Just Don't Get It. *Industrial Management,* 40 (4), p. 28.

Easterby-Smith, M. (1996) in Overell, S., Learning to Unlearn for a Flexible Future, *People Management,* 2 (9), p. 14.

Gonsalves, E. (1997) The Learning Organization, *Open Business Journal,* The Open University, Issue 6, p. 6.

Harrison, R. (1992) *Employee Development,* IPD Management (Series 2), p. 156.

Institute of Directors, University of Salford (1993–2002) Discussions with Directors attending the Diploma in Directorship, unpublished work.

Kets de Vries, M. (1996) The Leader as Analysis, *Harvard Business Review,* January–February, p. 158.

Keuning, D. (1998) *Management: A Contemporary Approach,* London: Pitman Publishing, pp. 174–85.

Kim, D.H. (1993) The Link Between Individual and Organizational Learning, *Sloan Management Review,* Autumn.

Kolb, D.A., Rubin, I.M, and McKintyre, J.M. (1974) *Organizational Psychology: An Experiential Approach,* Englewood Cliffs, NJ: Prentice–Hall.

Mandela, N. (2002) Interview with Oprah Winfrey, *Channel 5 Telelvision* (UK), 17 July.

Overell, S. (1996) Learning to Unlearn for a Flexible Future, *People Management,* 2 (9), p. 14.

Pedler, M.J. (1991) *Action Learning in Practice,* Aldershot: Gower.

Pedler, M.J., Burgoyne, J.G. and Boydell, T. (1986) *A Manager's Guide to Self Development,* New York: McGraw–Hill, p. 59.

Pedler, M.J., Burgoyne, J.G. and Boydell, T. (1995) *The Learning Company: A Strategy for Substantial Development,* New York: McGraw–Hill, p. 3.

Rogers, C.R. (1978) *Carl Rogers on Personal Power,* London: Constable.

Senge, P.M. (1990) The Learning Organization Made Plain, *Training and Development Journal (ITD),* 19 (54), p. 14.

Senge, P.M. (1991) *The Fifth Discipline: The Art and Practice of the Learning Organization,* New York: Doubleday.

Silverman, I. and Shulman, A.D. (1970) A Conceptual Model of

Artifact in Attitude Change Studies, *Sociometry*, No. 33, pp. 97–107.

Sullivan, B. (1996) in Overell, S., Learning to Unlearn for a Flexible Future, *People Management*, 2 (9), p. 14.

Thomas, K.W. and Tymon, W.G. (1982) Necessary Properties of Relevant Research: Lessons from Recent Criticisms of the Organizational Sciences, *Academy of Management Review*, No. 7, pp. 345–52.

Tichy, N. and Devanna, M.A. (1986) *Transformational Leadership*, New York: Wiley.

Williams, I. (1997) The Learning Organization – a Flawed Theory, *Open Business Journal*, Issue 7 (Spring/Summer), The Open University, p. 4.

Leadership for follower commitment 'recognition strategy'

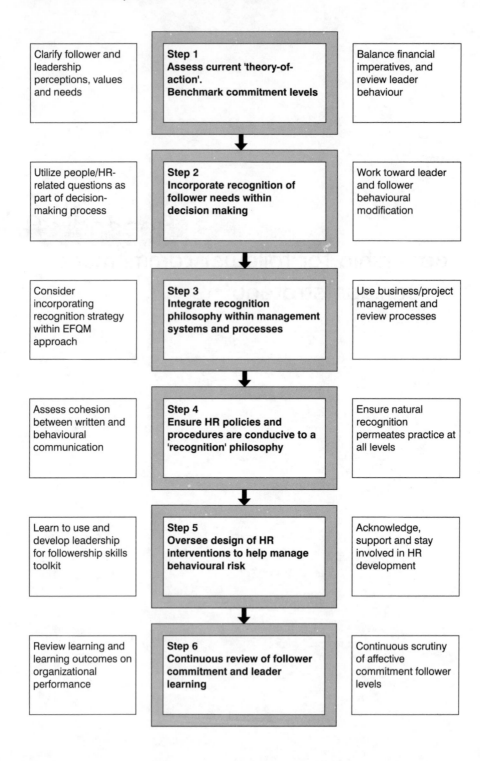

Clarify follower and leadership perceptions, values and needs	**Step 1** **Assess current 'theory-of-action'.** **Benchmark commitment levels**	Balance financial imperatives, and review leader behaviour
Utilize people/HR-related questions as part of decision-making process	**Step 2** **Incorporate recognition of follower needs within decision making**	Work toward leader and follower behavioural modification
Consider incorporating recognition strategy within EFQM approach	**Step 3** **Integrate recognition philosophy within management systems and processes**	Use business/project management and review processes
Assess cohesion between written and behavioural communication	**Step 4** **Ensure HR policies and procedures are conducive to a 'recognition' philosophy**	Ensure natural recognition permeates practice at all levels
Learn to use and develop leadership for followership skills toolkit	**Step 5** **Oversee design of HR interventions to help manage behavioural risk**	Acknowledge, support and stay involved in HR development
Review learning and learning outcomes on organizational performance	**Step 6** **Continuous review of follower commitment and leader learning**	Continuous scrutiny of affective commitment follower levels

The Organizational Commitment Questionnaire

1 I am willing to put in a great deal of effort beyond that normally expected in order to help this organization be successful.
2 I talk up this organization to my friends as a great organization to work for.
3 I feel very little loyalty to this organization. (R)
4 I would accept almost any type of job assignment in order to keep working for this organization.
5 I find that my values and the organization's values are very similar.
6 I am proud to tell others that I am part of this organization.
7 I could just as well be working for a different organization as long as the type of work was similar. (R)
8 This organization really inspires the very best in me in the way of job performance.
9 It would take very little change in my present circumstances to cause me to leave this organization. (R)
10 I am extremely glad that I chose this organization to work for over others I was considering at the time I joined.
11 There's not too much to be gained by sticking with the organization indefinitely. (R)
12 Often, I find it difficult to agree with this organization's policies on important matters relating to its employees. (R)
13 I really care about the fate of this organization.

14 For me this is the best of all possible organizations for which to work.
15 Deciding to work for this organization was a definite mistake on my part. (R)

Responses to each item are measured on a 7 point scale, with point anchors labelled: (1) strongly disagree; (2) moderately disagree; (3) slightly disagree; (4) neither disagree nor agree; (5) slightly agree; (6) moderately agree; (7) strongly agree. (R) denotes a negatively phrased and reverse scored item.

Source: Mowday, R.T., Steers, R.M. and Porter, L.W. (1979) A Measure of Organizational Commitment. *Journal of Vocational Behaviour*, 14, p. 228.

NB: This instrument can only be freely used for research purposes.

Follower satisfaction survey

1 I have confidence in senior management.
2 My needs and those of the organization are similar.
3 Senior management shows they are considerate of the needs of the workforce.
4 I am satisfied with the contact I have with my senior management.
5 I am content with company policies that are related to employees.
6 I feel my immediate supervisor/manager is competent in making work decisions.
7 I feel senior management are competent in making work decisions.
8 Senior management consider employees when making major decisions.
9 Senior management are only interested in getting the job done.
10 This organization is only concerned with making profit.
11 My job makes good use of my abilities.
12 I receive appropriate training and development.
13 My company encourages educational fulfilment.
14 My job is important to me.
15 My job provides steady employment.
16 A major satisfaction in my life comes from my job/role in this organization.

17 I find job-related tasks boring.
18 In my job, I get to do different tasks from time to time.
19 I feel empowered.
20 I have far too much responsibility.
21 I receive appropriate feedback about my job performance.
22 I find it difficult to make career progressions.
23 I am satisfied with my chances for advancement.
24 I have other activities more important than my job.
25 I am satisfied with my working conditions.
26 I work in a safe working environment.
27 I get praise for doing a good job.
28 Non-verbal praise (for example a smile of approval) is frequently seen.
29 Achievement by individuals is formally acknowledged.
30 In general, I feel my efforts are recognized.
31 I am satisfied as to how my colleagues get along with each other.

The above questions can be used to form part of a general satisfaction survey. A 7 point scale is recommended.

Case study discussion

Case study 1: Sven-Goran Eriksson

The case would not be regarded as providing confident and supportive evidence of great man theory. It may provide some evidence that certain traits and perhaps people skills are appropriate. However, the clear indication that these elements may be situation-specific provides a significant counter-argument.

It is clear that Sven-Goran Eriksson's style of leadership works toward the establishment of trust by means of having empathy with players. Comments such as 'I told the players first' strongly indicate a wish to sustain a close relationship. Sven's early success as England coach, however, is also related to his ability to pick a suitable and complementary coaching staff as well a team captain able to typify the need for commitment on the field – David Beckham. Sven is atypical when compared to previous charismatic leaders. Perhaps the most appropriate measure of Sven's leadership style is that it is task orientated by means of behaviour that is totally based on the personal but distanced approach.

The England football team performance is governed by the fans' need for the team to win. This is similar to a business and commercial need to make profit in order to keep shareholders content. The need for England to perform will also be the deciding factor as to Sven's continued success or demise. The media is very changeable and will alter their view within a small timeframe. This is perhaps typified by references to 'Sven' and sometimes 'Eriksson' depending on whether England have gained the desired result. Many observers feel that Sven's eventual demise must occur and that he will become another victim of circumstance. None the less, the Sven case clearly illustrates the importance of building relationships, to have empathy with players/employees, and to recognize and be considerate of emotional needs.

Case study 2: Conventional theory-of-action?

Results support the notion that senior managers are generally high achievers. Additionally, achievement for senior management is strongly associated with the task of their position. Task for these managers was strongly focused on the need to increase and/or sustain profit. Moreover, senior management tended to give far more consideration to task-related aspects as compared with employee-related aspects. This finding supports the view that rational-economic goals are likely to predominate within the boardroom. Such indications provide at least partial evidence that a conventional theory-of-action has been adopted as part of the overall organizational management approach.

If Sven-Goran Eriksson took over as Chief Executive Officer, we might expect people-related issues to be more prominent in the boardroom. Perhaps greater involvement of staff within decision-making forums might also arise. From experience, personality traits of managers can change over time – perhaps very gradually. The reason for this is that personality profiling is based on self-assessed knowledge of the behaviour the person would adopt in certain situations. If the context changes, and it might if a different style of the Chief Executive was adopted and asserted, the self-assessed weighting of traits such a caring, consideration, demo-cratic, empathy etc. might become more prominent in the boardroom.

Case study 3: Anita Roddick

If leadership requires passion, commitment, determination, per-sistence and caring, then perhaps Anita Roddick should be regarded as a leader. The important issue, however, is whether she was able to enthuse followers. Again, if followers are motivated, share the leader's vision and are satisfied that their needs are being catered for, then employees (and others) are likely to be following Anita's vision. Given the ecological and social rights issues that surround Body Shop products, it is likely that at least some suppliers and franchisers share the vision. However, value-based leadership whereby other stakeholders share your own values may not be appropriate in all organizational settings. Clearly, social ethics and human and animal rights issues will not be so specific to many other firms. Moreover, in terms of potential employee followers, readers might refer to this extract from Chapter 2 (see p. 42), which reads:

> *Wheeler and Sillanpaa conducted a detailed survey of 2200 Body Shop employees as part of a wider social audit. The survey found that while most employees endorsed the group's values, they had reservations about the everyday realities of working for the company. Fewer than half the employees agreed that the company's commitment to being a caring company was apparent to them on a day-to-day basis (also see Arkin, 1997).*

A vast amount of information about the company is readily available in the public domain. For some, The Body Shop organization is a 'well-led' visionary concept. To others, the enterprise has successfully exploited an idealistic theme. All depends on the observer's perception. None the less, Anita Roddick's philosophy of management might be repeated in other organizations to good effect. Of course, this book would argue that to gain follower commitment, philosophy must be substantiated in practice.

Case study 4: Follower commitment?

The results of the quantitative surveys suggest that the most important reason for employee dissatisfaction is related to their perception of how well the company values them, and the pay they receive for the job they do. In comparison, most of the other items received a positive response. Perhaps the conclusions provided in Chapters 2 and 3 might provide substance for advice.

In reality, the company did respond to the feedback employees had provided. Attempting to counter survey findings, the organization espoused the need for management to be more visible and 'walk the job'. Senior management requested all management levels to talk to people and force themselves to 'listen to their needs'. They were also requested to meet regularly and 'keep information flowing up and down'. Senior management espoused the view that 'management of people should involve the promotion of staff development, the acknowledgement of staff and a willingness to delegate responsibility'. Furthermore, they urged employees to be open, truthful and consistent and to 'think about the need for change'.

Of particular interest were the changes required of the management board. The board accepted that there was a need for them to be committed to people, to 'empower' staff and to urge action. They also accepted that the communication issue needed to be addressed. Senior management categorized the practice of showing commitment as incorporating visibility, listening, action, good use of resources and stressing the need for quality. Action was categorized as the need for new business ventures, and efficient use of resources and to provide reward and praise.

Follow-up reflections several months later as to the outcomes of company surveys suggested that little had changed in relation to addressing the key issues of disequilibrium between employees and employer. Senior management team behaviour still reinforced the need to give priority to rational-economic issues. Only a narrow view of employee motivation was considered.

The author is able to relate that during a short period where profit margins were squeezed, the company reacted by decreasing training and development expenditure. Job reductions also increased. Furthermore, the organization delegated additional responsibilities to employees at all levels while productivity payments were minimal. Appraisal systems focused on achieving task-related targets, and the organization was restructured putting greater pressure on employees to change. As for the employee satisfaction survey, it appeared that senior management shelved many of the accepted findings. Thus, the process fell into disrepute.

In times when the survival of the organization is in jeopardy one would expect the above response by senior management. Nevertheless, the short-term need for profitability seemed a greater imperative than long-term employee commitment.

It is considered, however, that the most serious negative effects leading to poor commitment could have been avoided. What the organization failed to do was to adapt a mechanism at senior management level that recognized the psychological needs of employees.

Case study 5: Student case study

This case study is designed to assist consolidation as to the themes, ideas and techniques contained in Chapter 4. Answers to all questions are contained within the chapter. However, as a general guideline, readers might wish to reflect on the following:

- Material for Question 1 can be found in Chapter 2.
- Material to assist answering Question 2 can be found in Chapter 3.
- Appendix A and information contained in Chapters 3 and 4 will assist answers to Question 3.
- Additional material for Question 4 can be found in Chapter 1 and Chapter 5.
- Answers to Question 5 will use information contained in Chapter 4 and possible use of the Occupational Commitment Questionnaire (OCQ) by Porter *et al.* shown in Appendix B. It is not necessary to get permission to use this instrument for research.

Index